D0330730

The Make-or-Break Year

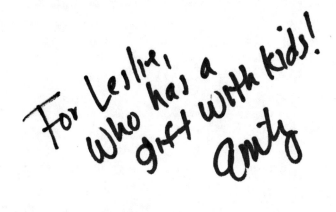

For Leslie, who has a gift with kids! Amy

The Make-or-Break Year

SOLVING THE DROPOUT CRISIS
ONE NINTH GRADER AT A TIME

Emily Krone Phillips

THE NEW PRESS

NEW YORK
LONDON

© 2019 by Emily Krone Phillips

All rights reserved.
No part of this book may be reproduced, in any form, without written permission from the publisher.

Requests for permission to reproduce selections from this book should be mailed to: Permissions Department, The New Press, 120 Wall Street, 31st floor, New York, NY 10005.

Published in the United States by The New Press, New York, 2019
Distributed by Two Rivers Distribution

ISBN 978-1-62097-323-3 (hc)
ISBN 978-1-62097-324-0 (ebook)
CIP data is available

The New Press publishes books that promote and enrich public discussion and understanding of the issues vital to our democracy and to a more equitable world. These books are made possible by the enthusiasm of our readers; the support of a committed group of donors, large and small; the collaboration of our many partners in the independent media and the not-for-profit sector; booksellers, who often hand-sell New Press books; librarians; and above all by our authors.

www.thenewpress.com

Composition by Westchester Publishing Services
This book was set in Minion Pro Regular

Printed in the United States of America

10 9 8 7 6 5 4 3 2 1

For Tom, Caroline, and James

CONTENTS

Author's Note   ix

Introduction   1

Chapter 1   19

Chapter 2   45

Chapter 3   78

Chapter 4   109

Chapter 5   135

Chapter 6   162

Chapter 7   191

Chapter 8   217

Chapter 9   241

Chapter 10   282

Epilogue   303

Acknowledgments   315

Notes   319

AUTHOR'S NOTE

The idea of this book originated when I was working as communications director at the University of Chicago Consortium on School Research, one of the country's oldest and most respected partnerships between university researchers and educators. Over the course of two decades, the UChicago Consortium conducted research on the Chicago Public Schools (CPS) that profoundly influenced district policy and practice. One of the most influential strands of their research pointed to the importance of supporting students during their ninth-grade year, which helped spur large improvements in graduation rates in Chicago. A privilege of working at the Consortium was getting to interact frequently with educators and policymakers at every level in the system in Chicago. From them I heard the stories of students, teachers, and schools transformed by the research on freshmen year. I realized those stories needed to be told more broadly, in part to help answer the questions that were being posed to me about how and why these improvements had occurred, and in part because the general public needs to hear about things that have gone right in public education and in the public sphere more generally.

The Spencer Foundation provided me with a generous grant, which allowed me to spend more than a year reporting from Chicago schools and interviewing past and present CPS teachers and administrators. I spent the 2015–16 school year at Tilden High

School, sitting in on staff meetings, tutoring sessions, and classes, and interviewing Tilden students as well as the teachers and staff who work with them.

When introducing myself to students, I explained that I was writing a book about the importance of freshmen year for future academic success. The students were eager to share their stories and often expressed their desire to improve freshmen year for other students. I have changed the names of all minors (but not adults) in this book, as well as certain identifying details, in order to protect their privacy. Most of the scenes in the Tilden chapters of the book I witnessed firsthand. For those that I did not, I relied on the accounts of at least two people who were there, and generally three or four.

The chapters in the book that tell the history of the Freshman OnTrack movement at Hancock High School and across Chicago rely primarily on my own personal interviews with students, researchers, teachers, administrators, and others who work in or for schools. They also draw on research conducted in Chicago schools by UChicago researchers and on news accounts from the time.

While I was reporting this book, students revealed personal details about their friendships, families, neighborhoods, hopes, fears, goals, and academic struggles and triumphs. Throughout the narrative, I disclose these details in so far as they influenced students' academic trajectories. The Freshman OnTrack movement in Chicago, which has transformed relationships between teachers and students, is predicated on the recognition that students' personal and academic lives are inextricably linked. It therefore seemed crucial to include details about students' private lives in order to illustrate the work of Freshman OnTrack in all its complexity. It is my sincerest hope that the depictions of students' lives inside and outside of the classroom will help educators unleash the potential of ninth graders nationwide.

INTRODUCTION

Average. That was how Eric thought of himself as he began his freshman year at John Hancock College Prep High School on Chicago's Southwest Side in the fall of 2014. Average student. Average athlete. Depressingly average build, despite an early growth spurt that had given him false hope that he might harbor some recessive height genes.

He hadn't always thought of himself in those terms. In eighth grade he had nursed the dream of attending one of the city's selective enrollment high schools, those educational crown jewels reserved for Chicago's academic elite who earned top grades and test scores in elementary school. Like many of his friends from elementary school did, Eric applied and was rejected. The rejection stung more than he let on, reinforcing his fears that he was not particularly smart or talented. And so he recalibrated his expectations and went looking for a high school that was thoroughly average. "I just wanted the most mundane school I could find," Eric said later. "I wanted an 'I-can-get-by-without-any-trouble'-type school."

He believed that Hancock, a small neighborhood high school near his home, fit the bill. Established to relieve overcrowding at nearby schools, Hancock was never meant to inspire—as the newly constructed selective-enrollment schools, with their glass, light, and sparkle were meant to do—instead, it was meant to accommodate.

It was housed in an aging building that had once held an all-girls Catholic school. Eric's older brother, a senior at Hancock, encouraged him to enroll. And so he did. He planned to keep his head down, work just hard enough to get by, and, upon graduation, leave school behind for good.

From the outset, though, Hancock's teachers and students seemed determined to upend his plan. He attended the freshman orientation before the start of the school year and was bombarded with overtures from upperclassmen who invited him to join their after-school clubs and activities. Teachers, too, seemed friendly and approachable. They quizzed him about his interests, his family, his goals, his learning style. On the first day of school, his math teacher, Mr. Castillo, screened *Stand and Deliver*, the classic film based on the story of Jaime Escalante, an East Los Angeles public-school teacher who took a ragtag group of underachieving, working-class Latino students and in a year taught them enough advanced math to enable them to pass the rigorous AP Calculus exam. After the movie wrapped, Raul Castillo addressed his own class full of low-income Latino students, vowing to help them reach new academic heights if they exhibited the same type of *ganas*, or drive, as the students in the film had.

Eric did not know what to make of it all. "I thought everyone was really friendly, but some people were kind of too friendly," he recalled. "Me and my older brother, we don't really trust people who are too friendly." He ticked off a list of traumatic events that had contributed to his trust issues: His half-brother's father's deportation. The Christmas Day when a family member attempted to kidnap his half-brother and reunite him with his father in Mexico, stabbing his mother and stepfather in the process (both survived). His own father's inconsistent presence in his life.

But Eric pinned most of the problems he experienced when he first arrived at Hancock on his own "laziness." "I was expecting to coast and that just didn't happen," he said. By the start of the fourth quarter of his freshman year, Eric was on the verge of failing three classes. He had D's in Environmental Science and French, plus an F in Mr. Castillo's Honors Algebra class.

This did not bode well for his academic future. Researchers have shown that freshman year is the "make-or-break" year for high school graduation. Students who receive more than one F in a semester during their freshman year are very unlikely to graduate, even if, like Eric, they posted solid academic records before high school. And if ninth grade is the make-or-break year for high school graduation, then it is also the pivotal year for a shot at the middle class. High school graduates earn roughly $670,000 more over the course of a lifetime than high school dropouts do. They are more likely to vote, volunteer, and participate in other aspects of civil society. They are less likely to live in poverty or be institutionalized in a prison or mental hospital. They are healthier. They live longer. In short, a high school diploma is the first line of defense against the corrosive effects of poverty. For Eric and the students whose lives are chronicled in this book, it is no exaggeration to say that ninth grade is a life-or-death proposition.

But Eric was lucky. Lucky to go to school when he did and lucky to attend Hancock, which by the time he entered high school had become one of the best schools in the city at supporting freshmen. It wasn't always this way. If he had attended Hancock—or any number of Chicago's public high schools—just a decade earlier, chances are good that he would have dropped out.

For many consecutive years during the 1980s, 1990s, and early 2000s, ninth graders entering Chicago's public high schools had roughly the same odds of dropping out as of graduating. If a student struggled freshman year, as Eric did, those odds increased exponentially.

This was no silent epidemic. Beginning in the early 1980s, dozens of studies documented the size and scope of the city's dropout crisis. Each subsequent report triggered paroxysms of publicity and finger-pointing, and served as further confirmation that Chicago's schools were broken, perhaps beyond repair.

"Nothing has shown us the dismal state of public schooling in Chicago as clearly as the most recent estimates of how many high school students fail to graduate," a 1985 *Chicago Tribune* editorial lamented. The Hispanic dropout rate constitutes an "intellectual genocide of a people," the head of the Chicago Board of Education's Dropout Prevention Bureau warned that same year. "African-Americans leave city's public schools at staggering rate," a 2003 front-page headline decried.

While there was near-universal consensus that the dropout rate in Chicago was indeed a crisis, not to mention a disgrace and black eye for the city, there was absolutely no agreement on its root causes or how to remedy them. Academics and educators, pundits and policy-makers, concerned citizens and at least one specially convened task force put forth dozens of theories, many of them contradictory and most of them implicating the rampant poverty in Chicago and its attendant social ills. Experts blamed broken families, broken communities, illiteracy, crime, drugs, street gangs for boys, and teen pregnancy for girls. Most of these challenges were complex, entrenched, and entirely outside the control of high schools. In short, they appeared insurmountable and so, therefore, did the dropout crisis.

It wasn't.

This book will tell the unlikely and largely untold story of how a simple idea—that ninth grade is the "make-or-break" year for high school graduation, and that teachers and schools must organize to support students during this treacherous transition year—transformed Chicago's dropout epidemic into a manageable, albeit chronic, disease and annually propelled thousands of additional students like Eric toward a spot in the middle class.

In the late 1990s, researchers at the University of Chicago Consortium on School Research identified an interesting statistical relationship. Students who passed their courses in ninth grade almost always went on to graduate. Those who failed more than one semester of a course almost always dropped out, even if they had excelled in elementary school. Subsequent research found that freshman-year academic performance was by far the best predictor of whether or not a student would persist to earn a high school diploma. Students who were "on-track" after freshman year—that is, students who failed no more than one semester of a core course and had at least ten semester credits—were more than three-and-a-half times as likely as students who were "off-track" to graduate. This finding prompted the UChicago Consortium to develop the "Freshman OnTrack" indicator, which came into wide use in Chicago schools and, eventually, beyond and proved more predictive of eventual graduation than prior academic achievement or background characteristics, such as students' race or gender or the level of their family or community resources did. In fact, it proved more predictive than all of those factors combined.

These findings suggested that students do not drop out because they are poor or black or illiterate, as conventional wisdom posits. They drop out because, for a constellation of reasons, they struggle at age fourteen and don't receive enough support to bounce back. The implications for practice were intriguing. High school educators have no control over the background characteristics of the students who arrive at their doorstep, but they can influence how students perform once they get there. The research suggested that freshman year offered a crucial intervention point for those working to reduce the number of dropouts.

In the 2008–09 school year, when Arne Duncan was the "CEO" of Chicago Public Schools (CPS), its administrators announced a major push to improve freshmen's on-track rates. Every high school in the city was to be held accountable for the percentage of freshmen that ended the year on-track to graduate. Schools began to receive real-time data reports on how their freshmen were faring. Teachers, principals, administrators, policymakers, researchers, and nonprofit organizations across the city began to create new strategies for supporting freshmen. Some strategies came from what's known as Central Office, some from classroom teachers, and others from the many nonprofit organizations that worked with schools.

Each school was free to choose its own path for supporting freshmen. Freshman OnTrack was neither a policy nor a program—it was a focus area that became a movement. Through trial and error, schools figured out what worked best for their students. Educators swapped information on what worked and what flopped, borrowing ideas from one another and modifying the ideas to fit the context of their schools.

As strategies bubbled up from the bottom, trickled down from the top, and moved laterally from school to school through formal and informal networks, citywide on-track rates for freshmen began to climb. After hovering for years in the mid-50s, the percentage of CPS freshmen finishing the year on-track to graduate reached 89 percent in 2017. Subsequent research by the Consortium (which also came to be known as the "UChicago Consortium") tied these improved freshman rates to record graduation rates three years down the line. Crucially, these improvements were not the result of students being "passed along" or awarded D's rather than F's. Since 2007, the percentage of students earning A's and B's has increased, and ACT scores have risen slightly, despite nearly seven thousand additional students taking the exam annually (at the time, the state administered the ACT to all juniors as part of required state testing). Perhaps most remarkably, given the well-documented tendency for education reforms to benefit higher-performing schools and leave the others behind, Freshman OnTrack efforts produced the largest gains in the lowest-performing schools and for the system's lowest-performing students.

In a 2014 press conference announcing record on-track rates, Chicago mayor Rahm Emanuel noted, "We're the biggest turnaround. We're on our way. And not just as a city—all these kids now, because of being on track for high school, they're on track to a life of possibility."

If ever there was a Chicago school that exemplified this trajectory from worst to first, it was Hancock. In the 2007–08 school year, the year before the district's push to improve freshman course performance began, Hancock's on-track rate for freshmen was just 58 percent. By the time Eric arrived at Hancock in 2014, the rate was a remarkable 94 percent.

One of the keys to Hancock's success was its "Freshman Success Team," a group of teachers who met regularly to keep tabs on individual students and monitor overall failure rates by grade level and class. This team approach figured prominently in most of the successful Freshman OnTrack initiatives across the district, transforming relationships among teachers and between teachers and students.

In the spring of Eric's freshman year, the teachers who made up Hancock's Freshman Success Team devoted part of their semimonthly meeting to discussing his struggles. Erin Neidt, a Freshman Physics teacher (and the school's Freshman OnTrack coordinator), kicked off the meeting. "Thank you, freshman team, for being here and being on time and being fully present for our meeting today," she said. "It's really important to be fully present so unless you have been asked to take minutes for the meeting or you are using it to look at data of specific students, please refrain from using a lot of technology today."

Organized, composed, and fiercely committed to helping students succeed, Neidt was an obvious candidate to lead her peers in the work to support freshmen. Her meetings ran smoothly and efficiently and concluded with concrete plans for helping struggling students. Also, like the products of any good physics teacher, her graphs and charts were impeccable.

On the overhead projector, Neidt flashed a bar graph that included up-to-date data on freshman course failures. "So here are current failures by grade level across the freshman courses," she said.

There were very small bars next to English and Human Geography and much larger bars next to Introduction to Computer Science. Also, 6 percent of students were failing PE, which was a higher rate than usual. "Let's take a minute to reflect on this. Talk amongst yourself in small groups."

The first half of Freshman Success Team meetings generally focused on overall trends in failures. The goal was to make sense of whatever patterns showed up in the data and then to problem solve accordingly as a group. Often, teachers could provide insights into why failure rates might be particularly high in a specific subject area or class. When failure rates were high across the board, they might consider new school-wide systems, policies, or structures to address the problem—a new attendance policy or grading system, for example.

The second half of Success Team meetings was devoted to discussing one or two struggling students. A photo of Eric, a baby-faced student with close-cropped hair and a shy half smile, was projected onto a screen at the front of the room. The team dove into the process of sharing their particular experiences with and knowledge of Eric.

After roughly ten minutes of discussion, the teachers determined that he was failing not because he was incapable of doing the work but because he wasn't applying himself. Eric's comments in class could be on point and insightful, but he had neglected to turn in numerous assignments and often seemed distracted, especially since March, when he had begun dating one of his classmates—a smart, motivated student who teachers believed could be an ally in their cause to get Eric back on-track. Michael Marzano, Eric's science teacher, and Jeschelyn Pilar, an English teacher, decided to stage an intervention—and to enlist the help of Eric's girlfriend in the process.

Much of the discussion in education reform centers on implementing new technology, curricula, and school models, and on attracting more investment and talent. Meetings where educators gather to talk about students? Systems and structures to ensure that

INTRODUCTION 9

students reliably receive the support they need? That's not on anyone's short list of cutting-edge, high-impact reform. And yet Eric would identify that single meeting of his teachers—and the plans that came out of it—as a turning point in his academic career, and maybe in his life.

On a fall day at the start of his senior year, Eric sat in a third-floor office, ready to chat about his experiences at Hancock. He was only vaguely recognizable from that freshman-year photo that had been flashed up on the screen two and a half years earlier at the Success Team meeting. His cheekbones were more pronounced. His hair had grown shaggier. His smile was broader. His handshake was firm and confident.

"Yeah, I was such an idiot freshman year," he said by way of introduction. All this time later, Eric vividly recalled the intervention with Ms. Pilar, Mr. Marzano, and his girlfriend. Ms. Pilar had tipped him off that a conversation was going to happen. Still, he was a little bewildered when they went into Mr. Marzano's lab classroom to talk.

Eric was embarrassed that the teachers were asking about his grades in front of his girlfriend. He knew she was serious about school, and he knew she thought he was not. She had been reluctant to date him, in large part because she thought he was too silly. "At first she friend-zoned me. It killed me," Eric said. He had spent a lot of time convincing her that he was different from his public persona. He didn't want this meeting to catapult him back into the "friend zone."

He was careful to blame himself—not her—for his academic struggles in that meeting with Marzano and Pilar. He admitted that he could probably work a little harder in French. He simply had never had to apply himself before in a language class. In elementary school, he had taken Spanish and hadn't had to work at it much since he already knew the language. Math was a different story. He was trying, but he was struggling to understand the concepts.

As a group, they decided Eric would start attending math tutoring regularly and commit to turning in his missing French assignments.

Pilar hounded him to attend math tutoring during lunch. Marzano checked in regularly about his French grade and stayed on him to complete assignments. And his girlfriend kept tabs on his academic progress as well. "She's like my second mom," Eric admitted ruefully.

Eric ended up passing both classes. "French wasn't hard. I honestly just had to sit down, look at it, read it, comprehend it. One class I actually needed help in was Algebra. I ended up passing with a D. But Mr. Castillo knew I worked really hard in the end."

After the intervention his grades improved, but in retrospect, that was just the start of an overall transformation in how he viewed himself and school. "That was when I started becoming more of a student leader," Eric said. "I started becoming more conscientious of my decisions. I thought before then that they only affected me. I think I realized after that that people actually cared and were mindful of what you do. As a freshman I thought teachers were just teachers. They do their work and go home. I didn't realize that teachers stay behind. The special thing about Hancock is that students are so prioritized as individuals. And it's not just certain individuals. It's all. If you don't want help, it's forced. It's honestly forced. I've been forced to do so many things that eventually helped me in the long run."

For example, he had been pressured to join Becoming a Man, a mentoring group run by a local nonprofit which has been shown to be quite successful at keeping students in school and out of trouble. The other students in BAM became "like my second family. I consider them brothers." And they got him through a tragedy sophomore year when one of his friends, a fellow Hancock student, was shot while he was walking to school. "When Victor died that was a big outlet for me. They were always asking, how do you feel emotionally, mentally, physically? Where are you right now? A lot of us, where we were wasn't stable. But because I was able to overcome it quicker than some people, I was able to help more people."

Eric became a peer mentor and also a volunteer at Freshman Connection, the orientation for new students (at which he himself had once been so overwhelmed by the friendly overtures of Hancock students). He saw freshmen who were angry and scared and insecure, just like he had been, and he wanted to help them. He started to envision a career in social work or teaching, though he felt a little sheepish about it sometimes.

"I think when I graduate from college I want to be someone who helps the youth," he said. "Because—it's kind of selfish, I guess— 'cause I've always had so many great influences, like teachers and mentors, that I want to be that person for someone."

He pictured himself doing someday for other students what Ms. Pilar, Mr. Marzano, Mr. Martinek, and others had done for him. Andrew Martinek, a social studies teacher, ran the school's Model UN Club, where Eric had become a policy wonk, arguing economic and weapons policy with classmates and students from other schools. As a senior, he was named secretary general of Hancock's team.

Martinek had taken Eric and his classmates on field trips to visit colleges, and he pushed him to take advantage of opportunities that were available to the city's teens. Over the years, Martinek had become an honorary member of Eric's family. "I've known him since my freshman year and he lives a block away from me," Eric said. "My mom has invited him to family parties. He's seen we can party until three a.m. I think he understands who we are and who my family is as a whole."

Mr. Martinek knew that Eric not only participated in Model UN, Becoming a Man, peer mentoring, the school's cheerleading team, and its tech squad (which provided IT support to teachers and staff), but also took care of his two-year-old sister every day after school and worked weekends at a grocery story on the city's North Side, a four-hour round-trip train ride away. There had been a time at Hancock, before the Freshman OnTrack movement really took root, when some Hancock teachers had looked down on

Hancock students and their families for appearing to prioritize work and family commitments over school. But Eric felt nothing but support from teachers for his balancing act.

"I take care of [my sister] because my stepdad works at night. After school I go home, I pick up her stroller and walk to her daycare. My teachers are like, 'That's such a great job.' But I'm humble. That's my everyday work. That's what I do. I don't complain about watching my sister. I love my sister a lot," Eric said, with a wide grin. "And she loves me the most."

It's hard to reconcile that doting big brother, responsible Model UN general secretary, and spirited cheerleader with Eric's description of himself in elementary school. "I was way, *way* different then," he insists. "In seventh and eighth grade I was, I guess, a bully. I was an angry person. My confidence was really low. I went through puberty really fast in fifth grade. I had acne everywhere. . . . I had a negative body image. Coming into high school, I felt like, I'm nothing."

Eric said he had a "big shift in mentality between the end of eighth grade and the end of ninth grade." He attributed that shift to having teachers who believed in him and propped him up until he experienced some successes and began to believe in himself. "It took a LOT of people to tell me I had promise and that they saw promise in me to believe I was smart," Eric said. "In elementary school people always labeled me—like, 'He has dyslexia. He has ADHD. He can't sit still.' I think they started saying that so much that I started believing them."

He paused, trying to find the right words for how he thought of himself now, as a senior. "I'm still pretty average, but I'm content with being average in high school. I'm just an average student. But in terms of extracurricular, things I do to provide for the school, I excel in that, and in helping other people."

Eric concluded the interview with a plea to tell Hancock's story in a way that captured what a special place it was. "I just want to emphasize that the teachers here don't get enough credit," he said. "I think this is one of the best schools in general on the South Side. It took

Hancock a while, and a lot of hard work, especially to help students who have always been told they are average."

This was actually a pretty good encapsulation of the Freshman OnTrack movement in Chicago—a lot of hard work, sustained over time, to help students who had struggled academically to believe that they could succeed in high school. As unlikely as it seems, that work, occurring in dozens of high schools across the city, permanently altered the trajectory of many thousands of lives. Freshman OnTrack in Chicago changed an entire system—school by school, principal by principal, teacher by teacher, and kid by kid. The change happened not just in the city's elite selective-enrollment schools or magnet programs; not just in a smattering of beating-the-odds schools manned by extraordinary individuals; but in, as one CPS administrator put it, "regular-ass CPS schools with regular-ass CPS kids." Kids like Eric, who didn't turn out to be just average after all.

By 2014, Chicago's improving on-track and graduation rates had attracted national attention, and educators wanted to better understand the Freshman OnTrack movement in order to replicate it in their districts and cities. UChicago Consortium researchers could explain that freshman year seemed to hold the key for high school graduation. And they could say that on-track rates were improving across the district and driving record graduation rates. Still, plenty of unanswered questions remained. The first group of questions centered on why freshman year was so predictive of later outcomes. Why did students who were on-track tend to remain on-track in subsequent years? And why did failures during freshman year prove so crushing? Another group of questions concerned what Freshman OnTrack was. If it wasn't a program, and it wasn't really a policy, then what was it and how did it spread?

A more pointed question, which often came from journalists familiar with Chicago's public reputation for dysfunction, was some form of: How did this happen in Chicago, of all places, which between 2007 and 2018 experienced eight different superintendents' tenures, a teachers strike, and the largest single mass school closure in the nation's history? Consortium researchers' tongue-in-cheek response was that if it could happen here, it could happen anywhere. But system shifts in education of this magnitude are rare anywhere. It is crucial to understand why this reform made a measurable impact at scale when so many other reforms have failed, and not simply so that other districts can replicate Freshman OnTrack and address their dropout crisis, but also so that educators in other cities and states can bring the principles of Freshman OnTrack to bear on *other* seemingly intractable problems. There are many hundreds of small pockets of excellence and improvement in education. And there are many more examples of failures. This is the rare story of improvement at scale, of an idea that triumphed in a system once labeled as the worst system in the nation, in schools typically the most impervious to reform, and among students who for many years had been written off.

This story follows three threads. The first trails a group of freshmen as they navigate what may be the most critical year of their lives. These students attend Tilden Career Community Academy in Back of the Yards, the former home of Union Stockyards, made famous in Upton Sinclair's *The Jungle*. Tilden serves some of the city's most vulnerable students. All Tilden students qualify as low-income, and one in five does not have a permanent place to call home. The students chronicled in this book all began the 2015–16 school year, their freshman year, at something of a personal crossroads. They were, as their English teacher put it, "still trying to decide whether to break good or break bad."

Throughout the course of the year, the teens stumble repeatedly. They cut school, show up forty-five minutes late to class, mouth off and storm out, forget assignments, and generally drive their teachers to distraction. They also make up missed assignments, persevere through personal trials, speak lovingly and admiringly about their favorite teachers, confide their secret ambitions to leave their neighborhood and pull their families out of poverty, and noticeably mature throughout the year.

Through it all, a dedicated group of teachers, staff, and administrators fight to keep all of them on-track. They meet regularly to problem solve around individual kids, stage interventions, call home, and give second, third, and fourth chances—all based on the philosophy that just because some freshmen arrive at high school not knowing how to be a good student, that should not mean that they never get the chance to become one.

The Tilden chapters delve into research on school transitions to help explain why ninth grade is such a pivotal year in students' academic careers. Research on adolescence shows that freshman year is critical for determining whether students persist to graduation. It is during this period that students either form an attachment to school and become part of the larger school community—or begin to drift away. The teenage brain is hardwired to connect with and conform to peers, even as it pushes back against authority. Freshman year helps determine how teens define their peer group and themselves. Students like David, who becomes increasingly involved in the school community over the course of the year, are likely to stay connected for the rest of high school. Others, like Aniyah, interpret their failure as proof that they don't belong in school. When Aniyah receives her third-quarter report card with all F's, her immediate response is "See, this is why I'm gonna be a stripper."

Emerging research on the teenage brain also helps explain why Tilden's students—and teenagers generally—so often behave in ways that seem inexplicable to adults. New technology has allowed scientists to track brain growth and make connections between brain function and behavior and, overturning many assumptions, to reveal that a young person's brain does not begin to resemble that of an adult until the person is in her early twenties. As Sharon Holmes, the Tilden English teacher and Freshman OnTrack coordinator, frequently reminds her students, "Your cerebral cortex is not fully formed! You make bad choices!" In fact, the cerebral cortex, which is responsible for thought and memory, looks very different in adolescents than it does in adults. The parts of the cerebral cortex responsible for controlling impulses and planning ahead—key aspects of school success—are among the last to mature, making Tilden's teachers' commitment to second chances and intensive support all the more crucial.

The book's second thread follows Hancock's teachers, students, and principals over an eight-year period as the school goes from being one of the worst in the state to being among the top in the city. The Hancock story shows in great detail how Freshman OnTrack worked at Hancock and became increasingly sophisticated and effective. It shows what it took to get there—the hit-and-miss experimentation, the philosophical debates, the throw-down arguments, and strategizing, arm-twisting, and swapping ideas and theories. It shows how Freshman OnTrack was just as much an intervention for adults as it was for students, forcing the staff not only to do their jobs differently but also, in some cases, to change their entire belief systems.

Though some of the specifics are unique to Hancock, the broad outlines of Hancock's story will help explain how and why Freshman OnTrack became such a powerful organizing principle for high schools citywide. It depicts the considerable challenges that Freshman OnTrack and most other initiatives which are introduced in very low performing schools have to overcome: a jaded workforce nursing a "this too shall pass" attitude toward reform; union rules that undermine change; deeply held beliefs about what poor and minority students are capable of achieving; relentless political pressure to demonstrate measurable progress on metrics that teachers and principals have no idea how to influence; policy initiatives enacted from on high that are tone deaf to the realities on the ground; and frequent teacher and administrative turnover that make it exceedingly difficult to maintain promising programs or learn from past mistakes, to name a few.

Amidst these challenges, Freshman OnTrack thrived among educators. It got teachers and principals, who for years had been working in isolation, working as teams for the very first time; it allowed teachers to tailor the work to the needs of their school and their students; and it made a dispirited workforce feel successful. Indeed, it so permeated the marrow of the school that it survived even when the principal who had catalyzed the initial Freshman OnTrack work retired, and also when, two years later, the mayor turned Hancock into a selective enrollment school, which upended both the school's mission and its student body. Broadly speaking, and in contrast to many other initiatives, it worked for Hancock teachers and Hancock students. And because they could see that it worked, teachers and principals kept working at it, day after day and year after year.

Finally, the third thread zooms out to place Freshman OnTrack in a larger historical and political context, showing how the initiative survived in Chicago from 2009 to the present day despite dysfunction, turnover, and competing agendas at district and city levels. The citywide story helps illustrate those aspects of Freshman OnTrack that allowed it to make a measurable impact at scale—a critical insight, given that most ideas in education fail entirely, or fail to spread beyond a few exceptional schools. It shows the power that teachers, principals, and policymakers working together have to solve a common problem, in contrast to the typical reform script in which solutions are imposed from above, without much thought given to the complexities on the ground. And it shows the power of networks, which were responsible for building educators' capacity to do the work (often an afterthought in education reform) and for keeping the initiative alive as the district's leaders hopped from one priority and crisis to the next.

Freshman OnTrack also beat the odds because it managed to avoid the "killer binaries"—debates without a middle ground—that so often polarize education reformers. It was neither purely "top down" nor purely "grassroots"; it combined the expertise of teachers, administrators, researchers, and policymakers. It hinged on accountability and data, both of which are championed by "business-minded" reformers who believe that schools should run more like corporations do. But by using data to pinpoint students' needs during a crucial developmental period, it also appealed to those who lament that the growing emphasis on accountability in schools has crowded out the human and relational elements of education.

Like most ideas, when implemented, Freshman OnTrack has had unintended consequences and mixed effects. It worked better in some schools and for some kids than for others. It repeatedly bumped up against competing priorities, political agendas, and district pathologies. And without fail, a new group of freshmen arrived every September, carrying with them all the promise and heartache that being fourteen entails, and the work began all over again. It's these struggles that make Freshman OnTrack such a compelling story. And it's the ability to overcome these struggles—some combination of which nearly any new idea in urban education is likely to face—that makes Freshman OnTrack such an instructive narrative for anyone interested in understanding how to improve schools and, most intriguingly, how to turn research on what works in education into a social movement that transforms lives.

CHAPTER 1

In the nineteenth century, Fall River, Massachusetts, was known as the textile capital of America. By the time Melissa Roderick attended high school there in the late 1970s, the city had fallen on harder times, but living-wage factory jobs were still attainable and, for many Fall River teens, were a lot more appealing than suffering through another year or two of high school. Teens who did manage to secure a factory job were permitted to sign out of class. "Most would just stop going to school because they were so miserable and they were failing everything anyway," Roderick recalled. "In high school, I don't think I learned anything. I don't think I even wrote a paper."

Roderick graduated from B.M.C. Durfee High School and went on to Bowdoin College, a selective liberal arts college in Maine. Others in her tight-knit group of friends dropped out. "They had terrible ninth-grade years. Tenth grade was a disaster. And by the end of tenth grade, I was the only one still in school," Roderick recalled.

Fall River had marked Roderick with a pronounced Boston accent, a blue-collar sensibility, and a deep affinity for the underdog. She insisted that her lackluster high school experience was actually "the best thing that ever happened to me, because it left me with this conundrum." Untangling that conundrum—why some students persevere through high school and college, while others drop out—became her life's work.

In the mid-1980s, Roderick was a graduate student in public policy at Harvard's Kennedy School of Government, working part-time at a dropout prevention program for Boston teens. The Summer Training and Education Program (STEP) provided teens with academic help, part-time work, and classes on topics such as pregnancy and drug use over a two-month period during the summer between middle school and high school. The goal was to prevent summer learning loss and teen pregnancy and eventually improve students' chances of graduating. The program seemed so promising that it was replicated in one hundred sites in fifteen states, reaching more than twenty thousand students between 1987 and 1991. But Roderick and some of her colleagues had noticed a disturbing trend. By all accounts, the summer program had been a success: the teens had been engaged and seemed poised to do well in high school. And yet, as soon as school began in the fall, word began trickling back about students who had already dropped out or were seriously considering doing so, one disheartening report after another. "No matter what we did, we lost kids in high school," Roderick said. "You could just never predict. The kid would look fine, then he got to ninth grade and bombed out."

As the program wound down, STEP's staff and community sponsors convened to discuss its future. Soon, a heated debate developed. On one side was a faction insisting that the program had not reached students early enough in their academic careers and needed to shift focus to the middle grades, a time when students' attachment to school often begins to fray.

Another faction insisted that it was students' experiences in high school that played the larger role in determining whether they graduated or dropped out. This group argued that the kids in the summer program were, by and large, just fine until ninth grade. Roderick was partial to this argument, in part because she had seen many of her own friends struggle with the transition to high school.

It isn't hard to discern why Roderick made it even as her friends stumbled. Her family placed a premium on education and public service. She joked that you could pinpoint the Rodericks on a Fall River census map because her mother and father were the only ones in the neighborhood with advanced degrees. Her mother, Marilyn, was a teacher at the local elementary school and served on both the city council and the school board for the better part of four decades.

It was clear from an early age that Melissa Roderick was destined for a world beyond Fall River. In high school she was assigned to gifted classes. She was a voracious reader and also remarkably determined and socially aware from a young age. As a teen she managed to talk her way onto the board of directors at the city's halfway house, coordinate the local chapter of Mo Udall's 1976 Democratic nomination campaign for the U.S. presidential race, and work thirty hours a week delivering newspapers.

Paradoxically, Roderick's subsequent research on dropouts, inspired by the debate that took place in that Boston meeting room, would help shift the national conversation about dropouts away from the qualities that students had or did not have. She would go on to spend most of her professional career arguing that properly run schools could keep students from dropping out and that students should not have to be preternaturally gifted or gritty to graduate from high school. Indeed, her message could be boiled down to the simple idea that a student should not have to be Melissa Roderick to graduate from a high school in a low-income area.

Born in 1961, Roderick is about as old as America's dropout problem, or at least as old as the dropout problem as we conceive of today. Throughout most of American history, high schools were considered to be elite institutions, and they were designed to serve and graduate only a small fraction of the population. It wasn't until 1940 that even half of the nation's high-school-age students were earning diplomas. There was little public hand-wringing over this state of affairs. Those who did think that universal education was an economic or moral necessity in a modern democracy tended to concentrate on elementary education.

But as a larger and larger share of teenagers began delaying entrance into the workforce, high schools became the dominant institution serving American adolescents, and the public's expectations for high schools changed dramatically. By 1960, the percentage of teenagers earning a high school diploma had reached 70 percent. It was also at this time that the public became convinced that the ranks of students who had *not* earned a high school diploma constituted a grave national problem, and the issue began to receive headline status.

In a 1963 speech taped for television at the White House, President John F. Kennedy emphasized the toll that dropping out takes on the individual and the nation. Kicking off a summer campaign to stem the tide of dropouts, President Kennedy warned, "Today an education is not a luxury. It is a necessity. The uneducated and untrained person is seriously handicapped, economically, socially and culturally. . . . School dropouts constitute a serious national problem, one deserving of the attention and efforts of all segments of our society—educators, clergymen, businessmen, labor leaders, and above all mothers and fathers."

Kennedy's singling out of mothers and fathers reflected the popular understanding that dysfunctional families were at the root of the dropout crisis. In 1960, *Life* magazine ran a two-part photo-essay titled "Dropout Tragedies," which detailed the "sad individual stories" that seemed to lay behind the dropout statistics. The article lamented, "There is often little help at home. Many parents praise 'good money,' scorn 'book learning.' Others do not care, or frequently in the case of minority groups, are just not able to help. And many homes are crippled by divorce, sickness and poverty."

The *Life* article reflected and reinforced the stereotype of the dropout that was emerging in popular culture at the time. Historian Sherman Dorn, who wrote the definitive history of America's relationship to its dropout crisis, argues that the way in which Americans have portrayed high school dropouts for the past half century is based more on recurring anxiety that the youth of the nation are going to hell in a handbasket than on any clearheaded analysis of the causes or effects of dropping out of school.

In the popular imagination, Dorn points out, dropouts were seen to be deviant somehow, either too dim to keep up with their peers academically or too dense to recognize the dire consequences of dropping out. If they weren't delinquents, then they were at the very least knuckleheads. Indeed, the very term dropout, which came into popular use in the 1960s, puts the onus for leaving school squarely on the students.

Conventional wisdom about dropouts didn't change much in proceeding decades, though the depictions of them changed with the times. In the early 1960s, the dropout of popular culture was a disaffected tough guy. In the late 1960s, the dropout was depicted as a Timothy Leary–style "flower child," "turning on, tuning in, and dropping out." In the 1980s, the dropout was often portrayed as a drug-dealing black or Latino male or as a pregnant black or Latina female. But even as the particulars of the stereotype evolved, the common denominator remained. Dropouts were a particular type. They came from particular families. They made particularly ill-advised choices.

The resulting assumption was that there was not much that schools could or should do to save these youths from themselves. Indeed, those community groups and activists who suggested otherwise sometimes came under scathing attack. In 1984, a group of Latino parents picketed the Chicago Board of Education, demanding the resignation of then-superintendent Reggie Love. They argued that the soaring Latino dropout rate—pegged somewhere between 50 and 75 percent at that the time—amounted to educational malpractice.

Legendary Chicago columnist Mike Royko, a Pulitzer Prize winner who was widely considered to be the "voice of the people" in the City of Big Shoulders, shot back with a column in the *Chicago Tribune* telling the protesting parents to go stick it. If they wanted to point their fingers at someone, they should "look in the mirror." "The fact is," Royko asserted, with characteristic cantankerousness, "there isn't much that anybody in the school system or in City Hall or in the state legislature or in Washington, DC, can do about the dropout rate. They can study it. They can provide statistics, and charts. They can hold hearings and blab about it and write long reports about it. But there's not much they can do to reduce it."

Royko ended his rant with a barrage of rhetorical questions aimed at the protesting parents: "Do you ever talk to them about their schoolwork? Do you encourage, reward, stimulate? Do you set up rules? Do you at least turn off the damn TV or the cassette player?" He concluded, "That's your job. And if they fail, it's your fault, not ours."

In many ways, Royko's assessment jibed with the academic literature on dropouts. Because dropping out of high school is such a complex, multifaceted process, studies are rarely able to pinpoint the precise reason that a student leaves high school without a diploma. Instead, they tend to unearth common associations between the characteristics or experiences of dropouts and the act of dropping out.

Studies label these factors "predictors" or "risk factors," and researchers have offered up many dozens of them, from low self-esteem to poverty to race and ethnicity. Dropout rates are higher for Latino and black students than for Asian and white students. They are higher for males than for females. They are higher for students living in poverty than for middle-class students. They are higher for children from single-parent homes than those from two-parent homes.

The problem was this research didn't provide much useful information for Roderick or the other educators and policymakers engaged in earnest debate over the best way to help young people. If students dropped out because they were poor or black or from a single-parent home, there wasn't a whole lot that a summer program was going to do about any of that.

Eventually, the debate in Boston about which direction the dropout prevention program should take reached an impasse. It was then that the head of Boston's anti-poverty agency turned to Roderick and asked her a question that would eventually change the course of her academic career. "You're the hotshot researcher," she said. "What does the evidence say about this?"

Not a lot, it turned out. Unable to uncover much evidence to inform her colleagues' debate, Roderick decided to embark on her own study to try to answer the question. Initially, she tried to conduct research within Boston Public Schools, but when she failed to get data from them, she turned to Fall River, where her deep roots in the community opened doors.

Fall River Public Schools provided an excellent laboratory to study the dropout crisis. Though considerably smaller than major urban school systems like Chicago's or New York's, it shared many of their challenges. In 1980, Fall River's median educational level was less than nine years, the lowest in all of Massachusetts. The school system served roughly twelve thousand students, 60 percent of whom were labeled as low-income. One-third of its students were racial or ethnic minorities, primarily Portuguese immigrants or native Portuguese speakers.

Fall River also provided Roderick with an opportunity to get data that was hard to come by at the time. In the early 1980s, school systems did not have the sophisticated data systems that are now a staple in large districts, tracking everything from attendance to grades to college admissions. A popular dataset was the federal government's High School and Beyond Survey, which did include transcript data but did not begin until students' sophomore year. It would be a coup for Roderick to get access to transcript data for students over a larger portion of their academic career.

In the basement of an old administrative building, Roderick unearthed the elementary school transcripts of Fall River's students who were seventh graders during the 1980–81 school year. Then she went over to the high school and uncovered those same students' high school transcripts, matching them to the elementary transcripts using birth dates and home addresses.

The results floored her. Most students had been chugging along nicely before high school, and then, seemingly without warning, they dropped off an academic cliff. The drop-off was so precipitous, she assumed she had made an error somewhere in her analysis. "The first time I read the means, I was like, 'Oh *man*, I screwed up, this is terrible! I can't believe I just hand-entered all these transcripts, and I made a mistake,'" she said, slapping her head for effect. But she hadn't made a mistake. "Ninth grade *was* a disaster. And it was real."

Roderick discovered that dropouts in her sample could be sorted into two buckets. The first were those who dropped out during or before ninth grade. She called these "early drops," and they accounted for about 35 percent of dropouts in the study.

Meanwhile, a much larger percentage of dropouts were what Roderick called "late drops": students who left school in tenth, eleventh, or twelfth grade. For most of their academic careers, these late drops had not earned significantly lower grades than the students who would eventually graduate in the bottom third of their class. The average fourth-grade GPA among late drops was 2.26, compared with 2.27 among those who graduated from high school in the bottom one-third. Though the grades of dropouts and those of the bottom one-third of graduates both declined dramatically from elementary school to high school, late dropouts had the steepest drop. The transition to high school seemed to do them in.

At the time, she had believed what the popular stereotypes and studies had suggested—that dropouts were fundamentally and academically different from graduates, and that those differences would show up long before high school. But if most drop-outs were virtually indistinguishable from graduates until they entered high school, then perhaps it wasn't the high school dropouts themselves who were the problem, but rather the actual high schools, or something about the transition to them. Her Boston colleagues had their answer—they should begin to focus more intensively on ninth grade, rather than on eighth. But it would take another couple of decades and a series of studies in Roderick's adopted hometown, Chicago, to figure out why.

In April 1995, Roderick and a team of researchers from the University of Chicago began interviewing ninety-eight Chicago eighth graders as they transitioned to high school. She was now an associate professor at the university, teaching statistical research methods to graduate and undergraduate students. The study, which she called the Student Life in High School Project, would begin to provide answers about why ninth grade seemed to be such a turning point for so many teens. At the time, Chicago students were as likely to drop out as they were to graduate. Fifty-fifty odds. A coin flip. Why, at a time when a high school diploma had become a virtual prerequisite for a shot at the middle class, was the average Chicago student unwilling or unable to stay in school long enough to earn a degree?

The Fall River study had provided a starting point—clearly something was happening to students in the transition to high school. But what? Answering that question, Roderick decided, would require talking to students and spending time in schools. She developed a plan to follow Chicago students from the end of eighth grade to the end of tenth grade. She and a team of researchers would interview students once every three months, collect transcript data, and survey their teachers and parents. She hoped these conversations would provide her with some theories about dropping out that she could test quantitatively.

The study got off to a shaky start. Roderick had deliberately chosen to follow students from relatively high-performing elementary schools. Since the average Chicago student who dropped out did so in high school, Roderick wanted to follow average students who seemed like they could go either way when they got to high school. After the first round of interviews in eighth grade, her team panicked, worried that they would not learn anything about the dropout problem by studying these particular students. They were too smart, too motivated, too *good* to drop out.

One clear standout was Malik. More than twenty years later, Malik remains "the kid," the one Roderick names first among all the students who have helped her see children and schools differently. She has taught his case to a new group of graduate students every year for the past two decades.

Malik lived with his father and younger sister on Chicago's South Side. It was a perilous time and place to be fourteen years old. The crack epidemic that had infiltrated Chicago's neighborhoods in the late 1980s was still exacting a deadly toll, particularly on the city's teenagers. The previous year had been the most violent year on record for Chicago's youth. In 1994, 278 children and young people between the ages of eleven and twenty were killed citywide.

Malik stood out among his peers and seemed poised to beat the odds. During his first interview in eighth grade, he came off as charming, confident, and determined. He had crafted an identity around being good—the best, even.

"What are your goals for high school?" one of Roderick's research assistants asked him.

"To be captain of the basketball team headed for valedictorian," he replied.

He said he loved learning and appreciated teachers who held students to high standards, "'cause it makes you wanna push to do better." He added that his friends called him "Little Malcolm X" because he "liked to read a lot of black books."

"How are smart students at your school treated?" the researcher asked.

"Most of the time, they happy for 'em, but some might try to talk about 'em and call them nerds, and things," he explained. "In a way, it's a compliment, 'coz they admittin' that I'm smarter, and it's kind of like they're a little jealous."

"What does that do to you?" the researcher probed.

"It makes me want to do even better and make them even MORE jealous!"

Malik's eighth-grade teachers generally saw him as he saw himself. They identified him as a standout, even though his grades and test scores in elementary school were just average. In a study survey they were asked to complete about Malik, they unanimously agreed that he was likely to go to college and very unlikely to struggle in high school. "Malik is an acute student. He does his work," one teacher noted. "Academically he does well."

During eighth grade Malik had moved in with his father because, as he put it, his mom was drinking and acting "kind of wacko." Loving and strict, Malik's dad made sure Malik attended church regularly and contributed to household duties. He described his own strengths as a parent as "role modeling, work, responsibility, promptness, and consistency." He had dreams that Malik would be a lawyer, though he worried that he would "give up on education, following in his relatives' footsteps and have low motivation in the face of low opportunity."

Malik had opted to enroll at a vocational school on the city's South Side. With an entering class of seven hundred students, it was one of the largest high schools in the city, and it had a solid if not spectacular academic reputation.

Malik's first semester at "South Side High" was not a disaster, but neither was it a triumph. He played on the football team and earned mostly B's and C's—plus an F in algebra. During his interview after the first semester of freshman year, he uttered a line that

Roderick would quote for many years. "I used to be a good math student," Malik lamented. "I mean, I just wonder, how come I can't get that algebra? It just makes me mad that I can't get it."

Roderick loved the line because it neatly summed up the experiences of so many of the students she was following that year. The material wasn't that much different than the material they had mastered in elementary school, and yet they were struggling mightily with it the second time around. The problem, it seemed, actually had very little to do with academics.

In elementary school (most of the elementary schools in Chicago run from kindergarten through eighth grade), teachers taught the same students for much of the day and knew them all personally. They noticed when they were absent, badgered them to get their work in, and provided extra support when they struggled. In high school, students were far more anonymous, in part because there were just so many more of them to keep track of. At the time, the average Chicago student experienced a 500 percent increase in the size of their grade cohort when they entered ninth grade. They were expected to already know how to get themselves to class, turn in their work, seek help when they needed it, and to generally take charge of their own academic futures. The problem was, most of them had never been taught how to do these things.

During Malik's interview after his first semester in high school, he spent a lot of time talking about how much he was struggling with the freedom that had been foisted upon him.

"If you were giving advice to a current eighth grader about high school, what would you tell them?"

"To expect a big change," Malik replied. "The grammar school teachers are more on you about getting your work in. But in high school, if you don't get it in, it's your fault."

At the same time that Roderick and her colleagues were interviewing Chicago students, they were also collecting quantitative data from Chicago Public Schools that showed that Malik's experiences were not an anomaly. Roderick's colleagues at the UChicago

Consortium conducted biennial surveys of students and teachers. One of the striking patterns in the surveys was the extent to which students' engagement in school and perceptions of their teachers dropped off when they entered high school.

Eighth graders reported working hard to complete homework and grapple with new material, and they reported that most of their teachers held them to high standards and were willing to help them with academic or personal issues. As tenth graders, they were less likely to report that their teachers were willing to help them with personal problems, to expect them to do their best all the time, or to encourage extra work when they didn't understand. Like Malik, students across the district were struggling with their newfound level of freedom, which they interpreted as an invitation to work less. When no one seemed to notice or offer additional assistance, they withdrew further.

Derrika, one of the teens who participated in Roderick's study, seemed to speak for many of her classmates when she articulated how her relationship with her teachers had deteriorated during the transition to high school. She said she appreciated her elementary school teachers because "if you don't want to learn, they are going to make you learn." In contrast, her high school teachers seemed to think, "If you fail, you just fail. It ain't our fault. You're the one that's dumb."

After Malik returned from winter break, he started down a path that would lead him further and further away from his goals of being an athletic star and valedictorian. He began skipping classes, particularly his academic prep course, because he didn't like his teacher. His grades went from B's and C's first semester to D's and F's third quarter, making him ineligible to play basketball for the school team. Things got worse from there. During the spring quarter he missed eighteen days of Biology and eight days of Algebra, despite missing only one full day of school. He was almost always in the building—he just chose not to attend those classes, both of which he ended up flunking.

His freshman-year teachers described him in very different terms than his eighth-grade teachers had used. "Student has excellent potential. Student is lackadaisical and little motivated until the last minute to do his work. . . . He does not get serious until time for grades," one teacher wrote.

Malik conceded he had "played" too much freshman year.

"So, tell me about what happened second semester," the researcher prompted him in an interview over the summer between ninth grade and tenth grade.

"You see the problem was, I don't know why I started hanging around two guys and they got to playing cards and then it'd be, like, one of them, like, 'Aw, you can miss this class this one day to go in the lunchroom.' And I do it and that's what messed me up, this following them and trying to do what they do."

He also admitted that he was really struggling to understand algebra.

"Did you ever ask your algebra teacher for help?"

Malik confessed that his pride had prevented him from seeking out assistance. "It wasn't beyond me. I don't never think I need help in nothing."

Malik's dad was disappointed and attempted to right the ship, though by the time he realized just how deep a hole Malik had dug, the damage to his transcript had already been done.

"He been on me a lot and getting me on the right track and I'm on punishment until the end of time," Malik lamented.

"Until the end of time?"

"Until I move out of the house!"

Malik enrolled in summer school and earned his algebra credit. He started sophomore year determined not to repeat the mistakes of freshman year, but his resolution didn't last. Though he continued dutifully to show up at school, once there he only sporadically attended class. Again, he frittered away hours at a time in the cafeteria, playing Spades with friends. He recognized that he was sabotaging himself, but seemed powerless to reverse course.

"What would make you feel better about school?" the researcher asked him.

"Well, if I didn't play so much. If I could just come back, do what I'm supposed to do ... I don't know ... I'm not focused. I'm still really messing up in grades and that. I stay focused for a minute and then I get lazy."

"What do you think it's gonna take to help you get off that particular track?"

"To be honest, I just don't know."

Most of his teachers didn't care whether he showed up or not, Malik insisted. He was particularly negative about his English teacher. "He a white teacher. I guess he just come and occupies the class with the amount of time he's supposed to and then leaves! And you know, he's not too much worried about whether we get ahead in life or not. Every day no more than ten people come. He doesn't seem to care."

Roderick was coming to believe that one of the biggest problems in high school was just how easy it was for Malik and other students in her study to skip class, itself an indication of a larger pattern of benign neglect, if not of outright negligence. Often her subjects were hiding in plain sight—in the cafeteria, outside school, in basement corridors. In addition to Malik, there was Omar, who had a 95 percent attendance rate in elementary school but missed twenty-seven of ninety days in the first semester of ninth grade; and Oscar, who tested two grade levels ahead in math and had perfect attendance in elementary school, but failed freshman-year algebra after missing thirty-nine days of class second semester. During the second semester of freshman year, two-thirds of Malik's classmates across the district missed two or more weeks of instruction in at least one major subject like English or math. And these were not just disaffected students. Forty-two percent of the highest-performing ninth graders in the system missed at least two weeks of class during the second semester in 1996.

Of course, not every teacher took a laissez-faire approach to attendance or learning. Malik's relationship with his sophomore year geometry teacher was an example of how much one teacher could influence whether students engaged in coursework—or not. Malik rarely missed this teacher's class, he explained to Roderick, because she "makes you want to learn."

"She just comes and say, 'You all, I'm making sure you're all learning something. You all ain't gonna be sittin' here doing nothin'.' . . . Even people that don't never do nothin', they somehow find ways to learn. And it's fun the way she teaches us. She makes it a challenge against everybody. She told us at the beginning of the year, two cuts is an automatic F. Scared everybody. Class is full every day. Nobody misses her class."

Malik's geometry teacher came to appreciate him too. "Malik did very little work the first semester. This last marking period, Malik realized he was at risk of failing and has been making more effort, coming for help sometimes during lunch," she wrote in an end-of-the-year evaluation. "I have grown to like Malik a great deal and appreciate his enthusiasm and energy. However, he often frustrates me because, like most sophomore boys, Malik is often silly. But I have seen some growth from Malik this year, which gives me hope for his future."

Malik didn't share her optimism. He could no longer muster a fraction of the confidence that had so defined him in elementary school. His interview after tenth grade was somber. He resisted talking about his future and sounded depressed. "I'm just gonna have to wait 'til I get out of high school 'cause right now, I can't see myself in the future now," he confessed. He spoke almost inaudibly and avoided eye contact.

Malik was barely recognizable as the buoyant fourteen-year-old he had been two years prior. This Malik was talking about himself as if he were a stranger whose motivations were opaque and suspect. "It just feels awkward, not knowing which way I want to go," he said. "But I wanna do the right thing. . . . I know it just seems hard for me. When I was a little kid, I was so focused on doing good at school. But now in high school, to be honest, I don't even care about the future no more.

"You can get into the habit of not doing it right and then when you know it's time for you to do right, it's just so hard for you to do it. It's just like, 'I'm trapped, man!'"

He concluded his sad soliloquy. "I never wanted to be a lawyer anyway. That was my parents' dream."

In the winter of eleventh grade, Malik dropped out of high school. The researchers lost track of him, though they believe he went on to earn his GED from an alternative high school.

Malik's story neatly illustrates the findings from Roderick's Fall River research by showing that ninth grade was Malik's make-or-break year for high school graduation. Prior to ninth grade, there was no way to predict that a kid like Malik would drop out of high school.

Malik's experiences also help explain why ninth grade is such a pivotal year for students. At the very time he was trying to figure out who he was—as a student, a learner, and a person in this world—he had failed. He was no longer the "Little Malcolm X" to his teachers and friends. He was a screwup wasting his potential. Afraid that asking for help would signal that he wasn't smart enough, he remained silent, hiding out in the cafeteria, which exacerbated his academic problems.

Roderick knew something about how that felt. She had hid out too. The difference was, someone had found her. As a freshman at Bowdoin, she had felt like an oddity. She was a lesbian in a school that didn't admit its first fully coed class until 1971; a working-class Portuguese kid among the WASP-y offspring of doctors and lawyers. She had enrolled in a freshman seminar on James Joyce and couldn't understand a thing the teacher or other students were saying. She had no idea how to write a paper longer than two pages or to prepare for a class discussion. She went from being something of a local superstar to being miserable and close to dropping out.

On Friday nights she had a routine that she had carried over from high school. As her classmates partied, she would retreat to the

library stacks and read through the great works of American literature. The books tethered her to her life before college and reminded
her that there was a vast and varied world beyond campus. One
Friday night, a young, female African American professor found
her in the stacks. Roderick was reading a book by Alice Walker. The
two struck up a conversation. The professor was impressed by
Roderick's passion for literature, and a friendship developed. Roderick admitted that she was struggling in her classes. The professor
assured her that she was plenty smart—she simply needed to learn
how to be a student. She offered her help, and Roderick accepted.
The professor demystified *Ulysses* for her. She explained that it was
based on a Greek myth and that it was about transubstantiation, a
matter that a Catholic kid from Fall River knew something about.
She told Roderick to talk about her ideas and she would help her
get them on paper. She taught her to write a cogent essay and gave
her the confidence to speak up in class.

"She totally saved me," Roderick said. "She saved my life."

The fact that nobody had done the same for Malik appalled her.
More than two decades later, she still can't talk about the kids from
that study without getting very sad or angry. The initial panic
among the researchers, that the kids they were interviewing were
not the types of students who would struggle with school, proved to
be unfounded. Ultimately, about half the students Roderick followed
dropped out, almost perfectly matching the dropout rate for the district as a whole. It was good for the study and utterly depressing for
the researchers involved.

Among the most devastating case studies was the story of Alex,
the kid that Roderick became most personally invested in over the
course of the study. When Roderick met Alex in eighth grade, he
seemed betwixt and between, not yet an adult but no longer a child,
not particularly engaged in school but grimly determined to earn a
high school diploma and support his mom and four younger sisters.
Roderick jotted down these cursory impressions of Alex after their
first meeting: "Student is small and thin. Shaved head. Baggy clothes.

He seems very serious and appears more mature than his age. He appears to be the 'man of the family' and supports his mother. No father is mentioned in the interview. . . . Student appears to be struggling with gangs and his own discipline problems. It is also clear that he is very bright."

Alex lived on Chicago's West Side in a largely Latino neighborhood where more than a dozen street gangs battled for control. Over the summer between eighth and ninth grades, Alex lost two friends to gang violence. Despite loads of circumstantial evidence to the contrary, Alex claimed he was not in a gang. "Just because we live here, they think we're gangsters. I can't do nothing. I mean, I live here. That's all," he told Roderick. He worried about going to his neighborhood high school, "West Side," where he believed he would be a target. "I don't like it over there," he told Roderick. "There's a lot of gangs over there."

West Side was about a mile from Alex's house. The majority of its students, like Alex, were Latinos from low-income immigrant families. The fact that West Side wasn't doing well by its students was evident to even a casual observer. The school was huge and chaotic. It was on four different bell schedules, making it a constant struggle to work out where a particular student or teacher might be at any given time. Students came and went throughout the day, and teachers wheeled all their materials from classroom to classroom on portable carts. During one visit to West Side, Roderick recalled walking by seven consecutive classrooms and finding absolutely nothing going on in any of them, except a fight in one. The area surrounding the school was so dangerous that students would race from the school's parking lot to the bus stop at a dead sprint, moving as if their lives depended on it. Sometimes they did.

When Roderick went to conduct her first ninth-grade interview with Alex in October, she found him "beside himself." He told her that he was regularly being threatened and beaten up, both at school and around it. Someone had even pulled a gun on him and his brother while they were on their way to school one day. He sounded defeated, declaring there was no point in asking adults for help. No one at school could do anything, he said dejectedly. "I'm all alone." Later, Roderick found out that he had appealed for help from some adults at the school, but they had dismissed his concerns because they believed he was a gang member. Alarmed, Roderick sent her own memo to the principal informing her that Alex was being physically threatened in and around school. As far as she knows, nothing ever came of it.

Alex was also clashing with his teachers. He especially disliked his English teacher, whom he considered to be a bully. He was galled in particular by one incident that had taken place in that class. A physically imposing boy had started a fight with a much smaller boy. Alex said the whole class witnessed the larger boy beating on the smaller one, but the English teacher had blamed the smaller boy and sent him to the office. Alex was convinced that the teacher had sided with the larger boy because he intimidated the teacher.

Alex responded by disengaging in English class. "I don't do nothing, 'cause he don't respect me," Alex told Roderick. Though he continued to attend school regularly, he had already resigned himself to the likelihood of having to repeat classes in summer school. Alex ended first semester of freshman year with C's and D's in all of his subjects except English, which he failed. Second semester was worse. By the winter quarter, Alex was attending school sporadically and, by his own admission, rarely completing any assignments. He ended freshman year with D's in Biology and Typing and F's in History, English, and Algebra. In order to catch up, he would have to do twice the work, making up old classes while also staying on top of his sophomore-year classes.

When Roderick interviewed Alex during the summer between ninth and tenth grades, he appeared clinically depressed. He talked about gang pressures and his desire to switch schools. While he talked, he rested his head on the table, barely making eye contact.

"How about you? You have to think about yourself, including good, bad, or okay. How do you feel about yourself?" Roderick asked.

"I feel bad," he answered succinctly.

"Why?"

"'Cause, I feel like I ain't going nowhere," Alex said.

"So, what do you mean?"

"I'm in the same place," he reiterated.

"You're in the same place as what?"

"Like, I always live, I always live right here . . . ," he said, trailing off, the last part of his comment inaudible.

"And you've been feeling that way?" Roderick said.

"No, it just started."

"In the future you want to sort of get out of here, right?"

"Yeah, make something out of myself, that's what I'm trying to say."

"But why don't you feel like you're making something of yourself right now?"

"I don't know," Alex responded morosely.

He begged Roderick to help him switch schools, but she knew it wouldn't be easy. His grades disqualified him from most of the city's magnet programs, and most open-enrollment schools near his house were overcrowded. It was unlikely that a principal was going to take a chance on Alex. A week into the school year, Roderick received a message on her answering machine from Alex asking her to call him immediately. When she connected with him later that day, the story spilled forth. One of his best friends had been shot and killed days after being initiated into a gang. Gang members had also been harassing his brother as he walked to school. His mother was distraught and had ordered both boys to stop going to school. Again, Alex pleaded with Roderick to help him change schools.

Roderick stepped up her efforts and called in a favor from a colleague on the Board of Education. The board member called in a favor at the magnet school that Alex was eager to attend. The school had a strong arts program, a multiracial population, and an excellent principal. It also had a reputation for having teachers who reached out to students who were struggling. Roderick went with Alex and his mom to West Side High to formalize the transfer process. The vice principal told Roderick he was glad to see Alex go.

Alex didn't immediately thrive at his new school, but he did find teachers and administrators who were supportive of him and more willing to intervene when he was in trouble. When he told his counselor that he was being harassed by some gang members, she had security escort him to the bus. And when he told his gym teacher that he was thinking about dropping out, she encouraged him to stick with it. Alex described the difference between his old school and his new school in a hopeful interview with Roderick in the middle of sophomore year.

"I was talking to her and she's like . . . you know, 'Keep on coming to school,' you know. 'I know you're a smart guy.' So . . . I guess . . . I'm not really sure, but I guess if it wasn't for her, I mean . . . I don't know . . . so I really liked that and—"

Roderick interrupted, "Did she have any ideas about what to do with the gang stuff?"

"No, not really . . . but she just told me, you know, 'Keep it up' . . .'cause . . . and now . . . I've been doing good . . . so, yeah."

He also loved his English teacher, who gave meaty writing and reading assignments and kept the class engaged and laughing.

"So, in general it sounds like you're liking your teachers better than last year?" Roderick asked.

"Yeah."

"You certainly like this English teacher better than the last one!"

"Oh yeah. *Oh yeah*," Alex agreed, laughing.

"How about the school in general though? Do you think teachers are in general better or nicer or—"

"Mmm . . . I think they're better . . .'cause they get into it . . . they get into the students."

"They like the students," Roderick supplied.

"Yeah."

Roderick's final interview with Alex took place about a month before the end of his sophomore year. When she called to set up the interview, she thought he sounded excited to see her. When she arrived, she found him "ebullient." The principal at his school had recently established a night program for students like Alex who were many credits short of graduation. Alex was working hard in the classes and had also recently secured a job at a fast-food restaurant. He told Roderick that this school year had been "a good struggle." "He was beside himself with pride," Roderick recalled. He also was concerned about his friends and brother whom he had left behind at West Side.

"So . . . a lotta your friends have dropped out," Roderick ventured.

"Yeah. . . . They will tell me to go with them, to join with them," Alex admitted.

"Why'd they all drop out?" Roderick asked.

"Of West Side? Ahhh, 'cause of West Side!"

"And you stayed in [school]?" Roderick prompted.

"'Cause, 'cause I had you!"

"Right. . . ."

"It wasn't for you, I woulda been outside right now."

Roderick was flattered and also surprised that her efforts had meant so much to him. Alex concluded the interview with a plea to help some of his friends and his brother return to school. He was particularly concerned about his brother, who had recently been in trouble with the police. Roderick promised to try. The thing Roderick remembers most from that interview and Alex's earlier ones was his "care for other people, his constantly saying, 'This is not just about me.'" In interview after interview, he insisted that he did not just want to improve things for himself, but for all the kids at West Side High and in his neighborhood.

"Do you think your friends are pretty supportive of what you've done this year?" Roderick asked during that final interview.

"Yeah."

"They feel good about you?"

"Yeah, but I don't want that. I don't want them to look up to me. I want for all of us to go up together."

"Together," Roderick echoed.

"Right *now*."

A month later, he was dead.

On the last day of school, Alex left early and hitched a ride with friends to a park near his home. He stopped to talk to a group of his brother's friends gathered on the corner. Around 11:00 a.m., a car pulled through an alley. A boy jumped out and pointed a gun at his head. He shot twice. Alex lived one more day. They never caught his killer, though there was speculation that the shooting might have been payback for something involving his brother, who had become increasingly enmeshed with gangs while at West Side.

On his last report card, Alex received an A in English, a B in History, and C's in his Computer and Geometry classes. His history teacher said of his performance, "Alex went from an F quarter one to a C quarter two, and quarter three to a B. He has improved tremendously. I'm not sure why." Roderick thought she did know the secret behind Alex's turnaround. Alex hadn't changed, but his surroundings had. He had found a school where he felt known and supported, where adults focused on the best, rather than the worst, version of him, a school determined to prevent failure.

Based on the interview data and quantitative data on all the ninth graders who had entered high school in fall 1992, Roderick and other UChicago researchers published *Charting Reform in Chicago: The Students Speak*, a scathing report on the state of city high schools. The report found that freshman year in Chicago was, in a word, disastrous. Ninth-grade failure was so widespread, so routine, that it had to be considered an institutional breakdown. Fully 42 percent of freshmen failed at least one course freshman year. Half of all males failed a course during their first semester. At one particularly troubled high school on Chicago's far West Side, 70 percent of the freshmen failed a course first semester of freshman year. Across the entire system, students who entered high school performing *at grade level*, precisely where they should be from an academic standpoint, still had a 30 percent chance of failing a class freshman year.

The study had uncovered a litany of challenges: vulnerable students, a treacherous transition to high school, and a total disconnect between students and staff at many high schools. Teachers didn't really know their kids, and kids didn't really know their teachers. The report's final paragraph is at once an indictment of Chicago's high schools and a call to action. "The overall picture that emerges from this analysis is one of broad-based institutional failure in response to students' needs—a failure to help students succeed during the transition, a failure to help students recover when they encounter difficulty, and more broadly, a failure to encourage students to form strong attachments to their school and build upon their strengths. Unless these deep-seated problems are addressed, the future for many students will be in jeopardy."

Roderick's takeaway from the study was one part analytical, one part moral outrage. Students were not ready to navigate the underregulated, often chaotic world of high school, and it was indefensible that nobody was helping them learn. "No one said to them, 'You're super smart, man. Let's just catch you up. You just don't know how to do the work—yet.' And they just imploded. We do this to kids all the time," Roderick reflected bitterly. In her opinion, the adults in the building had a moral obligation to do everything in their power to prevent students from failing, and they had failed.

Obligation, the notion that to whom much is given, much is expected, is one of the virtues that run through Roderick's stories, which are always teetering on the edge of parable. During an interview in her Chicago home, Roderick explained that she uses the case studies from the Student Life in High School Project to teach about the limits of personal resiliency, particularly the resiliency of teenagers. "You can't be resilient *all the time*," she railed, her voice rising. "Communities *have to come together*." This reminds her of another story about the need to create systems and structures that ensure young people succeed, rather than expecting them to manufacture their own success, which was one of the key lessons she learned from Malik and Alex and their classmates.

"There's this amazing story," she began. "I was interviewing kids from North Side High. The principal grabbed me and said, 'I have a big problem. My valedictorian, who is homeless, got rejected from college.' So I called up Penny [Sebring, a colleague] from Grinnell [College] . . . and the Grinnell president fell in love with her. She got a full ride. Graduated two years ago. And one day I told the story to M.A. [Pitcher, another colleague], who started yelling at me, 'LISTEN, are you going to save ONE KID AT A TIME, or create a SYSTEM that saves THEM ALL?'"

CHAPTER 2

"Afraid"

I tried to put those pants on
But they just didn't anymore
As I remember the 80 pounds that I patched on under
     my skin
Over the last 8 years
They were misfits
Individually missed understood

The best or the worst
The last or the first
The hunger or the thirst
The blessing or the curse
Not sure what to expect from this relationship
Uncertain of words should part my lips
I try to put on the pants again
But they still would not fit

I don't know what I want
But I know how I feel
All I want is to fit the pants I love
But pants promoted me

As my waist got bigger I
Trained
The question is will I take the risk to

Feel the beats of your heart
And listen to the sound
Interpret the rhythm
Let the music to speak to mind
As I relish the thought
That I am older now
Short summer
High School
New people
Different Colored Walls

Afraid I am
I am afraid
I must admit
I must admit

—Maurice Swinney

Fourteen-year-old Maurice Swinney went right ahead and called Ms. Strickland a bitch. In 1994, Strickland was a math teacher at Walter L. Cohen High School in New Orleans, and Swinney was a smart freshman with a smart mouth. One day midyear he disrupted her class, not for the first time, and she ordered him to move seats. "I ain't movin,' no fuckin' way," he declared. He got suspended. His mother was called to school and chewed him out. When he returned from suspension, Ms. Strickland told him, "You sit next to me now." The next few days she made a point of stopping by his desk and making sure he was able to complete his makeup work. Soon after, his English teacher, Ms. Murray, invited him to join the school's Future Teacher's Club. She and Ms. Strickland had formulated a little plan for Maurice, a born leader who for better or for worse could set the tone for the entire class. "You love to talk," Ms. Murray observed. "This is where you belong."

Two decades later, Swinney, thirty-seven, was the principal of Edward Tilden High School on Chicago's South Side. It was possible—indeed probable, if history was any guide—that one of his students would call him a bitch or worse this school year. When that happened, he would remind himself that it wasn't personal, just as it hadn't been personal when he had cussed out Ms. Strickland. Twenty-one years later, he can still remember how discordant he felt that day, the notes in his head all sharps and flats, "like I was 'on 10.'"

During his freshman year in high school, his mother left his father and moved with Maurice and his siblings to live with his grandmother in public housing. The night before his flare-up with Ms. Strickland, his father had come looking for them. He banged on the windows for what seemed like hours, calling his mama's name for all the neighbors to hear.

Now, when a student cussed Swinney out, he would try his best to remember how he felt that day when he walked into Ms. Strickland's classroom, like a hammer looking for a nail to pound as hard as he could until he didn't feel like pounding anything anymore, not even his dad. He would try to remember that Ms. Strickland had managed to look at his "little punk ass" and see a future teacher. And he would try very hard to remember, because it was easy to forget when being an educator came so naturally to him, that he could have just as easily not been the first in his family to graduate from college, not managed to secure a comfortable professional lifestyle, not landed on a career that challenged and inspired him. Then he would shift a benevolent gaze onto the kid who had just called him a motherfucker, and he would squint until he was able to see a future firefighter or entrepreneur or educator.

On a cloudless day in mid-August, the type of day that compels Chicagoans to soak up enough sunshine to sustain them on blustery

El platforms in February, Swinney had sequestered himself inside his second-floor office with the windows shut and the air conditioning humming. It was a month before the start of the 2015–16 school year, Swinney's fourth at Tilden.

Tilden is located in the Canaryville neighborhood on Chicago's South Side, about six miles south of the city's bustling downtown and four miles west of the city's sparkling lakefront. Its massive three-story brick building reflects both the lofty aspirations of public education and its sometimes bleak realities. It was built at the beginning of the twentieth century to serve the sons of middle-class managers and the growing immigrant workforce of the nearby Union Stockyards, made famous by Upton Sinclair's *The Jungle*. At the time, the Union Stockyards was at the heart of the city's meatpacking industry; Chicago was Hog Butcher for the World; and Tilden was the neighborhood jewel, a technical high school for boys, meant to train the next generation of architects, engineers, and tradesmen who would bend and shape the City of Big Shoulders into a more perfect version of itself.

Tilden's grand classical design testifies to the community's ambition at the time to "furnish facilities for the very best instruction, and in a neighborhood where the children are eager for an education and appreciate every privilege afforded to secure the same." The entryway is flanked by elaborate stone pediments and Ionic pillars, which stand like concrete commitments to the children who pass through them. The entryway leads to a soaring foyer with murals depicting famous midwestern architects and engineers and with inspirational quotes about the value of hard work and artistic passion. In one mural, the city's skyline stretches toward pastel clouds of early dawn. Underneath, a quote from famed Chicago architect Daniel Burnham exhorts:

MAKE NO LITTLE PLANS
THEY HAVE NO POWER TO STIR MEN'S BLOOD
MAKE BIG PLANS
AIM HIGH IN HOPE AND WORK

But Tilden's glory is now mostly faded. Though the murals have recently been refurbished, the rest of the building cries out for a new coat of paint. The exterior limestone is graying, the sidewalks surrounding the building are cracked, and the first-floor windows are covered in chain link. The classrooms are usually too cold, except during the first and last few weeks of school, when they are too hot. A metal detector has been a fixture in the foyer since 1992, when a Tilden student smuggled a gun into the school and fatally shot another student over a gambling debt incurred during a dice game in the school washroom. The Tilden shooting prompted a citywide security crackdown in schools. Ever since, students and visitors at Chicago high schools have been forced to empty their pockets, place their bags on a moving X-ray machine, and step through a metal detector that screens for guns or knives. It can be positively vertigo-inducing to contemplate the entryway murals while walking through the Tilden metal detector.

Swinney has worked to put his own imprint on the school and exorcise some of the Ghosts of Tilden Past. One of the first orders of business he undertook when he became the principal was to remove the portrait gallery of paintings of former Tilden principals that lined the main office. "I was like, 'Take it down. We're not about to be looking at old dead people all day,'" he recalled. Now an informal painting done by a student hangs over the entrance to the main office.

Inside Swinney's private office, which is painted Mardi-Gras purple and yellow, a large whiteboard with boxes, arrows, and other dry-erase hieroglyphics on it neatly mapped out roles and responsibilities for the year ahead. The markings represented a valiant effort to stave off the chaos Swinney knew would ensue when students returned in September. When Swinney is anxious, he organizes and tidies. On this day, every surface in the office was clear, save for a few neat stacks of paper.

He was nervous in particular about his incoming freshmen. Swinney had arrived in Chicago already thoroughly convinced that freshman year was the make-or-break year for succeeding in high school and beyond. His first administrative post was as the ninth-grade associate principal at St. Amant, a high school outside Baton Rouge, where he was responsible for shepherding five hundred students through "Year 9," as they called it in Louisiana. Swinney understood how freshman year forced students to reinvent themselves, and how precarious that reinvention could be.

He penned the poem at the beginning of this chapter after his first year at St. Amant, drawing on his students' experiences and his own. He remembered how high school had made him feel unfamiliar in his own skin and how Ms. Strickland had presented him with a new identity—future teacher—that fit just right. He wanted to do the same for his freshmen.

Trying on and shedding identities is a hallmark of adolescence, and one of the reasons why ninth grade is such a critical inflection point for students. "Contrary to naïve but widely held beliefs that identities represent stable, intrinsic properties, humans, including and especially teenagers, develop their identities in a fluid process through interactions with other people over time," writes Robert Crosnoe, the chair of the Sociology Department at the University of Texas. Crosnoe wrote the definitive book on how students' social lives impact their educational trajectories. Identity is the "linchpin" between the social aspect of high school (relationships among students, and between students and teachers) and academic performance. Students who believe that they do not belong in high school tend to adopt coping mechanisms, such as skipping school, that harm their academic performance.

Other researchers have also found that identity plays a key role in determining whether students remain in school or drop out. In a study of Latino teenagers at a Chicago high school conducted around the same time as Roderick's Chicago study was conducted, researcher Nilda Flores-Gonzalez found that teenagers who stayed had defined themselves as "school kids," while those who left had defined themselves as "street kids." Like Roderick, Flores-Gonzalez found that schools could "make or break the school-kid identity by offering different educational experiences to students," such as challenging classes or close, personal relationships with teachers.

Ninth grade, in particular, presented an inflection point for teenagers because they were exposed to a whole new set of social relationships and cues about who they were and where they belonged. For Malik, the "Little Malcolm X" from Roderick's study who had aspired to be valedictorian, the transition to high school led to a gradual fraying of his relationship to school and a dramatic shift in how he saw himself as a student. But ninth grade could work the other way, too, offering students a fresh opportunity to craft a new identity and connect to school in new ways.

Swinney had learned through trial and error in Louisiana that a critical step in that process was binding students to the larger school community right from the first day of high school. "Year nine is one of the most critical in determining success in school, and in life," Swinney had warned St. Amant freshmen and their parents in 2011, exactly four years ago to the day, back when he had been an associate principal at the Louisiana school. The families had crowded onto the bleachers of the Golden Dome, St. Amant's gym, for freshman orientation. Called Swamp Fest, the day was part information session, part pep rally. Even the local newspaper was on hand to cover the festivities. Peer mentors, dressed in mud-colored fatigues and orange sweatbands, guided the freshmen under a balloon-covered archway as cheerleaders in gold and black uniforms executed well-choreographed cheers.

Later, the freshmen broke into smaller groups and the peer mentors led them in getting-to-know-you games that were mostly silly and a little self-revelatory. They answered questions like "Would you rather be sucked up by a tornado or swallowed by a blue whale?" and "Is there anything you want to change about yourself?"

The peer mentors also walked the freshmen through the highlights of St. Amant's *What Every Freshman Should Know* handbook, which included a map and such critical information as the location of the pizza line in the cafeteria. To parents, Swinney would explain the ins and outs of credit accumulation, the various diploma paths, and St. Amant's Freshman Academy, a school within a school for freshmen that was designed to make sure ninth graders didn't get lost in the shuffle. "We want every student to belong, and ninth grade is about figuring out what works for each student," he assured them.

By the time Swamp Fest rolled around, Swinney would already be well on his way toward figuring out what worked for each student, even if he couldn't yet pick any of them out of a crowd. Each summer, he visited St. Amant's elementary feeder schools to interview principals and teachers. From these conversations he would collect a few key facts about every student, from their favorite activities to their home situations. The information he gathered figured into class assignments and allowed him to flag students who might need a little extra support during the transition to high school.

At St. Amant, Swinney had considered himself to be very good at his job. Ninety percent of his freshmen went on to graduate from high school, and two-thirds enrolled in college directly from high school. But in Chicago, he was less convinced of his effectiveness. "In my first year, I think I failed, I've got to be honest," Swinney said during the interview in his office. Analytical and self-reflective, Swinney was usually hardest on himself. When he talked about successes, he tended to say "we." When he talked about failures, he reverted to "I." He wasn't convinced that he was meeting his own considerable expectations for what Tilden could and should be.

One challenge he faced was that many of the strategies he had developed in Louisiana simply didn't translate to Chicago. Swinney's Louisiana students grew up knowing they would one day attend St. Amant High School, the sole public high school serving the unincorporated community of St. Amant. Most of his Tilden freshmen had no affiliation with the school until the day they enrolled. As many large urban districts in recent years had done, Chicago had instituted school "choice," which allows students to crisscross the city in search of the best fit, rather than assigning them to their neighborhood school. One result has been that traditional feeder patterns no longer apply. Tilden drew students from dozens of elementary schools across the city, and many of those students did not make a final decision until weeks or days before the first day of school, or, in some cases, well after the first day of school. The most current roster that Swinney was in possession of could optimistically be described as an educated guess.

"It's pretty freaking interesting, right? Neighborhoods have been completely deconstructed in terms of education," Swinney said, walking toward the office bookshelf that housed his professional library. "All my learning from Louisiana sort of went out the window."

The titles on the shelf provide a glimpse into his personal and professional priorities. Many are about motivation—how to motivate teachers to work together, how to get struggling students to try, and how to encourage teens raised on a steady media diet to engage in serious academic work. Some of the books are technical, some religious, some closer to self-help—from Rick Warren's *The Purpose Driven Life* and *Start with Why: How Great Leaders Inspire Everyone to Take Action*, to *Hip-Hop Generation* and *Chicken Soup for the Teacher's Soul*. The lone fictional works are a volume of short stories by African American writers and Harper Lee's *To Kill a Mockingbird*. From the shelf, he took down a large binder that he had received as part of a leadership course at the International Center for Leadership in Education. "This is one of the books that really helped develop my thinking around the ninth grade," he said. Its premise is that every freshman should feel "known, valued, and inspired." He'd had a knack for doing just that for St. Amant's kids, as grateful letters from former students—many tacked up to his office bulletin board—attested.

Figuring out what worked for Tilden's students was trickier, primarily because many of them had had negative experiences with school in the past. "We have to take away the option to fail, which is very hard," Swinney reflected. "Many of our kids are like, 'I've had an F before, this doesn't hurt me.' It's kind of like watching movies and watching people get shot in the head. We're so desensitized to it." While his St. Amant kids had fallen all along the academic spectrum, Tilden students were mostly concentrated at the very bottom in terms of their elementary grades and test scores. Chicago's public schools, long highly segregated by race and class, had become even more stratified since the city had embarked on its radical experiment in school choice.

Traditionally, the American public education system has been defined by strict neighborhood attendance boundaries for every school, with students assigned to the elementary and high schools closest to their homes. But in the 2000s, many school districts, particularly in large cities, began to challenge the supremacy of geography in school assignment. Policymakers argued that neighborhood boundaries disenfranchised low-income families, who were often stuck in the lowest-performing schools. They argued that doing away with boundaries would allow parents to access higher-performing or specialized schools that were the best fit for their children, injecting competition into what some considered to be a public monopoly. The hope was that school choice would spur broad-based improvement as schools were forced to compete for students and funding.

Chicago was at the forefront of the school choice movement, pursuing what Paul Hill at the University of Washington Center on Reinventing Public Education termed a "portfolio approach." As part of CPS CEO Arne Duncan's "Renaissance 2010" plan, the city opened more than one hundred new schools, mostly through charters that allow public funding to flow to privately operated schools that admit students via random lottery. The city also opened new selective enrollment schools, which drew the top performers from throughout the city. And the city established magnet schools and specialized programs within existing schools, from military academies to career and technical education programs. In 2004, Chicago had 88 high schools and 99,275 high-schoolers. In 2015–16, the city had 140 high schools for 100,670 students. Less than one-quarter of Chicago's high-schoolers now attend their neighborhood high school. Many ride public transportation for more than an hour to attend high school.

Whether or not school choice has spurred academic improvement in Chicago is an open question and a source of highly contentious debate. But one clear result is a school system that is more segregated than ever before by achievement and by parents' ability to navigate an increasingly complex system.

An implicit citywide pecking order among schools has developed. Selective enrollment schools occupy the top spot, and draw from the entire city. Next are the high-performing magnet schools with specialized programs, many of which also have performance requirements and often fill up quickly. Charter schools, particularly those in well-established charter networks, are next. They choose their students via lottery and often have long waiting lists. These schools rarely have to accept students after the first day of school, as Swinney does.

At the bottom—at least in terms of public perception—are neighborhood schools like Tilden, located in high-poverty neighborhoods. Neighborhood schools must take all comers from within their boundaries, as well as students from outside their boundaries so long as there are openings, which there generally are, particularly on the South and West Sides in predominantly African American neighborhoods. Chicagoans have taken to calling these "schools of last resort." "CPS is a caste system, and we're at the bottom," Swinney acknowledged.

Only a handful of high-school-age students who live within the school's geographic boundary actually attend Tilden (8 percent in 2015–16, down from 28 percent a decade prior). Swinney knew that the local elementary schools advise students not to attend Tilden. "Tilden has a terrible reputation because of things that happened in the '90s," Swinney conceded. "I am always hearing stories about things that happened years ago. I tell people I'm the principal at Tilden, and they're like, 'Oh my God!'"

In many ways, that reputation is out of date. Since Swinney arrived, college enrollment rates and ACT scores have improved slightly. Attendance is way up and fights are way down. The hallways often seem deserted, since just 311 students attend a school designed to hold 2,000—one consequence of school choice has been the radical depopulation of certain schools—and rarely particularly chaotic. The school's library now houses Tilden's "Convergence Academy," a welcoming, high-tech space featuring Apple computers and tablets, digital cameras, a recording studio, and 3-D printers. The Academy, a partnership with Chicago's Columbia College, is designed to turn Tilden students into savvy creators and consumers of digital media.

Moreover, Swinney has worked hard to make Tilden a school that specializes in serving students living in extraordinary circumstances, which most Tilden students do in one form or another. Nearly all Tilden students are considered low-income, meaning that their families receive public assistance or they are eligible for free- or reduced-price lunches, or they live in foster care. Most CPS students are poor by this definition, but Tilden students generally face a constellation of challenges that compound the effects of poverty. Swinney estimates that 90 percent of his students have experienced some sort of trauma—abuse, homelessness, or gun violence, for example. Forty percent have a designated learning disability. Twenty percent do not have a permanent place to call home.

In order to get these students on the path to graduation, Swinney must prevent the typical academic dip between eighth and ninth grade that Roderick's research had documented. Yet more challenging still, he must help them perform significantly better than most of them did in eighth grade. Two years prior, he and his staff had been wildly successful. In the 2013–14 school year, 82 percent of Tilden freshmen had finished the year on-track to graduate, above the district average despite Tilden's serving a much more disadvantaged population.

Swinney was already worried that he wouldn't be able to duplicate the success of previous years, in part because he simply did not have the resources he had relied on to get the job done. In 2013, the district had moved to a student-based budgeting system where dollars follow kids to school. His shrinking enrollment meant a shrinking budget. Moreover, a federal grant that had provided the school with $6 million over three years had expired. Swinney had used the grant to pay for a full-time Freshman OnTrack coordinator and other supports for students. This year he gave the role to Sharon Holmes, an English teacher who already had a full course load.

"There's some vulnerability. I have to say, I don't know how we're going to do all this again. We're probably going to slip a bit," he said. "You experience compassion fatigue. You get tired. And you have to run the race until the end." Now there was a new race to run with a new group of freshmen.

Swinney had finished the previous school year feeling depleted, and the summer had done little to boost his reserves. When he wasn't planning for the upcoming school year, he was working on his dissertation for his doctorate in education. The topic of his dissertation was how to re-engage youth who had dropped out of school. He had spent a few weeks home in Louisiana over the summer, but that hadn't been particularly restful either. His father was terminally ill with cancer, and his grief was complicated by their difficult relationship.

Swinney took a deep breath and flashed his signature smile, which was wide and warm and made his eyes crinkle. "I think what's keeping me going—what's keeping us going—is that we have become better at recognizing that if we don't give kids the chance now, they might never get it," he said. "The anguish is worthy of the outcome."

In a sea of khaki pants and blue-collared Tilden shirts, Marcus stood out. He was handsome, with short, tight dreadlocks, large almond-shaped eyes, and a wide, perfect smile. Newly fifteen, his physique had recently rounded the corner from baby fat to solid muscle. He wore a diamond-shaped stud twice the size of his earlobe and a bedazzled crucifix. He had two tattoos emblazoned on his arms honoring family members. From the first week of school, the other freshmen seemed to orbit around him, trying to catch some of his light. After one all-school assembly, he performed an exuberant front flip off of the stage. He stuck the landing.

One day during this first week of the 2015–16 school year, Swinney walked alongside Marcus in the hallway and placed a friendly hand on his shoulder. Marcus was visibly startled. "Are you okay?" Swinney asked. "Yeah, I just don't like to be touched," Marcus responded politely but firmly. Swinney couldn't recall another student reacting so viscerally to a pat on the back. He wondered about the history behind that reaction.

Swinney didn't have much to go on at that point. He knew Marcus had opted to come to Tilden at the last minute. His transcript revealed that he had attended two different elementary schools, one of which had expelled him, and had earned top grades until partway through elementary school, when A's turned to D's and F's. Marcus and two other freshmen boys from the neighborhood had come to Tilden together and moved as a pack through the halls and cafeteria, roughhousing and posing for selfies that often included a raised middle finger or coordinated gang signs.

Ms. Holmes, the Freshman English teacher, also took special notice of Marcus, although not because of his exuberance. During the first month of school, he cried nearly every day in her class. Some days he would put his head down on his desk for the entire period. Only the occasional sniff revealed that he was crying, not sleeping. On other days, he would stare straight ahead as silent tears leaked from his eyes and wound a circuitous path down and around his cheeks. He seemed unembarrassed, never bothering to hide them or wipe them away. Other kids were mercilessly teased for such public displays of emotion, but not Marcus. His classmates gave him a wide berth and tactfully ignored his tears. Holmes would make a point of acknowledging that he was upset. "I see you," she would say. "Let me know if you need some space." Once in a while he would say, "Ms. Holmes, I need to step out." Then he would pace up and down the hallway. Sometimes a loud clang of his foot or fist hitting a locker would reverberate through the empty corridor.

One October day, about a month into the school year, Holmes spied Marcus smoking a joint on a corner a mile from school as she dropped off a couple of students she had taught the previous year at their houses.

"Marcus," she shouted out her window. "What are you doing? Put that cigarette out!" She knew it was marijuana but thought it imprudent to holler at him across the street about illegal drug use.

"Oh, it's not a cigarette, Ms. Holmes," Marcus called back sweetly.

"I'm going to choose to believe that is a cigarette, and I want you to put it out *right now*," Holmes insisted. "And you're going to stop smoking because I don't like that."

"All right, all right, Ms. Holmes," Marcus conceded with a smile. He put out the joint.

The next day in class, Marcus said, "Ms. Holmes, you gotta be careful when you roll up on people like that. You could get shot."

"Oh, I wasn't worried, Marcus. I knew you would take care of me. But I'm real glad you put that *cigarette* out," she said, with a wink.

He let out a big laugh. From then on, Ms. Holmes could ask him to do just about anything, and he'd do it.

Holmes was a teacher who conceptualized her role broadly. Her job wasn't simply about teaching students how to write a five-paragraph essay, it was also about convincing students that they belonged in school. To that end, she tried to make every interaction with students a positive one, even when she stumbled upon them smoking a joint. This philosophy was why Swinney had made her the leader of Tilden's Freshman Success Team, a group of teachers and staff responsible for ensuring that every ninth grader earned enough credits to advance to sophomore year. The creation of such a position was a key development in Chicago's movement to improve the number of freshmen on-track to graduate.

Holmes knew the story behind the story of every kid at Tilden. She was, as she put it, always "ear hustling," eavesdropping on students' semi-private conversations. She lurked unapologetically on their Facebook pages, and chastised students who posted selfies smoking pot or flashing gang signs. She teased, cajoled, and sometimes yelled at them, and they loved her for it. Her class inevitably started five minutes late as she emptied the room of students who were not in fact assigned to her class that period but had popped in to receive a hug, to gossip, or just to linger silently, eager for acknowledgment. Occasionally, students would wander into her class mid-period and plop themselves down at an empty desk, having ditched or been booted from another class. "GO! Shoo! *Shoo!* Where are you supposed to be? Get out of here! I don't *LIKE* little kids!" she would say with mock exasperation. "*Byyye*, Ms. Holmes," they would sing playfully, sure of her affection.

The first assignment Holmes gave out to her freshmen every year was the "This I Believe" essay, a personal statement about their core values. It allowed her to quickly assess their writing and communication skills and also provided surprisingly intimate glimpses into how they viewed and defined themselves, two pieces of information she considered crucial to doing her job well.

Holmes was pleasantly surprised. This year's batch of essays had been uniformly stronger than in years past. Most of the freshmen had basic grammar and punctuation down and a few were clearly advanced thinkers and writers. But Marcus's essay gave her pause. It was titled "Born Bad":

> Some of my family said "You were born bad." I never understood what they were meaning. My mother said they say that because I used to take things that I want and when I can't get them I would cry or annoy you until you give it to me. I don't remember any of that. My mother also said no one could stop me from crying but her ex

boyfriend. It was like he was my dad instead of my real dad. Wherever he went, I went. He was like my real dad. My father was never in my life. Now I don't know where he is, but he took a responsibility that was not his. I appreciate him. I respect him as a man and as a role model.

Holmes wasn't entirely sure what to make of the essay, which she graded in her West Side home as her two children slept. Somehow, Marcus's essay had made her even sadder than the other essays did, many of which touched on gun violence and poverty in the city. Did he truly believe he had been "born bad"? Holmes knew right then that a large part of her job with Marcus this year would be convincing him that he had not, in fact, been "born bad" and that he could be a "school kid" rather than a "street kid." The next day she addressed him before class as she fiddled with the overhead projector that never seemed to project. "Marcus, I was really surprised by your essay," she said casually. "You're always very respectful in my class. I don't see you the way you described yourself at all."

"No, Ms. Holmes," Marcus replied seriously. "For real. I'm really bad."

Despite the claim in his essay, Marcus hadn't always seen himself as bad. He talked longingly of the old Marcus, a chubby, churchgoing mama's boy. These reminiscences often made it sound as if he were talking about a long-dead friend, rather than about a slightly younger version of himself. Occasionally he posted throwback photos of himself on Facebook at eleven or twelve wearing an oversized T-shirt over his protruding belly and an ear-to-ear grin. He always added a self-deprecating "I was fat" comment and the laughing–crying emoji alongside these photos. They were a sharp contrast to the newer ones of himself, shirtless, tattooed, sinewy— and often armed. "#hardbody," he wrote next to these.

As a boy, he had been a regular at a Baptist church in his neighborhood. "Most people wouldn't see me as a church boy," Marcus said, smiling. "But I used to be suited and booted every church day. Dress shoes, dress pants, my tie all nice, buttoned-up shirt. I used to love going to church." He loved listening to the preacher preach and the sense of community and order the church provided. He loved going to church up until the day he got banned for fighting. Now he wouldn't go back, even if they would have him. "It would just start something up," he said regretfully.

He started getting into regular fights in seventh grade, which was also around the time that his relationship with his mom and siblings began to deteriorate. She was out of work at the time, and the family was living in a house without heat or hot water. Sometimes there wasn't enough food. He decided that if she couldn't take care of his needs, he would take care of them for himself, and he did. "I used to steal. Snatch somebody's phone and run. Put a gun on them and rob them. Steal cars. Stuff like that," he said. His mom was scared for his future and frequently angry at him.

One particular incident from around that period had a profound effect on the way Marcus viewed himself and the world. When he was twelve, he watched a man die. "Someone tried to rob him, right in front of the church," Marcus recalled. "I watched him gasping for air. They really wouldn't let me outside. When I stepped out the door, my uncle pulled me back inside and told me the guy was stabbed. I was just shocked. I couldn't really feel nothing. I was just like, 'Dang, he's dead?' For a week straight, I was like, That's going to happen to me someday. Sometimes smells still remind me of that day. I'll get a whiff of a smell, and dang, it's exactly what I smelled in that moment.

"That's when I really jumped off the porch, when I started really going outside, really gangbanging. After that I'm like, Hey, I'm going to die someday. I can't be scared to be outside. I'm a guy, not a girl." He became a Moe, a faction of the Black P Stones, one of Chicago's most notorious street gangs. He was a Moe because most of the boys his age on his block were Moes. These were the boys who knew the chubby, churchgoing Marcus, the ones he called his "blood brothers." "And after that I stopped worrying so much about dying. Now I look at it, everybody going to die someday, so why be scared of it? I started being exposed to stuff I'd never seen."

During those years, school, like church, began to lose its allure. Marcus described the origins of his disillusionment with school in an essay he titled "Smart Little Cookie":

> When I was in second grade, my mom noticed something different about me. I had straight A's. She told me I was very smart and I needed to show that. So the next day at school I quoted my mother, "My mother said I'm very smart and need to show it." I was showing it without trying. I answered all the questions in class and they were the right answers. I shined like a lighthouse on the lake. I was the smartest cookie out of the bunch. But after sixth grade my shine stopped. I got a B. I was so upset I stopped doing my work. That B went to a C and it went downhill from there.

A single B might seem like a minor setback, but coming when it did, as Marcus was questioning his relationship to church and family and the other anchors of his childhood, it was devastating.

Marcus said the B made him think maybe he wasn't so smart after all. "To me it wasn't good enough, that's why. Because I was a straight-A student. After I got that B, I just stopped trying. I was like, Ain't no point. I probably can't even bring it up to an A." His comments were similar to those Malik had made in Roderick's study two decades earlier. Like Marcus, Malik had derived considerable pride from his reputation as a "smart cookie," or, in his case, as "Little Malcolm X." And like Marcus, he began to question that identity when faced with academic adversity.

Renowned social psychologist Claude Steele refers to the process of disengagement from school that Malik and Marcus experienced as "dis-identification," and he argues that minority students are especially vulnerable to it. Steele argues that African-American students, in particular, often stop identifying with school in part because of the way society views them and in part because of the way they see themselves through society's eyes: "Doing well in school requires a belief that school achievement can be a promising basis of self-esteem, and that belief needs constant reaffirmation even for advantaged students. Tragically, I believe, the lives of black Americans are still haunted by a specter that threatens this belief and the identification that derives from it at every level of schooling."

Certainly this specter, the "devaluation of black Americans" in every facet of American life, was as evident in the 1990s, when Steele wrote this essay and Malik dropped out of high school, as it was when Marcus and his classmates were students in 2015.

The world that these freshmen inhabited was more dangerous and hostile to them than at any other time Holmes could recall during her teaching career. Donald J. Trump was running for president, and the students talked constantly about what might happen to them and their families if he was elected. Her Latino students were concerned that their families might be sent back to Mexico or other countries. Somewhere along the way her black students also became convinced that he might send their families back to Africa.

The news story dominating the Chicago headlines that fall was the shooting death of Laquan McDonald, a black teenager who had been just a few years older than most of the freshmen. Like them, McDonald had lived on the city's South Side and had attended Chicago public schools. He had been killed the previous year by a police officer—shot sixteen times. The officer claimed it had been self-defense. The fall that Marcus entered high school, the dash-cam video of the fatal shooting was finally released. It clearly showed McDonald brandishing a knife but walking away from police at the time he was shot, contradicting the official claims of self-defense. Many Tilden students had watched the video, seen McDonald's final pirouette as bullets ripped through his body, and watched the officer kick the knife out of McDonald's hand as he lay on the ground, dying. For many, it had confirmed their worst fears about the police and about authority generally. Marcus had been jumped by a group of boys near his house the summer before freshman year. His brother had wanted to call the police. "But really that was the stupidest thing you could do," he recalled later. "That was 2015, and all the killin' was going on *with* the police."

Marcus's freshman year would also be the most violent one in Chicago in more than a decade. In the mid-1990s, when the murder rate in Chicago was at its apex, the killings were primarily connected to street gangs and the drug trade. Now that the hierarchical gang structure and drug trade had been disrupted, murders were as likely to be about revenge or petty insults on social media, or seemingly about nothing at all. It had bred a sense of fatalism in many of Holmes's students. "They say, 'Why does this matter? Because I'm going to be dead in five years anyway,'" Holmes recounted.

Holmes had identified this freshman class as the most academically skilled class she had taught at Tilden—and the toughest. "Five weeks into school, I was like, What's *up* with this group of kids? I think these kids were more alienated and more apathetic than in the past. They just really truly did *not care* about stuff. They were not buying into anything that we were selling. I don't know if that came from home or if that came from looking at the world as it is," Holmes said.

Holmes had read the research. She knew that freshman year might be the best and last time to reach these students. "It's really true," she said. "If you pass ninth grade, your chance for success really grows. If you have just a little pocket of success, and then that snowballs, and then you have a change in mentality, and then you become the first in your family to graduate high school, and then the first in your family to graduate college . . ." She trailed off. "So yeah, it really is saving lives."

One of the first friends Marcus made at Tilden was a regal-looking freshman with a coterie of admirers. If Marcus was the freshman class's alpha dog, Sierra was its queen bee. Everyone noticed Sierra the first month of school—teachers, students, and especially the senior boys. Sierra reveled in their attention. She spent much of the school day posing for selfies with Marcus and a new constellation of friends. One Tilden staffer said it was as if the Kardashians had descended on 47th and Union.

Sierra had a heart-shaped face, amber complexion, and stately nose that elevated her look from conventionally pretty to striking. Undeterred by the dull constraints of Tilden's dress code, she always managed to appear fashion forward. She wore her hair straightened or in thick, ropelike braids that extended the length of her back, and she carried a rotating selection of small purses that matched her footwear. Her eyes were often rolled dramatically upward toward her neatly arched eyebrows. She had perfected a look of near-permanent and profound ennui.

Despite her cool exterior, which was sometimes mistaken for aloofness, Sierra initially found high school thrilling. Previously she had attended the Stagg School of Excellence, which was run by the nonprofit Academy for Urban School Leadership. AUSL schools in Chicago were "turnaround schools," chronically low-performing schools that the Board of Education had handed over to private management in an effort to improve student learning. AUSL had a reputation for creating orderly, often rigid, environments for students. At Stagg, Sierra walked in lines from classroom to classroom. Her teachers told her what to do and when to do it. Immediately she felt more adult at Tilden with no one monitoring her every move. "It was fun, just really fun 'cause they gave us a lot more choice," she recalled with a wide smile. "It just felt like I was having more freedom and getting more and more older, finally doing what I wanted to do. I wanted to go to school more and more."

When she arrived at Tilden, she only knew one boy who went there. Her home was six miles southeast of her new school, nearly an hour-long trip on public transportation. None of her older siblings had gone to Tilden, but her grandmother had enrolled her—she wasn't entirely sure why—so she went. So far, she was very pleased with her choice. Her classmates seemed nice, and Sierra put a premium on friendship. She loved books with fierce female protagonists who were uncompromising in their quest for love, particularly those by Sister

Souljah. Her Facebook page was populated by posts about loyalty, integrity, kindness, and the type of friends, both male and female, she was yearning for. She was hopeful she would find them here.

From the start, she liked most of the adults at Tilden. At Stagg, she had had a mentor who had closely monitored her attendance (which was spotty) and who came to care about her a great deal, even dropping by her new school to check in with her. She seemed on her way to developing similar relationships at Tilden. She had established a rapport with Ms. Scott, one of the office clerks, and she loved Ms. Holmes's class, where she got a "very good vibe." The assignments seemed manageable, and Ms. Holmes was funny and sarcastic in a nice way. Ms. Holmes liked Sierra, too, though she worried about her from the start. It was clear that Sierra knew she was cute (or "cute as hell," as she sometimes wrote on social media), but she didn't seem to believe that she was smart, too.

As much as Marcus and Sierra stood out, David Solis faded into the background at Tilden. Part of it was his appearance. He was short and skinny, all knees, elbows, and shoulder blades. At fourteen he could easily pass for eleven or twelve, save for the recent patchy growth on his upper lip, which could charitably be described as a two o'clock shadow. He rarely spoke in class, and when he did, it was generally a well-timed aside to his neighbor. During passing periods, he ambled through the hallways with his hands in his pockets and a dreamy half-smile that seemed to say, "I'm here, but really I'm not."

Only Tania Dominguez had him on her radar, and that was due to his chronic absenteeism. Ms. Dominguez was Tilden's attendance coordinator, responsible for monitoring and preventing absenteeism. Students who were chronically absent were usually the students who were most in danger of becoming a "street kid" if no one from school intervened. By monitoring attendance, she was the de facto monitor of students' attachment to school, which made her a key line of defense against students' dis-identification with school.

She began each school day standing by the metal detectors, chatting with students as they swiped in electronically using their student IDs. By 9:00 a.m. she would have an electronic attendance record for the day. Then she and other staff members would divvy up the names of absent students—often as many as eighty or ninety in total—and start making phone calls to the parent or guardian of each and every one. As a general rule, she reached voicemail half of the time, a disconnected number a quarter of the time, and an actual human the other quarter of the time. When she did speak to a parent or guardian, she recorded the conversation in a log, which she would review with a team of Tilden staffers that met every other week to strategize about increasing attendance. When she couldn't reach a parent of a chronically absent student, she'd track down a friend and ask him to send an inquiring text. She offered bribes and prizes for students who pulled their attendance up. She grabbed students in the lunchroom and probed for the reason behind the absence: Trouble at home? Lack of bus money? Childcare duties?

Dominguez sometimes wondered what her high school friends would think if they saw her now. In high school she had been a chronic truant, precisely the type of kid she spent her time tracking down at Tilden. Now thirty-eight years old, Dominquez had attended Chicago's Lake View High School in the 1990s, when Roderick was conducting her research on the freshman year. Her high school experience was consistent with the experiences of Roderick's research subjects. Like them, she had felt entirely invisible in high school. And when she had made bad choices, no one had bothered to put up a fight.

Around October in her freshman year, another ninth grader named Gloria approached her at her locker and asked her to go to a "daytime," a party during school hours at someone's house. She assured her that no one would even notice she was gone. She was right. From that day forward, Dominguez was absent as often as she was present, despite having been a model student in elementary school. She flunked multiple courses freshman year. By senior year, significantly behind her classmates in credits, she dropped out.

She still vividly remembers the day she officially dropped out, too embarrassed to continue the charade of school when she was so many credits behind. "I'm here to drop out," she recalled saying timidly. The counselor, whose name she didn't even know, asked for her school ID, handed her a form and a pencil, and wordlessly pointed her to a table in the far corner of the room. She signed the form and left it on the front desk. "No one even blinked," Dominguez recalled. Now, when students told her they were dropping out, she refused to let them. "No. Nope. That's not a choice," she would say. "If we aren't the right fit for you, find somewhere else. Go to an alternative setting. Somewhere."

She mused, "I don't know. Maybe it's weird that I tell them that it's not an option to drop out. But I do wish someone had done that for me. Because for me, no one called. I was one of those invisible kids who just left. So that's why I am so tough on them. I just want them to think of the future. Because I'm ten years behind where I should be because I wasted so much time."

David was at the top of Dominguez's list this year. After registering perfect attendance the first two weeks, he had reverted to an every-other-day plan of school attendance. Even on the days he showed, he rarely stayed the entire school day. Once or twice Tilden's security officers had managed to catch him in the act of cutting and had escorted him back to class, but Tilden's campus had plenty of hiding spots and means of egress. If someone was resourceful and determined to leave, it was nearly impossible to stop him. David was both.

During an interview in her office, Dominquez pulled up on her computer screen a student ID photo of David with his hair gelled and combed neatly to the side, looking like a much younger child forced by his mom to pose for a portrait at Sears. "Isn't he adorable?" she asked. "I show it to people all the time and they always say, 'Awww.'" Indeed, he was adorable, with rounded, childlike features: circular face; large brown eyes; dramatic lips and eyelashes; and smooth, olive-colored skin.

"His teachers say he's brilliant. He could be valedictorian as a senior," she said. "He's very pleasant, great manners, great kid all around. It's just SOMETHING lacking. I personally think it's his home life," Dominguez said. She had been trying and failing to reach his mother for weeks, leaving messages on her voicemail that went unreturned. She had offered David a free bus pass if he would show up every day for two weeks. So far, he hadn't made it one week. "When he comes back, he always gives me this little smile and shrug," she said. "I'm like, '*C'mon*, David!'"

While pondering David's circumstances, she noticed a freshman boy sitting unobtrusively at the table just outside her private office. "Hey, Alejandro," she said casually, and then she did a double-take. "Wait, what are you doing here?" she demanded.

"I couldn't do the work," he said.

"What do you mean you—"

"In Spanish class."

Dominguez threw up her hands in exasperation. "But you speak Spanish!"

Alejandro looked sheepish.

"Why do you guys do this?" she demanded. "Why are you out of her classroom? What are you going to do?"

"I don't know. Just go home."

"Home, *why*?" Dominguez demanded. "Why don't you want to do the work in her class?"

"Can't."

"What do you mean, can't? *No entiendes*? You getting frustrated?"

"Yeah."

"Okay, I'll go back up to her classroom with you," Dominguez offered reluctantly. Alejandro smiled widely.

She walked out of the office with him, shaking her head. "Lord, give me patience."

It was a plea that Tilden teachers would repeat to themselves silently and aloud throughout the year, for if Freshman OnTrack required teachers to bind students to school in new ways, it also required from them much higher levels of skill and empathy—and patience.

On a Thursday morning a month into the semester, Ms. Holmes struggled to get the attention of her first-period English class. The noise level was at 10, though nearly half the class was either absent or late. The teens talked over, above, and around one another, accompanied by the whir of the electric pencil sharpener, a favorite destination for students looking for an excuse to stretch their legs. Ms. Holmes had already shooed several students who belonged in other classes out of her room and had denied three different students use of the bathroom pass.

She did a quick head count. Just ten students today, including David and Marcus. Sierra was not assigned to this class, though she might as well have been since she had already popped in twice to see Ms. Holmes, who promptly sent her back to math class with a wave and an air kiss.

"Where is everyone?" Holmes asked.

"In grammar school this is considered a retarded class," opined Michael, a heavyset boy with short dreadlocks and an A average.

Holmes fixed him with a look. "Uh, no," she said. "Just 'cause some people decided not to come to class today doesn't by default make you retarded."

"This *is* the retarded class," Michael insisted. It was unusual to spend any extended period of time with Tilden students without them questioning the intellectual capacity of their peers. Dumb. Retarded. Stupid. Slow. They lobbed these insults at one another all day long. Holmes sometimes wondered how much more she might get done every day if she didn't have to spend so much time repairing her students' images of themselves.

"All right. So, let's get going," Ms. Holmes shouted over the din. "I'm going to give you five minutes for your 'Do Now.'" She spotted a girl staring blankly at the paper on her desk. "Wait, why don't you have a pencil?" she demanded. "You remember your cell phone but not your pencil!" Holmes heaved a big sigh, then passed out pencils to everyone who had come to class without one.

There was a loud knock on the door and Ms. Holmes went to open it. "Hello, Ms. King. It's very nice to see you today."

Makayla King plopped herself next to one of her girlfriends, who promptly began to brush Makayla's hair.

"You need to stop that right now!" Holmes ordered.

"What's wrong with that?" asked a boy from the back of the room.

"Because we need to get started, number one, and number two, it's not beauty school!"

"She told me to brush it!" the girlfriend explained.

"I don't care! If she told you to jump out your window, would you jump?" Holmes turned her attention to Makayla. "Where's your binder?" she demanded.

"Can I go to the bathroom?" she replied.

"No! You just got here!"

On the board, Ms. Holmes had written a quote from *The Absolutely True Diary of a Part-Time Indian* by Sherman Alexie, the story of a teen growing up on the Spokane Indian Reservation. The class had been reading the book for the past week. "I draw because I feel like it might be my only real chance to escape the reservation," the quote read.

"Write your reaction to that quote," Holmes says. "What does it mean? See if it sparks anything in you."

After a few semi-quiet minutes passed, Holmes asked for volunteers to share their work.

Jordan, a popular freshman who favored high tops and baggy pants, waved to a senior in the hallway and moved to follow him outside. Jordan said she had come to Tilden because she wanted to play basketball there, but she had quit during the preseason after seeing how much running was expected. Her elementary teachers were disappointed when she told them where she was going; they said she was too smart to go to Tilden.

"Jordan! Sit *DOWN*," Holmes ordered.

Jordan sat down and narrowed her eyes at Holmes.

"You are the most compliant gangster I've ever seen," Holmes said, narrowing her eyes right back at Jordan.

"Explain that," Jordan snapped.

"Because you act so gangster and so hard, yet still you do everything you're supposed to do. You come to school every day. You sit down and do your work every day."

Holmes was masterful at reframing students' antics. She acted as if their negative behaviors were nothing more than elaborate hoaxes to cover up their true selves. She offered up a string of positive identities and hoped they would adopt one for themselves. Often, they did. As if to confirm Holmes's assessment of her, Jordan began to saunter out of the classroom, her boxers peeking out from beneath her khaki pants, and then pivoted abruptly and returned to her seat with a dramatic flop.

A tall, rail-thin freshman entered the classroom just as Jordan was completing her pantomime insurrection.

"Martin!" Holmes addressed the new arrival. "Sit down. You're late."

Martin took a seat next to David, who had shown up for school on time and, this being first period, had not yet contemplated ditching.

"Young *people*," Holmes nearly shouted. "Can I get someone to volunteer to share out your Do Now? What was your response, Ms. King?"

"Drawing is a calm-down strategy," Makayla said.

"That's right. It's a way to calm himself down, deal with his emotions," Holmes said approvingly.

"Drawing could make him forget everything that's happening in his life," Marcus offered, briefly raising his head up from his desk.

Holmes probed, "But how does that help him escape the reservation? Does he mean that figuratively or literally?"

Marcus placed his forehead back on his desk.

"Literally," others in the class chorused.

"Okay," Holmes said, "but I think you all are thinking figuratively, like you're saying it helps you get [mentally] away. But how can some talent help someone literally escape a reservation?" Holmes asked again. "Because I propose some of you live on reservations."

"Do you live on a reservation?" Jordan shot back.

"I *used* to—but not anymore," Holmes replied. One of the reasons her students loved her was that she tried to connect the work they were doing in class to their lives, and their lives to her own.

"What does 'reservation' mean?" David asked.

"Good question," Holmes said approvingly. "What is a real definition of a reservation?"

"A group of people living in an area based on something about them—based on their culture," Jordan supplied.

"Which culture?" Holmes asked.

"Indians," Jordan answered.

"Right," Holmes said. "A reservation is set aside for Native Americans to live in," Holmes said. "We have about three hundred and four reservations in the United States today. But I propose that a reservation could be housing projects, could be ghettos, could be any place where you are told you have to live."

Holmes began to introduce the day's writing assignment: a paragraph describing the book's narrator. Before the class split off to complete the assignment, she asked them to generate some adjectives to describe the narrator and use textual evidence to support their claims.

"Why are we reading about Indians?" demanded Jordan, ignoring Holmes's request for textual evidence.

"Yeah, I'm not Indian," chorused Makayla.

"Some things are universal," Holmes countered, "and his struggle is probably something you all might relate to—he's a kid going into the ninth grade. You guys are in the ninth grade. He's going to talk a lot about his identity, and a lot of you are trying to figure out who you are."

"I'm David."

"I'm Michael."

The class snickered.

Holmes persisted. "He talks a lot about how being poor has impacted his life— *Michael*!" Holmes admonished.

"I'm not even talking!"

"You are talking!"

Holmes tried again. "He talks a lot about how being poor has affected his life in terms of his education, in terms of the opportunities he has had; and some of you are poor, and being poor has affected those things for you as well."

"Who poor?" Jordan demanded indignantly.

"I said a lot of you were poor, I didn't say you were poor," Holmes clarified. "You sounded kind of defensive about that. I don't want you to be defensive because I grew up poor. I grew up on a farm in Alabama. We *grew* most of our food. We were that kind of poor. During summertime we were pickin' peas, shuckin' peas, and my mom would preserve those peas in a mason jar, and that's what we ate during the winter. My mama killed my pet pig!"

"You all used to eat cows and pigs???"

"YES! Don't y'all eat hamburgers? Steak?" Holmes inquired. "I ate rabbit. I inadvertently ate squirrel. My mama cooked it, and I didn't know what it was, and I ate it—"

Another late entrance interrupted the food tangent. This time it was Justin, wearing large headphones and bobbing to a beat only he could hear. Justin was the oldest of ten children. At home, he was often responsible for taking care of his brothers and sisters. At school, he was often responsible for disrupting class. Seemingly incapable of sitting still, he exuded a manic energy that upped the chaos quotient of every room he entered. He also had a quick, highly associative mind that connected every situation to a song or movie lyric.

"Good morning!" Holmes greeted him. "Take off your headphones, sir! It's nice to see you. Take off your headphones."

Justin complied with Holmes's request. Then he settled in next to Michael and punched him in the shoulder. Michael returned the playful jab.

"Justin! Michael! HUSH!" Holmes commanded. "So anyway, we went off on a tangent. I didn't mean to do that. What is your evidence for him being poor?"

A tall Latino teen with a thatch of curly hair walked through the door. "It's nice to see you, Mateo," Holmes said. "Now go see Ms. Parsons. Hurry up. You're missing math." Mateo exited the room, just as another teen attempted to slip into the room unnoticed.

"JALEN! WHERE HAVE YOU BEEN?" Holmes demanded.

"Home," Jalen said.

"Dude, I just saw you fifteen minutes ago. You passed back and forth. I saw you passing by my door three times."

"I had to go to my locker," Jalen replied.

"Okay, now you're here. Whatever," Holmes said wearily. She pointed to the assignment on the board. Jalen rummaged through his backpack. Holmes wordlessly flipped him a pencil.

"Okay, so as I was saying, you can use the quote about his big head from page three to say—"

"That's what I was going to say!" Jordan said.

"Great minds, Jordan," Holmes replied with a wink.

A girl wearing a black T-shirt, sparkly gold UGG boots, and a high ponytail sauntered into the room. It was 9:05 a.m., an hour after the first bell. She grabbed the binder Holmes kept for each student and sat down.

"Kiara! It is SO good to see you! I feel like I haven't seen you *forever*!" Holmes enthused. Even if she hadn't seen a kid in a week, even if she knew the kid had been ditching, she always tried to make her first interaction of the day a positive one.

"For the *first* time in *forever* . . ." Justin crooned, quoting Princess Anna from *Frozen*.

Mateo poked his head in again, having ignored Holmes's previous admonition to go to his math class. "GO TO CLASS, MATEO!" Holmes shouted.

The constant stream into and out of the classroom had made it nearly impossible to maintain any kind of momentum for the lesson. Holmes surveyed the room. Less than half of the students had begun their paragraphs. Jalen was seated at his desk with his backpack still on. Justin was sharpening a pencil. Holmes snapped.

"One, two, three, four. . . . Five of you strolled into my classroom late to my class today," Holmes said, taking a quick inventory. "So I'm going to talk to Mr. Swinney today, and I'm going to ask for permission to have lunch detention for my class."

A lusty chorus of boos followed.

"Let me explain why," Holmes said, straining to make herself heard. "We are writing this paragraph. Some of you are already behind and can't catch up. Tomorrow we are going to keep going on this essay, so you guys are going to need lunch to catch up."

"Why not just let them decide?" Michael asked.

"NO! And let me tell you why," Holmes said. "Because at fourteen, fifteen years old, your brain is *not* fully developed! You don't always make the best decisions . . . so I'm not asking your permission. I'm telling you what I'm going to do."

"How about people have to live with consequences, how about that?" Marcus asked.

"You know what? You are talking about this like it's a discussion! It's not a discussion! I am doing this for *your own good.* At fourteen your frontal lobe where you make all your decisions is not fully developed. It's a shame that at fourteen years old you are making decisions that are going to affect you when you're forty. It's a shame, but that's reality. So I'm going to tell you all what's going to happen. You all are going to start coming to class on time, or resign yourself to spending that time with me in lunch detention. Goodbye." She gave them a little wave. "I'm done talking about it."

CHAPTER 3

Urban education reform is littered with failed ideas. Ideas abandoned too early and ideas abandoned far too late. Ideas that worked for these schools but not those schools. Ideas with mixed effects and unintended consequences. Popular ideas that attracted money and manpower. Polarizing ideas that divided and distracted. New ideas, and bastardized ideas, and musty old ideas repackaged and sold as new.

"If you look from 10,000 feet at education interventions, you can almost count on your hand the number of interventions that have truly scaled and established themselves," said Jerome D'Agostino, a professor of educational studies at Ohio State University. He led a meta-analysis of the ten thousand studies that have been reviewed by the U.S. Department of Education's What Works Clearinghouse, which had been designed to help educators select programs and practices that are backed by rigorous evidence. D'Agostino's analysis found only twenty-nine interventions that had had significant effects, most of them small. This is not to say that the reforms did not work in some places for some students, but rather that the chances of a program or intervention working for many different types of students across many different types of contexts was slim.

This hard truth—that much of school reform in recent years has amounted to so much wheel spinning—is succinctly summarized by the title of Rutgers University professor Charles M. Payne's book *So Much Reform, So Little Change: The Persistence of Failure in Urban Schools*. Payne wrote, "Reformers of every stripe got their butts kicked from one end of the 1990s to the other." Though he was referring to the 1990s, he could just as easily have been writing about any decade since the 1983 release of the *Nation at Risk* report, which touched off intense waves of reform activity in the United States. Produced by President Ronald Reagan's National Commission on Excellence in Education, the report employed doomsday language to warn that "the educational foundations of our society are presently being eroded by a rising tide of mediocrity that threatens our very future as a Nation and a people." American public education systems, particularly in urban areas, have been in perpetual states of reform ever since.

These reforms have tended to follow a common script: under tremendous public pressure to demonstrate turnarounds, leaders go big and fast with a new program or initiative that may previously have worked in another context but has never been tried in that particular school, district, or classroom. Anthony Bryk, a UChicago sociology professor who founded the Consortium and then went on to lead the Carnegie Foundation for the Advancement of Teaching at Stanford University, coined the term "solutionitis" to describe this phenomenon, arguing that "the propensity to jump quickly on a solution before fully understanding the exact problem to be solved" is rampant in education reform and accounts for many of its failures.

Often, in their rush to a solution, reformers fail to get buy-in from teachers or principals, who feel that reform is being done "to" them rather than with them. When the results of the program or policy turn out to be uneven—as is almost inevitably the case when lots of different schools try to implement the same program—policymakers abandon it altogether rather than building on its successes and learning from its failures. Finally, there is a general disavowal of the old and a frantic search for the next "big idea."

These failures are not just abstractions. They have sunk careers, squandered goodwill, and misspent billions. They have bred a pervading pessimism about the ability of school reform to make lasting, meaningful improvement at scale, an attitude particularly acute among teachers, many of whom long ago adopted a "this too shall pass" attitude to reform. Most damningly, reforms have failed the children they were designed to serve.

Freshman OnTrack is an important exception to this general trend. It is an idea that managed to take root, blossom, and cross-pollinate in ways that have positively impacted tens of thousands of lives in measurable ways: it is the rare education idea that made it at scale.

And yet, it very nearly didn't. The first time that the district acted on Roderick's ninth-grade research, it followed the predictable pattern of education reform: many solutions to the problem were generated in short order. Those solutions didn't account for the particular realities each school was facing on the ground. As a result, many of the solutions were unpopular or untenable to the people (the teachers and principals) charged with carrying them out. Schools implemented the reforms superficially, complying with the letter of the law but not its intent. The reforms failed to have their desired impacts. They were deemed spectacular failures, which helped to usher in a regime change.

Subsequent iterations of Freshman OnTrack would prove much more effective and sustaining. But to understand why Freshman OnTrack eventually beat the odds, we can look to how a similar impetus, based on the same research, with the same goal—to support freshmen during the transition to high school—fell so short. That story begins in the mid-1990s, when a new superintendent named Paul Vallas began shaking up the status quo in Chicago's public schools and making headlines in Chicago and across the country.

By the early 2000s, Vallas would be the national face of a type of education reform that borrows principles from the corporate world.

He would be called a "CEO," rather than a superintendent, and his system would emphasize accountability, privatization, and free market choice in education. After a six-year stint in Chicago, he would go on to lead the public schools in Philadelphia; Bridgeport, Connecticut; and post–Hurricane Katrina New Orleans. But in 1996, when Roderick's report was released, Vallas was still an education novice faced with the Sisyphean task of improving graduation rates and student learning in Chicago while also grappling with a gaping budget hole.

How Vallas fared would determine whether he kept his job as head of Chicago schools—and perhaps whether Mayor Richard M. Daley, the son of iconic Chicago mayor Richard J. Daley, would keep his. Daley had named Vallas, his former budget director, the CEO of Chicago's schools the previous July, just days after the state's Republican legislature and governor gave him broad authority over the city's schools. The 1995 overhaul gave Daley and his handpicked school board the power to name a superintendent, intervene in failing schools, and allocate resources in new and creative ways.

Mayoral control represented a break from the long-standing practice across the country of separating mayoral and education politics. An outgrowth of Progressive Era reforms, the separation was meant to buffer schools from the back-scratching that had so often characterized City Hall dealings. But that separation had created an uneasy power structure whereby the mayor had little direct control over the institutions that mattered most to many taxpayers and voters. With mayoral control, city politics would inextricably be linked to school politics. The schools would have to answer to the mayor, and the mayor, in turn, would have to answer to the public about the state of the schools.

In this new era, "accountability" became the new education buzzword. Chronically low-performing schools would need to show measurable improvement or face sanctions. Vallas was threatening to put schools with very low test scores on probation, which would allow him to make personnel changes, including removing principals. Students were also put on notice. Vallas made it clear that he was putting an end to the practice of "social promotion," whereby students automatically advanced to the next grade. Moving forward, students would need to demonstrate proficiency or risk being held back. Everyone was under the gun in unprecedented ways, from Daley to Vallas, to principals, teachers, and students.

So the timing of the release of Roderick's bleak portrait of Chicago's high schools was propitious, coming when the entire educational system and city government were finding themselves under pressure to demonstrate radical change. The report lit a fire under Vallas, who was touched by the stories of the individual students Roderick had chronicled. Vallas talked all the time about Clara, a pseudonym for one of the students whom Roderick had interviewed. "He talked about her like he knew her. And like her actual name was Clara," Roderick recalled, laughing. "We somehow figured out that by looking at these kids, people could understand. These were not bad kids. These kids were getting in trouble for something stupid or small."

The month that *Students Speak* was released, Vallas pulled together a task force made up of seven committees totaling 150 members drawn from reform groups, charitable foundations, academia, and CPS administration. He called on them to make "quick and lasting reforms" to the city's high schools. The task force included "just about every prominent player in education reform," including Roderick, although notably it did not include any teachers. After the union balked, Vallas added two teachers and seven union representatives. The union was only slightly mollified: "We squeak, and they put a little oil on us," Chicago Teachers Union vice president Norma White observed.

The seven committees returned after four months with reports that were compiled into a seventy-nine-page draft plan, which was basically a laundry list of concrete recommendations and sketchy aspirations that some dismissed as "pie in the sky." While Vallas technically opened up the document for public comment, critics complained that the hearings were cursory. He wanted to submit a plan to the Board of Education as quickly as possible, so that high schools would have the balance of the year to implement the ambitious plans. A series of community hearings were crammed into the month of December, including one on Christmas Eve. "It was a joke," said one teacher who attended the Christmas Eve hearing. "There was no information. They showed us into a conference room, we sat down, we wrote our comments, and that was it."

Four months later, the Board of Education announced a new "Design for High Schools" based on the recommendations that the committees had submitted. Vallas and his team trumpeted the plan, which came with an estimated $33 million annual price tag, as a game changer.

The plan had two key tenets: increase standards and accountability on the one hand, and increase support for students on the other. To increase support and personalization, the reform called for the creation of freshmen academies at every high school in the city. The board did not dictate what shape the academies needed to take—they could be a separate physical space, or simply a set of common supports and practices for freshmen. "The whole idea is to try," Roderick said. "If something doesn't work, try something else."

The other major initiative to increase student support involved mandatory advisories in every school. Modeled after a successful long-standing program at New Trier High School, which served some of Chicago's wealthiest suburbs, the advisories program required teachers or counselors to meet daily with a small group of students over the course of their high school careers. The advisor was meant to serve as a mentor/counselor to help students navigate both academic and personal issues.

The other key tenet of the new plan was increased rigor, which was to be achieved through tougher graduation and course-taking requirements. At the time, some Chicago high schools were offering as many as one hundred courses, many of them electives and remedial courses of dubious quality. Students would now be required

to take a college-prep course sequence of English, math, science, social studies, and foreign language in order to graduate. Meanwhile,
they would be tested regularly to ensure that they were being exposed to suitably rigorous material and that they were actually
learning it. The district developed end-of-course exams, which they
called the Chicago Academic Standards Exams (CASE), to be administered twice a year and to count toward students' final grades.
Ninth graders who flunked the test would be required to attend
summer school.

Expectations were high when schools started the following fall. "I
think people's confidence is being restored in the system," Vallas declared, the day before the start of the 1997–98 school year. "All the
initiatives that we've laid out in our education plan have either been
implemented or are in the process of being implemented."

Though Vallas presented the success of his reform agenda as
something of a fait accompli, the truth is that the implementation
stage marks the beginning—not the middle, certainly not the end—of
any reform project. Bryk, who co-authored *Students Speak*, sounded a
more cautious note. "The devil is in the details. . . . It's going to take a
while—more than one year—to determine if the changes are working." Bryk knew it is in the implementation stage, when sparkling new
ideas are superimposed onto the messy reality of schools, in which
details such as whether teachers buy into a common plan and have
the capacity to execute it often matter more than the policy itself
does.

Advisories and freshmen academies fell apart quickly. High
schools had scrambled to put advisories and freshmen academies in
place, shuffling around teachers and schedules to comply with the
new requirements. But teachers balked at the extra work without extra pay and the expansion of their duties into the non-academic
realm, where many felt uncomfortable and out of their depth.
Many complained—publicly and privately—that they had been hired
to teach subjects like math and science, not to serve as therapist or
counselor.

As is often the case in education reform, the one-size-fits-all mandate had not taken into account how the unique context of each high school—even something as simple as student and teacher scheduling logistics—could doom implementation. At Carl Schurz High School, for example, an overcrowded high school on the Northwest Side (and one of the city's oldest and largest), the school's staggered bell schedule made implementation of a single advisory period tricky. The way that Schurz's schedule was set up, it already was a challenge for some students to get the course credits they needed to graduate. The task became more difficult when the board increased math and science requirements and added the mandatory twenty-five-minute daily advisory period.

In order to accommodate the changes, the school day would have to be reconfigured, which required a union vote of approval. Schurz teachers were already demoralized by Vallas's decision the previous fall to put their school and thirty-seven other high schools on academic probation. That status allowed the administration to intervene in the daily operations of the school, and placed it one step away from being "reconstituted" with new staff. Schurz teachers opposed the schedule change on the grounds that they were being asked to pick up an additional class without being compensated for it. The school administration said it did not have the money to pay teachers for an extra period. The school's union delegate sent a strongly worded letter that urged teachers to reject the schedule change.

Schurz principal Sharon Rae Bender called a meeting to discuss the pending vote. She spent the meeting alternately appealing to teachers' duty to their students, and apologizing for a Central Office edict that she claimed no responsibility for. She began by talking about how much she had enjoyed getting to know her students personally when she had run an advisory back in her teaching days. "You develop a rapport with them," she enthused. Then she switched gears. "Sometimes I feel like I'm between a rock and a hard place," she continued. "As you know, I'm a former union delegate, and now I'm a principal. Twenty-five minutes of so-called advisory was not my idea. I have been instructed by Mr. Vallas and the board to prepare for this." Then she switched tactics again. "I believe you are professionals, and being professional is different from punching a time clock in a factory. . . . I'm not asking you to give blood. I really believe that this doesn't really faze most of you."

In a vote the following week, the teachers overwhelmingly rejected the reform-related schedule change by a vote of 122–10. Across the district, schools took similar votes. Many ultimately ignored the district's order to implement advisories. It took another year for the board and the union to resolve the issue. In November 1998, the board negotiated a new four-year deal with the union. Under the new contract, class periods were cut by five minutes each, freeing time for a paid advisory period. But while schools now had the time for advisories, they generally "were conducted out of a sense of compliance, not as a way of fostering closer relationships with and among students in a school."

Freshmen academies suffered a similar fate. In 1996, shortly after the release of Roderick's report but a full year before the board approved the high school plan, CPS had offered $100,000 and training for schools interested in launching an academy. These early adopters experienced some successes implementing the academies. But another large group of high schools declined to participate in the original pilot program, only to be drafted into it shortly before the school year began. These schools got a fraction of the money ($35,000) and little time to plan, resulting in programming that seemed "thrown together," according to some critics.

Not surprisingly, considering its hasty implementation, the freshmen academy plan never did get much traction in Chicago. Only a small number of high schools designated a separate part of the building for freshmen or assigned them to a specific group of teachers—what were supposed to be the defining features of the academies. Most schools simply paid lip service to the idea, referring to their freshman and sophomore classes as the "Junior Academy," without making any substantive changes.

Finally, there were the controversial CASE exams, which were both unpopular and ineffective. They were initially meant to determine part of students' final grades and whether ninth graders would be allowed to pass to tenth grade or would be required to attend summer school. However, after the first year few of the freshmen who failed the exam showed up at the "mandatory" summer school, and the board eliminated the promotion gate.

Teachers claimed that the test was a waste of time, poorly constructed, and confusing. They also argued that the multiple-choice questions favored simplistic responses over complex analyses. A question about *Romeo and Juliet*, for example, asked students to identify the "climax" of the play. To highlight the test's ambiguity, one reporter polled a high school English teacher, a Shakespearean actor, and a Northwestern University professor about the question, only to receive conflicting answers.

In protest, George Schmidt, an English teacher, printed portions of the test in *Substance*, his monthly newsletter that was sharply critical of the Vallas administration. School administrators, who had intended to reuse the test the following year, were livid. The board sued Schmidt, claiming he had violated copyright laws and stolen trade secrets. The legal battle dragged on for six years, and in the end the board got to fire Schmidt but had to drop its bid for financial compensation. By the conclusion of the lawsuit, Vallas was long gone and so were the CASE exams.

Even as many of the high school reforms limped along, Vallas managed to maintain a public reputation as reformer-in-chief. In January 1999, President Bill Clinton praised Chicago's schools as a model for the nation during his State of the Union Address for the second consecutive year. In May of that year, the *Chicago Tribune* editorial board declared "A Light at the End of the Tunnel," as high school students made significant gains on state tests. The percentage

of freshmen meeting national norms in math had more than dou-
bled, from 20 percent in 1996 to 42 percent in 1999.

But just two years later, in March 2001, Professor G. Alfred
Hess Jr. of Northwestern released a damning report that concluded
that the high schools had shown "little significant change" despite
the administration's reform efforts. The district had commissioned
the $1.8 million study, which had included an extensive review of
test scores and attendance and graduation rates, as well as qualita-
tive work that drew on classroom observations and interviews with
teachers and principals at high schools on probation. Hess concluded that while high school test scores had indeed improved, the
gains were due to students coming into high school more prepared
than they had been in the past. He also found that efforts to support
students during the transition to high school had generally fallen
flat. The Vallas administration had initially attempted to bury the
results of Hess's study.

A week later the UChicago Consortium released its own critical
report; it found that graduation rates had not budged since 1985.
Then, as before, 43 percent of students tracked from age thirteen
left school without a degree. "We still see the same dropout rate,"
said Bryk, the Consortium's leader. "I certainly wouldn't want to
use Chicago as a model for making national policy." Vallas dismissed Bryk's criticism as ideological rather than substantive. "Tony
[Bryk] has his own agenda," Vallas charged. "He was the champion
of the previous school reform agenda" (a 1988 reform that had decentralized the system and preceded mayoral control). But business
leaders, state legislators, and others who had formerly had two feet
in the Vallas camp began to defect. "Mayor Daley recently said we
ought to think outside of the box," said Republican state senator
Daniel Cronin, who had supported Vallas's reform agenda as chair-
man of the State Senate Education Committee. "Maybe we ought to
get away from that box entirely."

Two months later, in May 2001, another round of standardized
tests was released. These showed that elementary math scores and

high school reading scores had dipped. Three weeks later, on June 6, 2001, Vallas resigned. "Six years is enough," he was quoted saying in the *New York Times*. Some speculated that Daley had pushed him out because he had become too independently popular. Others claimed Daley was simply disappointed by flattening scores and wanted to shake things up. Roderick summed up the state of schools: "We don't stink anymore," she told the *Times*. "We've now got the problem of how do we really move ourselves up a notch." Hess, the Northwestern professor who issued the damning report on the high school redesign, added, "The biggest thing that Vallas . . . did was change the culture of the school system. It is no longer acceptable to say we can't expect poor children to learn." High school reforms may not have worked as well as intended, but the accountability Vallas brought to the system would be crucial to the success of the Freshman OnTrack movement down the road.

Chastened by the dismal outcomes of high school reform, Roderick and UChicago Consortium researchers set about redefining the role they played in school improvement in Chicago. In the future, they resolved to focus their research and outreach efforts on helping educators understand and solve their own problems through incremental, steady improvement, rather than on setting out to catalyze large-scale policy shifts. A simple indicator—which they called Freshman OnTrack—would make it possible.

The Freshman OnTrack indicator was developed in the mid-1990s by Consortium researchers to measure whether ninth graders were making basic progress toward graduation. Students who failed no more than one semester of a core course and earned enough credits to advance to sophomore year were considered "on-track." Preliminary analysis had suggested that the Freshman OnTrack metric was a good predictor of whether freshmen would go on to graduate. That is, those who were on-track were more likely than those who were off-track to graduate four years later.

The UChicago Consortium had originally developed the on-track measure at the behest of elementary schools and nonprofits that worked with eighth graders and wanted to know how their students fared when they entered high school. But in 2003, Arne Duncan, who replaced Vallas as CEO, moved to put the metric on the district's accountability framework, meaning that high schools would be judged in part on whether a large percentage of their freshmen were on-track to graduate. Duncan had been looking for a metric other than test scores to gauge how schools were doing with their underclassmen, and Freshman OnTrack fit the bill. The Consortium's staff panicked when they learned of Duncan's intention. They did not yet know enough about the metric to feel comfortable recommending it as something schools should be judged upon. As researcher Elaine Allensworth put it, "If OnTrack was going to matter, then we had to make sure it *really* mattered."

Allensworth was assigned to validate the metric. She was not initially enthused about the project; she had more methodologically complex projects she was looking to work on, and this new project seemed like a snore of a detour. Still, the entire purpose of the Consortium was to do research that really mattered to educators, even if it didn't appear to be the most cutting-edge work for academics.

The UChicago Consortium was founded in 1990 by Bryk, then a professor of urban education in the university's sociology department. Widely considered to be one of the country's top education researchers, Bryk bears a striking physical resemblance to Bill Gates and tends to talk in perfectly organized paragraphs. It is easy, therefore, to mistake him for a typical ivory-tower academic. He isn't. When he arrived at UChicago in the mid-1980s, Bryk was sharply critical of his colleagues who studied educational theory but never engaged with the people working in schools. He believed that the type of research produced by the academy was too often of little practical use to educators, and he was determined to bridge the gap between research and practice.

Bryk's Consortium was a new kind of education research organization. Its research agenda was driven not by the interests, expertise, or professional concerns of the researchers, but by the needs of educators. Its steering committee was composed of representatives from the teachers union, the principals association, local nonprofits, the school system, parent advocates, local philanthropists, and researchers—a deliberately pluralist group. "The first meeting, I remember thinking, 'I hope someone doesn't jump across the table and punch somebody else out,' because it was Chicago and it was pretty adversarial," Bryk said in an interview.

The Consortium's focus on a single district (Chicago) allowed its researchers to build lasting relationships and trust with local educators and policymakers, and deep institutional knowledge about the people and schools they were studying. It also allowed them to research a problem over time, with each study building on the last one. The Consortium's dropout research exemplified this approach. "There was an accretion that went on for years," said John Easton, who co-authored the early on-track studies and led the Consortium from 2002 until 2009, at which point Duncan appointed him to serve as the director of the Institute of Education Sciences in the U.S. Department of Education. "On the way to Freshman OnTrack there were little pieces here and there, and it took some time for it to come together."

Roderick had jump-started the Consortium's dropout research, focusing the organization on the importance of freshman year, and Allensworth was the perfect candidate to build on Roderick's initial findings. Roderick was the big-picture thinker, while Allensworth was more measured and precise, content to ask tightly defined questions. Freshman OnTrack cemented Allensworth's faith in undertaking more modest projects. "I realized," she said, "that sometimes the simplest analyses also produce the simplest answers."

Allensworth's analysis revealed that the on-track indicator was far more predictive of graduation than she had initially guessed. Students who were on-track at the end of freshman year had an 81 percent chance of graduating. Students who were off-track had just a 22 percent chance. Thus, being on-track seemed to increase a student's odds of graduating nearly fourfold. This finding was crucial, because at the time there was a perception that there was no way to predict who would graduate and who would drop out.

Initially, Allensworth had suspected that the on-track indicator might be predictive of graduation only because it was strongly related to test scores. Her analysis debunked this theory. "I ran the numbers and I was like, oh my God, there are a *lot* of students with really high test scores who are off-track, and they are not graduating even though they test really well," Allensworth recalled. What she had found was that Freshman OnTrack status was actually more predictive of high school graduation than test scores were. In other words, students' course performance during freshman year had more to do with their chances of graduating than how they performed on tests, the gold standard of proficiency in most education circles. Allensworth recalled hurrying over to John Easton's office to share her initial analysis. "I remember saying, 'Look at *this*.'"

Allensworth's findings were completely contrary to the dominant assumptions underlying education reform, then and now—namely, that test scores are the best predictor of future success and that the primary goal of educators and reformers should be test score improvement. The federal No Child Left Behind Act, signed into law in January 2002, both reflected and deepened this preoccupation with test scores. Under the law, schools were required to ensure that all students met standards on state tests by the 2013–14 school year or face sanctions. When Allensworth was conducting her analysis in 2004, schools across the country were frantically working to get as many students as possible over this proficiency bar.

Educators were inevitably taken aback by Allensworth's findings, often pushing back vehemently against this challenge to the supremacy of test scores. One chart in particular always garnered a reaction (see Figure 1).

What it showed was that off-track students with test scores in the top quartile nationally were far less likely to graduate than on-track

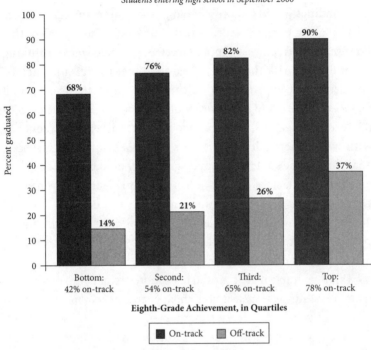

Four-Year Graduation Rates by On-Track Status After Freshman Year and
Incoming Reading and Mathematics Achievement
Students entering high school in September 2000

Note: Students who dropped or transferred out of CPS before the end of the school year are not included in these calculations.

Figure 1. Source: Elaine M. Allensworth and John Q. Easton, *The On-Track Indicator as a Predictor of High School Graduation*, Consortium on Chicago School Research, June 2005, 9.

students with scores in the bottom quartile. Indeed, the on-track students with the lowest test scores were 31 percentage points more likely to graduate than the off-track students with the highest test scores. And it was not as if just a handful of students with strong test scores were off-track. Fully 22 percent of students with eighth-grade test scores in the top quartile and another 35 percent of students in the second quartile were off-track. This suggested not only that schools needed to stop focusing exclusively on students with the lowest test scores, but also that they needed to stop blaming high dropout rates on students' low skills, a common excuse at the time. Accepting these findings would require a paradigm shift for many educators.

Just as important, Allensworth's analysis also revealed that Freshman OnTrack was a more targeted, accurate way of thinking about dropout risk than race, class, and other background factors. She performed an analysis that combined all of the background factors that she could measure about a student: race, ethnicity, gender, economic status, neighborhood poverty level, the frequency with which the student transferred schools prior to high school, and whether the student was overage for her grade. When she combined all these factors, she was still only able to identify 65 percent of all graduates. Worse, she was only able to correctly identify 48 percent of all dropouts—less favorable odds than a coin flip. In contrast, the Freshman OnTrack indicator by itself correctly identified 80 percent of all graduates and 72 percent of dropouts.

This one simple metric proved to be more predictive of graduation than everything else measurable about a student *combined*. And the relationship held for *every* subgroup of student at *every* school. Whether you were black, white, or Latino, from the South Side of Chicago or the North, attended a selective enrollment high school or a neighborhood high school, freshman year seemed to have the power to make or break your high school experience. This was an empowering finding for high school educators. They cannot control the race, ethnicity, income, or prior test scores of the students who walk through their doors, but they do have a shot at helping them pass their classes freshman year. At last, Freshman OnTrack offered them something to work on that was squarely within their locus of control.

Nationally, the conversation around dropouts was also shifting, with more emphasis being placed on the role schools had in promoting or thwarting graduation. In 2004, researchers Robert Balfanz and Nettie Legters from Johns Hopkins University released an ambitious study that attempted to determine the size of the national dropout problem and the percentage of high schools with high dropout rates. They found that two thousand schools across the United States produced the majority of the nation's dropouts; these were schools that had 60 or fewer percent seniors than freshmen. The researchers labeled these schools "dropout factories," a term that implied that schools were manufacturers of the dropout problem rather than recipients of it, and that placed the burden for fixing the problem on schools rather than on the students they served. The term "dropout factory" went viral, appearing in newspapers and magazines across the country, much as the term "dropout" itself had captured the public's imagination forty years earlier.

Of course, there was pushback against the idea that schools played a primary role in preventing dropouts. Critics of the "dropout factory" term argued that it ignored the difficult realities of educating students living in poverty and absolved students of their personal responsibility for making it through high school. Skeptics of Allensworth's on-track research, which was published a year later, argued that students who failed ninth grade were likely to be different from other students in some fundamental way that researchers couldn't measure. Gangs, drugs, teen pregnancy, a lack of family support: all could affect students' ability to stay in school, without showing up in any dataset. If this were the case, then schools couldn't do much to increase students' odds of passing their courses freshman year. "Principals and some teachers were *angry*," Allensworth said, "because there was this very firm belief that 'Yes our graduation rates are low and yes our on-track rates are low, but it's because of the *kids* not us,'" she said.

One figure in the Freshman OnTrack report generally gave these critics pause. It showed the on-track rates of every school in the district, adjusted for the students they served. In other words, it compared what a school's Freshman OnTrack rates would be *if* they all served students with similar background characteristics. As it turned out, the adjusted on-track rates varied significantly across the district. Schools serving students with similar background characteristics had widely divergent rates. This suggested that schools *could* significantly impact their on-track rates, with the right supports. And if they could influence their rates, then they might also be able to influence their graduation rates three years down the line. Thus, the Freshman OnTrack indicator seemed to have the potential to be used in two different and powerful ways: first, as a *predictor* of who might be at risk of dropping out and in need of extra services and support and, second, as a *direct lever* for improving students' likelihood of graduating.

A follow-up report in 2007 provided more actionable information to schools. It named the factors that were likely to move the on-track rate—crucial information if schools were meant to use it as a lever to improve graduation rates in real time. Specifically, it showed that attendance was as predictive of graduation as the on-track indicator was. Indeed, attendance was eight times more predictive of course failure than test scores, and just one additional week of absence per semester could decrease a student's chance of graduating by 20 percentage points (see Figure 2).

The report also found that schools with strong climates, as measured by surveys of teachers and students, tended to have better freshman attendance and lower course failure. Attendance was significantly higher, and course failure was significantly lower, in schools where students reported that they trusted their teachers and that their teachers provided them with high levels of personal support. This supported Allensworth's earlier finding that Freshman OnTrack was malleable; that is, it could be influenced by school practices. The Consortium and Duncan had their answer: the Freshman OnTrack indicator did indeed appear to be a metric that mattered, and the way to improve it was to work on improving grades and attendance throughout freshman year, especially by strengthening relationships between teachers and students.

"The stakes are just so extraordinarily high, if we're trying to stop dropouts in their junior or senior year, we've missed the boat," CEO

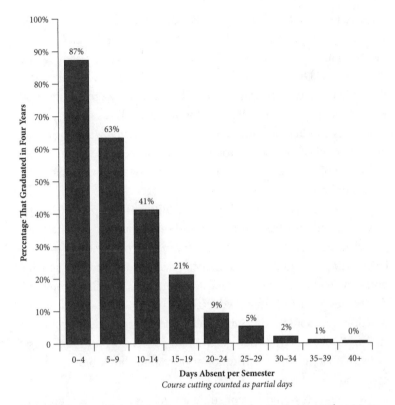

Figure 2. Source: Elaine M. Allensworth and John Q. Easton, *What Matters for Staying On-Track and Graduating in Chicago Public Schools: A Close Look at Course Grades, Failures, and Attendance in the Freshman Year,* Consortium on Chicago School Research, 2007, 7.

Arne Duncan said just before the start of the 2007–08 school year. CPS distributed highlights of the study to the homes of thirty thousand high school students before classes began. The handouts called freshman year the "Make It Or Break It Year" for graduation, and emphasized how even small improvements in attendance or grades during this pivotal year could dramatically increase students' chances of graduating.

Duncan's enthusiasm for Freshman OnTrack provided much of its early momentum. "Arne loved Freshman OnTrack, and everyone loved Arne," said Steve Gering, a CPS educational consultant. The responses of administrators and district officials to Freshman OnTrack ran the gamut, but no one at CPS could afford to completely ignore the metric if Duncan was championing it. "He made it really clear that this is what we're working on. This is what we're doing," said Paige Ponder, who led the district's Freshman OnTrack strategy as the head of its Graduation Pathways department. "If you were a principal or an area officer, you knew you were going to be asked about it, and you were going to be caught with your pants down if you didn't know your numbers."

When Duncan replaced Vallas as CEO, most people in Chicago viewed him as amiable, committed, and smart, but also politically inexperienced. A sociology major at Harvard and onetime professional basketball player in Australia, Duncan had returned to Chicago, his hometown, to run the Ariel Education Initiative, a philanthropic endeavor designed to increase educational opportunities for students on Chicago's South Side. Subsequently he served as deputy chief of staff for Vallas and ran the system's magnet schools program, positions that came with a fair amount of responsibility but not much direct political fire.

Yet Duncan would demonstrate a steely will and keen political instincts that belied his inexperience. "When Arne saw something that made sense to him, he *advocated* for it," Gering said. Duncan managed to survive at the helm of the system for seven years—a year longer than Vallas had—while championing a string of bold, controversial programs that might have sunk someone less politically adept, from closing low-performing schools and opening one hundred new ones, to instituting merit pay for teachers.

Unlike Vallas, whose primary lever for improvement had been turning up the heat on students, teachers, and schools, Duncan often spoke about the need to build the professional capacity of teachers and principals to meet higher standards. He tapped into private funds from the city's civic community to make large investments in training for early career and veteran teachers. He left

Chicago with a reputation as a pragmatist who was more interested in results than ideology.

The Consortium's reputation also helped Freshman OnTrack gain traction among competing reform factions and maintain a middle ground between the two. By frequently referencing the Consortium's research, CPS administrators were able to keep those on the ground focused on solving the particular problem of ninth-grade course failure, rather than fighting over the particulars of the district's approach to Freshman OnTrack. It was a sharp contrast to high school reform under Vallas, where the problem of the ninth-grade transition got lost amidst the rush to find a comprehensive solution to the array of problems plaguing high schools.

Those who became the biggest champions of Freshman OnTrack bought into the research first, *before* it was a graduation strategy. "When the Consortium brought out the OnTrack data and they talked about the freshman year, it was like a light bulb went off for me," said Sean Stalling, who was a principal at Manley High School on the city's West Side when the 2007 Freshman OnTrack report was released. "I started tracking through my experiences before I got to CPS, just as a high school teacher. . . . I remembered the numbers. We had one hundred and fifty freshmen, and then we had one hundred sophomores, and it was like, where do these kids go? You hear not many of those kids graduated, this kid is locked up, this kid is here, all these stories, but I never tracked each kid." Stalling would become a key champion of Freshman OnTrack after Duncan left the district and Daley appointed Ron Huberman, the mayor's former chief of staff, to succeed him.

The research prompted other educators to rethink their previous approach to freshmen. "I feel like the big 'aha' was the realization that the old-school, don't smile until Christmas, scare everyone straight approach—there are real implications to that way of thinking," Ponder said. "We moved into these deep transition discussions. Before that time there really wasn't any thought about the freshman year for anything."

Elizabeth Kirby, a principal at Kenwood High School on the city's South Side, recalled taping a photographed copy of a Consortium graph showing that one additional week of absences cut a student's probability of graduating by 20 percentage points to her computer. Every time she considered suspending a student for a week, she would look at that graph and ask herself whether the offense really warranted the potential long-term harm of the punishment. Usually the answer was no.

Meanwhile, as CPS administrators and Consortium researchers educated teachers and other key staff about the on-track findings, the Parthenon Group, a consulting firm hired to help develop a plan for improving graduation rates, worked with CPS administrators to develop a strategy for how schools could use data to improve on-track rates. For years, CPS's department of Dropout and Recovery had been a hodgepodge: credit recovery programs, academies for over-age ninth graders, alternative schools for students who had already left high school, etc. But all these programs were on the periphery, separate from the day-to-day work of high schools, and were largely aimed at the district's lowest-performing students—those who had failed eighth grade or were many credits behind the rest of their classmates. Freshman OnTrack would be a different kind of strategy, and more than an indicator. It would be aimed at helping the average kid, whom the Consortium had demonstrated was still very much at risk of dropping out.

It also differed from extant programs for dropouts because it was explicitly *not* a program. From the beginning, CPS administrators made it clear that they were not going to tell anyone precisely how to improve their on-track rates. Indeed, no one at that point had the answer anyway. Instead, with funding from the Gates Foundation, they established Freshman OnTrack Labs at six neighborhood high schools, which each had two full-time coordinators. The labs were meant to serve as incubators of new ideas and strategies. The hope was that these strategies would eventually be shared with schools across the district.

Ponder, the district's project manager for the OnTrack initiative, told the on-track coordinators that they needed to act as if they were researchers observing, analyzing, and experimenting to try to solve the problem of freshman year course failure. She developed a process to help guide their work. First, she said, take an inventory of all the programs and services already in existence at the school that could somehow be utilized to support freshmen. Get the lay of the land and create a strategy that takes into account the current realities on the ground. She also asked them to create strategic plans that listed what they were going to do, what they expected to see, and the data they would use to check whether what they were doing was working. She was trying to strike the right balance between giving on-track coordinators the autonomy to create their own plans and giving them enough structure to avoid spinning their wheels. "Because it's really easy to go into a school, and just get sucked into just the chaos of the school," she said.

While only six schools received full-time staff members devoted to improving freshman performance, every district high school began receiving new data reports on their freshmen that were designed to help them identify struggling students early in the semester and then track them throughout the year. A "Watch List," distributed to schools at the start of the school year, included students' eighth-grade grades and attendance. The list helped remedy the historic lack of coordination between elementary and high schools in Chicago.

A second report, released every five weeks, listed each student's grades and attendance. These "Success Reports" were meant to serve as "hot data," providing up-to-date information on which students were at risk of falling off-track. They allowed schools to craft individualized academic, attendance, or behavioral interventions for struggling students *before* they failed a course freshman year. Finally, a "Credit Recovery Report" provided information on those students who had failed courses during first or second semester. Schools used the reports to ensure that those students who had failed a course enrolled in summer school or other credit recovery programs, also a point in the system where students historically fell through the cracks.

It is difficult to overstate how revolutionary the five-week data cycles were in 2008. "It was just a totally new concept to be looking at data more than once a year," Ponder said. Prior to the Freshman OnTrack reports, there was no systematic tracking of students throughout the school year. Teachers might know who was failing their class, but there were no formal mechanisms for sharing that information until the end of the semester—when the failing grade was already in the books.

This was not a problem unique to Chicago. "One thing that became clear with this work was that there were weird fissures in most systems," recalled Bob Balfanz, the Johns Hopkins researcher. "Up to that point, no one was monitoring student data systematically. Students got report cards, and the data was all there, but that was a private thing. And even teachers never saw the data in totality. They put in their grades and sent in their suspension slips and attendance sheets. But no teacher saw a kid's complete report card. And no one was looking at data in actionable ways."

Gering, the education consultant whom Duncan had recruited to work with Area Instructional Officers (AIOs were essentially deputy superintendents overseeing networks of schools), became one of the chief constituents for the reports. He encouraged the AIOs who he worked with to pressure principals to analyze their data, set goals, and develop plans for reaching those goals, and then monitor their progress. It quickly became apparent, however, that the principals were having trouble seeing the forest for the trees. So much data on individual students was sending them in too many directions. They needed a summary measure.

Ponder's team responded by adding a "point-in-time" on-track rate to every success report. It told principals what their FOT (or Freshman OnTrack) rate would be if school ended that day. AIOs could also be held accountable for their rates. In the meeting area where the AIOs gathered, Gering posted the point-in-time on-track rates of every area, and of every school in the areas. The public displays were a visible reminder of the priority the district was placing on Freshman OnTrack and also a way to monitor who was making progress on the metric and who was not. "You could see at a glance where everyone stood," Gering said. "We wanted to get everyone's attention—and we did." Every five weeks AIOs would receive updated numbers to assess whether each area had met its goals and refine the strategy for the next quarter.

Like the Freshman OnTrack validation research, none of this was particularly thrilling. Watch lists. Data reports. Planning cycles. Teacher teams. Later, when Consortium researchers would try to explain the monumental shift that occurred around Freshman OnTrack, people would look at them skeptically, as if trying to figure out where the big idea was hiding. In fact, it was not that the big idea was hiding, per se, but rather that the big ideas most people tend to think matter most in education don't really matter all that much.

Education professor John Hattie, director of the Melbourne Education Research Institute at the University of Melbourne, has dedicated his career to studying what really matters for improving student achievement—and to debunking the popular misconceptions that swirl around the topic. Hattie argues that the things we argue about most in education, the hot-button education issues like performance pay, charter schools and school choice, technology, and curricular fixes, for instance, have little effect on improving student learning.

He calls the public's fixation on these unproven fixes "the politics of distraction," arguing that "many policy-makers and systems are persistently drawn to the wrong kind of education interventions." The politics of distraction rests on the faulty assumption that "there is a relatively simple intervention that can be defined and structured from near the top of the political system and that can then work its way through to positive effects for students." Using

Hattie's criteria, the vast majority of reforms instituted in Chicago during the Vallas and Duncan eras would have fallen under the heading of "politics of distraction."

These distractions cost lots of money and waste lots of time and effort, but even more crucially, they divert attention away from the factors that *do* have a large, measurable impact on student learning. These evidence-based factors aren't headline-grabbing and don't sound particularly groundbreaking. For the most part, they are hard to make policy around, except indirectly. Many involve getting teachers to work together effectively toward a common goal. They include "working together to evaluate their impact," "building trust and welcoming errors as opportunities to learn," and "getting maximum feedback from others about their effect." Hattie calls this kind of work the "politics of collective action." In the politics of collective action, educators form communities within and across schools that set a common goal, determine interventions to meet that goal, and use data to evaluate their progress toward that goal and determine where to go next.

The Freshman OnTrack movement in Chicago fit squarely within Hattie's definition of the politics of collective action. It provided a common, well-defined goal for teachers of freshmen to work toward: preventing course failure. The data reports provided teachers with regular feedback on the progress they were making. At the same time, the central office was encouraging schools to form teams that could make collective decisions about whether their interventions were working or not, and what they might try next. As they did this, they began creating "narratives of impact," as Hattie called them—stories about what had worked and what had not—that could be shared from teacher to teacher and from school to school.

"It wasn't this well-defined, sexy thing," recalled CPS principal Elizabeth Dozier. "It was building relationships with kids, finding ways to gather teachers to collaborate and talk about kids, making small plans, and then checking to see if the plans worked."

Before Dozier became something of a celebrity principal in Chicago and a leading character in both Paul Tough's bestselling *How Children Succeed* and CNN's docudrama *Chicagoland*, Dozier was a first-year assistant principal at Harper High School in Englewood, one of the most violent neighborhoods in Chicago. At Harper, her primary charge was to keep all 217 of Harper High's freshmen on-track to graduate from high school.

During the 2007–08 school year, the year before Dozier arrived at Harper, 57 percent of Harper's freshmen—142 of them—failed two or more core courses. And just like that, before they were even old enough to drive, they were virtually out of the running for a high school diploma and a spot in the American middle class.

Dozier wanted to draw a bright line for her staff between these dismal freshman outcomes and her students' futures. At the beginning of the year, she engaged all the freshman teachers in a visioning exercise. Where would the 142 off-track freshmen from the previous year be in three years? In ten years? Would they be in college? Working? Or standing on a street corner in Englewood? She reminded them that black male dropouts—and all of the 142 off-track freshmen were black—have a 70 percent chance of being incarcerated by their mid-thirties. "It was meant to tug at their emotional heartstrings," Dozier says. "If we're not careful, we can get desensitized to what this really means. These aren't just data points. This isn't just about Harper. It's about lives. It's about communities."

Without a specific plan or policy from the district, Dozier's initial approach to improving Harper's on-track rates was mostly trial and error. She created a community of freshman teachers who met weekly to review data on each student's grades, attendance, and discipline patterns. The group strategized about ways to support and motivate students academically and to provide additional help for those whose struggles had nothing to do with academics. To make the work feel more tangible, she created a board with every student's name on it and moved the student on- or off-track throughout the year. The team celebrated every small victory—a kid who went from failing to passing math; a chronic truant who started showing up regularly.

One challenge the group struggled with was how to help students take responsibility for their own learning and achievement. Many students interpreted failing grades as something that was done to them by teachers, not as something they had earned. The group needed a way to help students keep track of where they stood academically. Harper had an online student portal that included grades and assignments, but students rarely checked it. The group decided they needed something more public and easily accessible. Dozier made a giant color-coded board with every freshman's name on it and hung it in the main hallway for the entire school to see. She placed the students' names under one of three headers: green for on-track, red for off-track, yellow for "almost there." Making the names public went against CPS board policy, but she did it anyway. Brain research may suggest that most fourteen-year-olds will not be swayed by the potential long-term consequences of missing school or failing to turn in an assignment, "but what they do understand is social pressure," Dozier said. "One name would be the size of two napkins. You could read it from down the hallway. It became this thing. No one wanted to be at the end part. They'd say, 'Ms. Dozier, why am I off-track?' The older you get, it doesn't matter so much, but with these little ones, this public thing was very big for them."

Students began making connections for themselves between learning, the grades they were getting in the class, and their status on the "big board," which was a major breakthrough as far as Dozier was concerned. Dozier added, with a large smile, "I remember one time someone from CPS came and said, 'Take it down' and we said, 'Okay, sure. And, oh, when are you coming back?'"

One freshman student in particular stood out for Dozier that first year. He was a nice kid, she recalled, but something seemed off.

One day he got into a verbal argument with a teacher, and she told him, "Okay, we're going to your house." The principal advised Dozier to take Harper's football coach, who was born in Englewood, along with her. "It just completely put some stuff in perspective. We talked to his grandmother. She was completely cracked out. And that was the moment I realized how complex the work really is, and there's not a formulaic response for every kid. Maybe for a good portion you can use the public stuff, and incentives, and teachers meetings, but it totally changed our approach to the kids who are the most difficult to serve."

She described going to the next on-track meeting and telling everyone that the kid they had been struggling to reach lived in *that* house. "Everyone knew that house. It was where all the gangbangers hung out, where all the drugs were sold. Families and gangs used to fight right outside. I remember seeing a mob fight one day. Someone picked up one of those police horses and just threw it into the fight. And so when I said, 'This is where the kid lives,' there was a *whole* new perspective."

Dozier and her team started conducting regular home visits whenever a student was failing. She would gather a group of teachers, take along the football coach for security, and engage parents in conversations about their child. "Lots of these people had bad experiences with their high school, so they're not coming to the building," Dozier said. "So we said, Okay, we will bring school to you. It was really impactful for parents. They saw that the school really cares, and that is not typical. And it was also impactful for teachers because now you're not just driving down 63rd and going to the parking lot and going home. Now you're driving through the community. And it made a difference for the kids, because what they want to know is, 'Do you care about me? Do you have my best interests at heart?'"

At the end of the school year, Harper's Freshman OnTrack rate had risen 18 percentage points, from 43 percent the previous year, to 61 percent—roughly equivalent to forty additional students being on-track to graduate. One of those on-track students was the kid from "the house," almost certainly a student who would have fallen off-track in the past. Mayor Daley held a press conference at Harper to highlight the improvement there and the modest uptick in district-wide on-track rates (up 4.5 percentage points from the previous year). Dozier remembered a phalanx of city workers descending on the area before Daley arrived, cleaning streets and filling potholes. "It was really big for Harper. We had made this huge jump."

The press conference was sparsely attended, mostly by the small cadre of City Hall reporters who follow the mayor from one public event to another, asking off-topic questions only relevant to the major stories they are covering that day. A few local outlets briefly noted the Freshman OnTrack story and mentioned that Chicago schools were focusing on freshmen in order to improve graduation rates. And that was all. Just 4.5 percentage points district-wide hardly seemed like something to celebrate, and the on-track metric itself was still obscure. It looked like any other press conference in which data were marshaled to declare some minor victory in the ongoing political war over school reform. Instead, it was a precursor to one of the largest system shifts in Chicago Public Schools' history, a shift that came not from a high-level policy, trendy national program, or any of the big ideas that typically get discussed during debates around school reform, but from efforts that got teachers working together in new ways to solve problems that most of them had previously assumed they were powerless to affect.

It didn't happen overnight. Changing the way that teachers related to one another and to their students was critical to the success of Freshman OnTrack, but doing so could be arduous— particularly in very low performing schools, which is what Hancock High School was at the start of the 2008–09 school year.

CHAPTER 4

On its surface, Hancock High School did not look like a dropout factory in 2008, when Pam Glynn was named the school's fourth principal in five years. Located in a three-story yellow brick building that had once housed Our Lady of Lourdes Catholic High School, Hancock overlooked tidy rows of postwar brick bungalows in West Elsdon, a quiet working-class neighborhood on Chicago's Southwest Side, about a mile and a half from Midway Airport. West Elsdon's residents mow their lawns, prune their bushes, and decorate enthusiastically for Halloween and Christmas. They have ten-year-old minivans parked in the alleys, flowers in the window boxes, and statues of the Virgin Mary in their gardens. A 1991 *Chicago Tribune* article compared West Elsdon to "a picture postcard from the late 1940s . . . a scene of classic Americana."

The neighborhood might have evoked classic Americana, but its high school wasn't doing much to uphold its part of the American Dream. The vast majority of Hancock's students were children of immigrant parents from Mexico, who had come seeking better lives for their families. The students were "sweet, beautiful, compliant kids with complicated lives," as their principal called them, yet one-third of them never made it to high school graduation. Of those who did, fewer than half enrolled in a two- or four-year college. On an average day, a quarter of Hancock's student body failed to show up to class. The neighborhood had lost confidence in the school.

Even the principal of the feeder elementary school counseled eighth graders that Hancock should be their last resort for high school.

West Elsdon had undergone numerous ethnic gyrations over the past century and a half, before arriving at its mix of recent immigrants from Mexico and longtime homeowners whose parents and grandparents had come from Poland, Czechoslovakia, and Hungary. The neighborhood changed rapidly between 1990 and 2000, from slightly less than 10 percent Hispanic to 50 percent Hispanic. CPS began leasing Hancock's building in 2002 from the Sisters of St. Joseph to relieve severe overcrowding on the city's Southwest Side, a byproduct of these demographic shifts.

When Hancock was first moved to its location on 56th Street in 2002, students shared space with retired nuns who continued to live in the building's convent. Current and former students swear the school is still haunted by one of those nuns, whose footsteps are said to echo in empty hallways. Hancock teachers and administrators say it's not the specter of former nuns who haunt them, but the hundreds of students who, for a better part of the decade, did not receive the kind of education they deserved.

"There was just a culture of very low expectations for minority students," said Glynn. After having served as the assistant principal during the 2007–08 school year, Glynn took over for the previous principal, who had resigned due to an illness that turned out to be terminal. Glynn believed that much of the staff she had inherited were still mourning a bygone Hancock. The school began in a different location as a small elementary school and started adding high school grades in 1997 to relieve overcrowding at nearby high schools. The school's small original size had contributed to a cozy, collegial atmosphere. "We are a family," founding principal James Iles had told a reporter a decade earlier, "and that is what has helped us prevent dropouts and keep our attendance rates up." Its status as a magnet school also helped, allowing Iles to handpick students who would fit well with the school's culture. Iles said he didn't seek out academic superstars but instead "solid students with good attendance rates and reports from counselors that they were committed to learning."

Under Iles, Hancock became a "surprising success story," posting some of the highest standardized test scores in the city. But things had changed by 2003. Iles had retired, the school had been relocated to its new building in West Elsdon, and Hancock had dropped its middle grades and become a neighborhood high school, which meant that it could no longer control which students were admitted. Achievement plummeted, and so did teachers' expectations for students.

"There were things teachers would do that just curled your toes," Glynn said. "We had one history teacher who would show the *Transformers* videos for weeks on end in class. We had a math teacher who had the kids playing Twister. And they were convinced the kids loved them." She added, scathingly, "It was just because these kids are well-behaved and super docile, and you could shovel shit all day and they wouldn't rebel and neither would their parents."

Glynn identified strongly with these students and their parents, who were by and large immigrants and children of immigrants. She had grown up the second of six kids in a Polish immigrant family on the city's Northwest Side, where she had attended Taft, a large CPS high school that had a mix of children of professionals, cops and firefighters, and blue-collar workers. She often joked that, in Chicago, "Mexicans are the new Poles." Like the parents of many of her Hancock students, her parents did not speak English as their first language and never spoke about college as an option. But they believed strongly in education and hard work. "I remember hearing one Hancock kid say to another, 'What are you going to do when you graduate?' And the kid responded, 'I'm going to work. We're Mexicans. That's what we do,'" Glynn recalled. "And that was really true for the blue-collar people who went to Taft when I was a kid. We were all children of immigrants, first generation Americans. You were supposed to do the right thing."

Glynn clearly saw that same ethos in the Hancock students and their parents. However, she was convinced that most of her largely white, middle-class staff did not. Everywhere she looked—from the classrooms where "baby work" was taking place, to the staff rooms where teachers frequently complained about "those kids" and "those parents"—she found clues that her staff did not think Hancock students valued, or deserved, a first-rate education.

Glynn took over as principal in 2008–09, the same year that CPS began its district-wide push to improve the on-track rates of freshmen. The previous year, when Glynn was still serving as Hancock's assistant principal, just 58 percent of the freshmen ended the school year on-track to graduate, similar to the district average of 60 percent.

"It was so crushing to know how many freshmen were off-track," said Letty Hernandez, who began her career as an English teacher at Hancock in 1999, when Hancock was still at its former location. Hernandez's reaction to the data was precisely the type of response from teachers that administrators in Central Office were hoping for when they began making Freshman OnTrack information available to every school. The historical data conjured up names and faces of students who had passed through her classroom years before. Who *were* those kids who had slipped away?

Sometime during her first year as a principal at Hancock, Glynn decided she wanted to make Freshman OnTrack a key part of her rebuilding strategy. "I remember being at a meeting and hearing Melissa [Roderick] talk about how if we focus on freshman year, a lot of good things could happen, and I thought, that's a pretty good theory," Glynn recalled. Roderick had been worried that Glynn would be defensive about her school's dismal data. Instead, Glynn declared, "These numbers are my responsibility. And they're going to change."

Glynn was determined to improve them—but at the time she wasn't sure how she would do so. Freshman OnTrack as a strategy was not clearly defined at all. Like Dozier at Harper, Glynn was struck by the lack of specific direction around the initiative. CPS was pushing principals to pay attention to the metric, but they were not offering much guidance on how to move it. "People were left to their own devices," Glynn recalled.

She began by defining what Freshman OnTrack would mean for her school and her students, beyond simply preventing class failure during freshman year. Done right, she believed, it could be one of those reforms that have a "ripple effect" onto other areas of the school. At the first meeting introducing Freshman OnTrack, Glynn told her staff that they were going to focus on fixing freshman year at Hancock. She knew the reasons for the school's failure were myriad and complex, and it would likely take time—perhaps years—to unearth them all. But they would never get to the root of the problem if they just thought of FOT as a strategy for improving data. "One of the things I said right from the beginning was, I think we're going to unearth a lot of *other* things that were not on our radar at this point in time, but the one thing I want to be really clear about, this doesn't mean I just want you to pass kids; that's not what this is about."

She told her staff, "We don't want to be on-track for the sake of being on-track. We want to be on-track because we want to change outcomes for kids. That means we have to believe in them and believe they have it within their capacity to have a different future than what they initially thought." She added, with her signature bluntness, "Because a kid doesn't give a shit if they are on-track. That means nothing to them. *Big whoop.* But they might care if you say, we have research that says it's predictive of lots of good things and also it's *common freaking sense* that if you can stay the course and start out on a good foot, you can end on a good foot, and faster, and with lots more options."

Eventually Freshman OnTrack would transform how Hancock's teachers conceptualized their jobs and how Hancock's students saw themselves as learners and people in this world. It is the story of how a reform structured around collective problem solving can overcome—and even help remediate—the entrenched pathologies of a low-performing school by improving the school's culture and climate, thereby making a measurable impact on students' trajectories year after year after year.

Carlos Munoz can still vividly recall the hoopla surrounding freshman orientation in 2008. At the time, he was a junior at Hancock, and he was jealous. The Hancock marching band serenaded the new ninth graders. A giant chalk mural welcomed the Class of 2012. A cadre of spirited upperclassmen—the most positive, involved students Glynn could round up—greeted them with smiles and handed out Hancock T-shirts. Glynn met them at the door and ushered them inside. Everything about that first day was carefully orchestrated to communicate two messages: *You belong here. We care about you.*

In contrast, his freshman year, "It was just, 'Here's your schedule. Now go to class,'" Munoz said. When he arrived at Hancock, Munoz's primary support system was his older sister, Jessica, who told him how to get around the building, which clubs were worth joining, and who were the best teachers. Now freshmen could pick up this type of information at Freshman Connection, a month-long summer school program for incoming freshmen.

Freshman Connection, offered at all high schools across the city, was another aspect of the district's Freshman OnTrack initiative in those early years. The program gave students the opportunity to meet their future teachers and classmates, understand expectations around coursework and homework, and generally familiarize themselves with their new high school. Glynn tried to keep the activities lighthearted and to normalize the fact that everyone struggles a bit to learn the ins and outs of a new place. "We gave them their locker, and they had to practice with their locks just to make sure they could do it. We made it fun, how fast can you do it? How many tries does it take? I think that going from junior high to high school is *scary*, so we were just trying to do what we could to build the comfort level so that on day one they didn't walk into the building sweating bullets."

Both Jessica and Carlos agreed that prior to Glynn's arrival, Hancock had not been a terrible place to go to high school, but neither had it been particularly pleasant or inspiring. Adults yelled at students in the hallways—a lot. Much of the yelling was about students' violation of the uniform code, a code which was meant to create a more orderly environment but seemed to cause as many problems as it solved. Discipline was often very harsh—or totally lax. Security guards let students slip out the back door, so long as they brought them back a coffee from the nearby Dunkin' Donuts.

Though it wasn't a large school—Carlos's freshman class started with 230 students—it was easy to pass through Hancock anonymously. When students were absent, their parents received a "robocall." If they were absent ten days, they received a certified letter at home. Nothing felt personalized. Most of the students did not know most of the staff. "I never met my counselor," Jessica recalled. Neither recalled much support for students outside the classroom. A number of the girls on Jessica's softball team were coming out as gay and were struggling with the decision. There was a ton of tension in the locker room and at least one large lunchroom brawl as a result, but Jessica couldn't recall any adults intervening, even when she and other students appealed for help.

So many things about the school just seemed chaotic, from the attendance office (which never seemed to have the information or forms you needed) to the way after-school clubs were designed. "Art Club was like, 'Here's a paintbrush,'" Jessica recalled, laughing. "Gardening Club was like, 'Here's a hose. Garden.'" This culture of neglect had consequences. Carlos and Jessica both had a number of friends and acquaintances who stopped coming to school, kids they had grown up with, who quietly faded out of their lives. "Honestly, it was kind of expected during those years," Jessica said. "A lot of people were just dropping out, moving away. They were just like,

'I don't want to be here anymore, I want to get out of here,' and so they did."

Now here was Glynn walking through the hallways, greeting students by name, encouraging them to come out for the after-school art club, which she herself ran. She started requiring all freshmen to participate in a sport, a club, or an after-school activity to ensure that they immediately felt connected to the school. She held after-school dances that were just for freshmen. She also began reassigning her strongest, most positive teachers to ninth graders. She expected them to greet students warmly, build up to big assignments, and establish strong classroom organizational structures, from binders that helped students keep track of all their assignments to grading practices that were transparent and fair. In prior years, freshman year had been the dumping ground for inexperienced or ineffective teachers, while senior year had been the coveted assignment.

Glynn assigned Gayle Neely, one of Carlos's favorite teachers, to be the school's Freshman OnTrack coordinator, responsible for intervening when a student started showing attendance or grade issues. Neely hadn't "vibed" with the former principal, and Glynn had been warned when she arrived that Neely was a "troublemaker." But when Glynn talked to students about their favorite teachers, she heard over and over again that Ms. Neely was the teacher who always listened to them. Neely was one of the few teachers Carlos felt comfortable going to for support. He had only had Neely for one semester before he was switched into the honors track, but he often ate lunch in her classroom even after he was no longer her student. She, in turn, connected him to extracurricular and volunteer opportunities. She was particularly skilled at getting kids to cross boundaries and connect with one another. She convinced Carlos, for example, to volunteer at the events for the African American student club that she sponsored. She renamed it the Multicultural Club to try to build bridges between the school's large Latino population and its much smaller African American population.

When Glynn made her the Freshman OnTrack coordinator, Neely began working with those students who were flagged as orange, blue, or yellow on the student Success Reports from Central Office. Blue meant they had a D or lower during the first quarter of freshman year; orange meant they had missed three or more days of school during the first quarter; yellow meant they had done both. She would try to identify the sources of their struggle—whether it was purely academic or it had other dimensions—and then connect them with the proper resources. "I would ask them a series of questions to try to get to the root of the problem," Neely said. "Was it home related? A learning disability? An issue with a teacher?"

One consistent trend she identified was that students avoided asking teachers for help. "It was a cultural issue," Neely recalled. "They didn't feel comfortable voicing misunderstanding in front of their peers." Some said they felt it was disrespectful to ask too many questions of the teacher, thinking it would imply that the teacher had explained it poorly, so Neely began to urge teachers to post office hours to make it possible for students to seek help confidentially. "That was one hurdle we were able to get over," Neely said.

As she was expanding access to the personalized help that struggling students needed, Glynn was also creating what she called a "culture of celebration," particularly for freshmen. Like Dozier at Harper, she posted the names of every on-track freshman in the building. She put up photos of students who were "Most Improved." She had teachers write a little blurb about how much the student had improved, and she had the most improved student write a blurb about how he or she had turned things around. "It sounds nerdy, but kids would be stopping and looking at it," Glynn recalled. "It created a culture of 'We care about you.'" She asked every student to write what they hoped for in their future on an index card, and placed all the index cards on a giant bulletin board. When parents came in, she asked them to fill out their hopes for their children on index cards too.

She also reinstated all-school assemblies, which had been banned for the past three years following an unfortunate incident in which upperclassmen pelted freshmen with pennies, which had been enough for the former administration to pull the plug on assemblies indefinitely. When she took over as principal, Glynn said she wanted to hold an all-school assembly, a move that was met with skepticism. Glynn said she would personally guarantee that not one coin—penny or otherwise—would be thrown. They said it was her funeral. She held the assembly. No one threw anything.

When Glynn talks about Freshman OnTrack now, years later, she talks about reinstating assemblies, and the importance of the school's Gay–Straight Alliance and African American Club. She talks about working with the front office staff to ensure that community members and parents were greeted warmly every time they walked into the building. She talks about holding lock-in parties for seniors and car washes to raise money for undocumented students who weren't eligible for federal grants for college. She talks about all sorts of initiatives that weren't, on their face, related to preventing freshman course failure but were about binding all kids and their families to the school community.

"I just repeated and repeated, the one thing that is my job is to ensure everyone who walks through that door feels like this is a safe place, a place where you don't have to worry about being picked on, don't have to worry about people not caring for you, don't have to worry about not saying what you think or believe." She didn't see how Freshman OnTrack or any other type of reform strategy could bring about true change without this type of cultural shift. A school in which 42 percent of freshmen end the year off-track to graduate doesn't just have a freshman problem—it has a culture problem.

Still, freshmen faced special challenges, and Glynn was determined to "communicate the hell out of the message" to parents, in particular, that ninth grade was critical to their children's future. She created a presentation in English and Spanish for parents of freshmen with slides of the Consortium's research. "We told them this was *the* most important year of high school." It was the most important year, Glynn explained to parents, because it led to high school graduation, which led to college and other opportunities, which provided a path out of poverty. She gave the speech at the freshman orientation, and again at report card pickup, and again in parent workshops.

For Jessica, who graduated before Glynn arrived, the Freshman OnTrack changes did not come soon enough. She had worked hard in high school, earned good grades, and participated in loads of extracurricular activities—everything an American kid is supposed to do in order to have a shot at higher education and the middle class. But when the time came to apply to college, she received almost no support. She filled out the FAFSA form—the Free Application for Federal Student Aid—but had no idea that it had anything to do with money for college. She ended up at a community college, which seemed like a good option at the time. Years later, seeing what her brother and cousins who graduated from Hancock were able to do, she felt cheated. "I didn't know there were scholarships available. When I found out about the Posse scholarship [which identifies promising students from urban backgrounds and provides both tuition and extra support for them at highly selective colleges], I almost cried. I didn't know about it. We were new immigrants. We never met anyone who went to college," Jessica recalled. "My dad was fifteen when he got married in Mexico. He got amnesty. But still we were faced with those teachers who said, 'You're never going to college. You don't have papers.'"

Carlos had a totally different experience. Glynn immediately recognized something in him. She helped him craft his college essay during the senior seminar she taught. She recruited him for Gallery 37, the after-school art club that she ran herself. Most importantly, she made sure that the high school's college counselors actually counseled students like him. Then, after he had matriculated in college, she brought him back as an intern to earn extra money and to serve as an example to younger Hancock students who needed to see that kids like them could make it at college. Carlos graduated from Northeastern University and then earned his master's degree in school counseling at the University of Illinois at Urbana-Champaign. Carlos wrote Glynn a note after he graduated. "I am a Hispanic male from the Chicago South Side, this can only mean that I was doomed for a life that was limited; however, I had you to help me find windows of opportunity. Even though you are a non-Hispanic, you have done so much for the Hispanic community by helping every student get into college. I can only hope that I follow in your footsteps and help all communities like you. You have made the world slightly more beautiful by doing what you did for John Hancock."

Glynn treasured the note. She placed it in her "happy file" of artifacts that testified to Hancock's improvement under her leadership. She needed that happy file. Some days, it was the only thing that kept her going. Because while it's one thing to say that you are going to change the culture of a school, implement lots of new programs for the benefit of kids, and get the entire staff working together toward a common goal, it's quite another thing to do it.

Some of Glynn's early initiatives around Freshman OnTrack were the types of initiatives that were common in schools which experienced modest early jumps in their FOT rates: the Freshman Connection summer program, celebratory posters for on-track students, a part-time staffer dedicated to checking in with struggling students. They didn't require many extra resources or even much staff buy-in. They just required a bit of resource redistribution, intentionality, and ingenuity. If Glynn had left it at that, Freshman OnTrack would likely have had a small and fleeting impact at Hancock. She would have missed the opportunity for deep, lasting change. She would have also saved herself a lot of headaches and heartaches. "Those first few years, people hated my ass," Glynn said.

Richard Lietz, the dean of students when Glynn arrived, agreed with Glynn's assessment, though he phrased it more charitably. "It was just really hard when Pam got here. I had battles with her all the time. She just had a very strong personality. She was very committed to the cause, and she just didn't let up on it." The product of an all-male Catholic school, Lietz considered himself an "old school" disciplinarian. He handed out frequent suspensions and rode students hard if he thought they were troublemakers. He believed his tough-love approach was the best way to maintain order and keep students on the straight-and-narrow—particularly teenage boys.

Glynn believed that Lietz's approach was creating a hostile environment and turning kids off of school. She wanted the school's discipline to be less punitive and more restorative. It was a debate that was playing out across the country, as schools moved away from "zero tolerance" policies that led to mass suspensions and expulsions. In districts throughout the country, these policies disproportionately affected black and Latino students and students with disabilities. Critics say they created a "school-to-prison" pipeline that criminalized young people for acting in the ways most teenagers behave and then siphoned them into the criminal justice system. Lietz said he and Glynn both wanted the best for kids, but they had very different philosophies about how to get there. "I think in theory we were always aligned," Lietz said, "but practice is where we would generally butt heads. I think it really amounted to my background as opposed to hers."

When Glynn first introduced Freshman OnTrack to her staff, she said the initiative needed to be about improving outcomes for students and uncovering those systems, structures, and processes that were not working for kids at Hancock—from discipline policies to classroom instruction. To stay true to this vision, the staff needed to buy into two core beliefs: first, that Hancock kids were capable of much more than they were currently achieving; and second, that the actions of the adults in the building, from administrative staff to teachers to the principal, were contributing to that failure, and that it was within their power—indeed it was their obligation—to prevent students from failing. Karen Boran, who followed Glynn as principal of Hancock in 2012, called Freshman OnTrack a "mindset intervention for adults."

As Glynn would discover, changing teachers' mindsets is really tough, which is one reason why so many educational reforms fail. Like Freshman OnTrack, many reforms require teachers to fundamentally change the way that they think or act. Typically reforms introduce new structures, procedures, or materials, but they don't touch the instructional "core": "the relationships between teachers and students and the organizational practices that support those relationships."

The distinction is akin to the difference between dieting and adopting healthy lifestyle changes. A diet requires only that people follow a prescribed food regimen, much like a policy prescription handed down from on high. A lifestyle change requires that people fundamentally alter their relationship to food, exercise, and their own health. Diets tend to be short-lived and ineffective, much like the majority of surface-level school reforms in education.

Enacting deep change is particularly difficult in schools like Hancock with a history of failure. Sociologist Charles Payne's book on the difficulty of bringing about lasting change in "demoralized institutions," where staff has given up on the educational mission, the kids, and one another, describes the bleak reality of low-performing schools:

> They tend to be places governed by an overarching sense of futility and pessimism; where colleagues may distrust their supervisors and perhaps one another; where there can be a certain harshness in the way children and parents are dealt with; where many children seem to be disengaged much of the time, but not necessarily more so than the teachers; where the levels of human capital are at their lowest; where instruction is uncoordinated and uninspiring; where there are

too few resources, and those few are often badly used; where the curriculum is narrow, boring, and frequently changing; where teachers have profound skepticism about "programs"; where there is a general feeling of instability—personnel come and go, students come and go, programs come and go—all of it presided over by a dysfunctional bureaucracy.

He could have been describing Hancock when Glynn arrived. Payne argues:

> We have to think about demoralized schools as if they were clinically depressed individuals, people whose emotional state makes every task, even the smallest, seem overwhelmingly difficult, makes it difficult for them to do that which they would otherwise be capable of.

This type of demoralization is why the policy emphasis on exporting "best practices" and proven programs from one context to another so often fails. The entire educational apparatus is programmed to look for "what works" in education and spread it. The problem is that in a truly demoralized school, not much of anything is likely to work without expending a tremendous amount of effort to identify and fix the root causes of the demoralization.

Glynn was determined to use Freshman OnTrack for just that purpose. Freshman OnTrack provided the staff with a goal and a way of monitoring progress toward that goal. Data became key to all of Glynn's reform efforts. She used it to set goals, measure progress, and hold her staff accountable for making and sustaining change. "The joke kind of became that Pam started every sentence with either 'Research says' or 'Data shows,'" Neely recalled.

Glynn showed her staff data on the percentage of Hancock students who ended the previous school year off-track (40 percent). She showed them data on the percentage of freshmen who failed at least one course the previous year (58 percent). She showed them data on the number of Hancock students with above-average test scores who still ended the year off-track (33 percent). She showed them data on the percentage of freshmen who missed at least three weeks of school (31 percent). Some teachers, like Hernandez, saw the data and agreed it needed to change. Others got defensive and shifted the blame. Often, meetings devolved into finger-pointing and kid blaming. "Our students are lazy. Their parents don't care. They are unprepared," she heard over and over again. Sometimes she just lost it at people.

Shouting wasn't working, and neither, it seemed, were her more measured verbal appeals. To remove emotion from the equation, she tried to bring as much objective research as possible to the table. She countered the claims that kids were "lazy" with research showing that teachers impact their students' motivation. She responded to comments that Hancock students were undisciplined and impulsive with research on the teenage brain that showed they were actually behaving in typical adolescent fashion. She assigned them reading from Lisa Delpit's *Other People's Children: Cultural Conflict in the Classroom*, which chronicles how misunderstandings and stereotypes about minority students lead to ineffective instruction and frayed relationships between students and teachers, in order to inspire the teachers to reflect on how their own cultural biases and stereotypes—as a mostly white, middle-class staff teaching low-income Latino students—inevitably intruded in the classroom.

Glynn surfaced some of the ways she thought her staff were hurting Hancock students by seeing them through their own white, middle-class lens. She had overheard some of her staff criticize parents for asking kids to contribute to family finances. She told them, "You can't apply your middle-class upbringing to another group." She continued, "When you tell a kid that you need to quit your job because school is your first priority, and that kid has to help their family make rent and get food, you are essentially disparaging the noble act that that kid is doing going out there and helping his family." She heard teachers complain that the parents could not even be bothered to come to school for meetings. Glynn shot back, "Have you ever tried to survive on minimum wage?"

It was no coincidence, Glynn believed, that some of the most successful teachers at Hancock came from backgrounds that resembled those of the students they were teaching. Raul Castillo began his career as a math teacher at Hancock the same year that Glynn arrived. Like Glynn, he was immediately struck by the low expectations that the staff had for themselves and for their students. On his very first day, he was taken aside by a veteran teacher who confided that Hancock was a great place to teach—because he wasn't really accountable to anyone. "'No one's going to check on you at this school. If you're doing math or not, the right things or not, the right topics or not, no one will care,'" Castillo recalled him saying. The teacher added that the kids were nice—they wouldn't bother him either. As a new teacher, Castillo wasn't sure if this was standard operating procedure at most CPS high schools or not. He was sure, however, that he hadn't become a teacher just to coast.

Castillo had arrived in the United States from Mexico at age seventeen. He spoke very little English, but he had an affinity for math that transcended language barriers. At the CPS high school he attended, other students often asked him to tutor them in math. He wouldn't give them the answers. Instead, he would have them work in groups and help them arrive at the answer themselves. He was a natural teacher. "Everything I heard about Latinos in America was about cleaning or construction, not using your brain. I decided to get an education to keep helping other students," he said.

He received a full scholarship to the University of Illinois, the state's flagship university. But before he could enroll, his father died, which effectively eliminated the possibility of attending a university so far from home. Instead, he enrolled at Chicago State, a local public university that has come under fire for graduating only a very small portion of the students it admits. Initially, Castillo struggled there, failing the entrance exam three times because he could not pass the English test. "I passed it the fourth time," he recalled. "When you have a dream of something, you have to keep trying."

Hancock was full of teens who reminded Castillo of himself at that age, highly capable but insecure. He remembered how that Chicago State English exam had made him question whether he truly belonged in college, and he saw that many of his students had similar misgivings. Other math teachers at Hancock placed the students in rows and lectured through the entire period. He spent the first few minutes of class explaining the most complex concepts, then placed the students in small groups and let them struggle with it. Some of the students balked. "When are you going to *teach* us?" they would ask. He explained that it was like using a remote control. Someone could teach you to use it, and you'd probably forget. Or you could struggle with it yourself, and you'd likely remember.

A few months into school, Glynn called Castillo into her office. He was nervous. He had heard that the new administrator was tough. "So, what are you doing in your classroom?" Glynn asked without preamble. Castillo wasn't sure if it was a question or an accusation. He explained—somewhat tentatively—his strategy for splitting students into groups and having them teach each other the material. "Well, keep it up," Glynn said approvingly. "Your kids have the strongest scores in the department."

Glynn was happy with his performance but other teachers weren't. "They didn't like that I was doing things differently," he recalled. In very low performing schools, where teachers are accustomed to doing the minimum, those who go above and beyond are often shunned, much as the "rate buster" on a factory floor is shunned. Castillo was undoubtedly a rate buster. He was doing all sorts of things that other Hancock teachers considered well beyond their professional responsibilities. Castillo talked to his students' parents. All the time. He called in the beginning of the year to introduce himself, invite them to sit in on his class, and show them how to check their child's homework on the internet-based "parent portal" of posted announcements, grades, and classroom material. He called when students were acting up or failing to turn in homework. And he called when they were excelling, so that parents didn't think of him as only the bearer of bad news. He made it clear that they could contact him anytime with questions or concerns. "Sometimes my wife complains, 'You respond quicker to your students and their parents than to me.'" He admitted this was probably true. "I care for my students. I love what I do."

Castillo even made house calls, particularly if a student missed a number of assignments. The home visits were usually revelatory. Sometimes he found out that students did not have internet access and needed to have assignments printed out. Once he learned that a family had recently been robbed and the student was too preoccupied by the turmoil to concentrate in class. The home visits also made him realize how many of his students had obligations outside of school—to pick up younger siblings or to work, for example. He realized that his practice of telling students to come to him for extra help after school wasn't very effective for these students. He started offering extra tutoring during lunch.

Parents were often a little wary when he first appeared at their doorstep. Their first question generally was "What did he do?" By the end of the visit, though, they usually thanked him profusely for coming. He knew it helped that he spoke their language and understood their culture. Other Hancock teachers were under the impression that the parents were not invested in their children's education. Castillo knew this was not the case. "We as a Latino culture, we give a lot of credit to teachers," Castillo said. "We are more on the teacher's side than the student's. And usually, the freshmen are still a little afraid of their parents."

Castillo exhibited the two ingredients that Glynn repeatedly stated were necessary to improve Freshman OnTrack rates: a belief in students, and a willingness to do whatever it took to make them successful. Glynn needed a school full of Mr. Castillos. Short of that, she needed to imbue some of his belief system into the rest of her staff. Every day, in one form or another, Glynn was holding teachers' beliefs up to the light and asking them to do the same. Much of the staff did not appreciate the unflattering picture she was painting of them, and they weren't particularly interested in engaging in the type of dialogue she was suggesting.

Part of the problem was that Glynn was intimidating, even to people who liked and respected her. "I was like, 'Oh my God, who is this lady who came in like a tornado and set very clear expectations?'" Hernandez, the English teacher, said. "I was afraid of her, but I respected her." Neely, the original Freshman OnTrack coordinator, added, "It was a huge culture shift." Glynn had a strong personality and she did not suffer fools gladly. Neely observed, "I think the staff were intimidated by Pam. She's *really* smart and intuitive." She continued, "She was the type of administrator who ... was going to tell you what she saw. She had a very savvy way of saying it: 'You need to reflect. This is what needs to be done. I can give you the tools. If it's a skill issue, I will give you help. But if it's innate, if you're not doing it for the kids, but for a paycheck, then I will coach you out.'"

Glynn started popping into classrooms to observe, which prompted teachers to send a note to the Local School Council (LSC), which in Chicago is responsible for evaluating and selecting the school's principal, to ask if the principal was allowed in their classrooms. Historically, education has been referred to as the "second most private profession." In the past decade, there has been a push to make teacher practice public and to require principals to spend more time in the classrooms observing and evaluating their staff. But at Hancock in 2008, Glynn's presence in the classroom was viewed as an assault on teacher autonomy.

Particularly irksome to some veteran teachers was her decision to start auditing their grade books, which she suspected might hold the key to why so many freshmen were earning failing grades. Glynn found that the average teacher was failing 30 percent of his or her students. She believed the number should be closer to 15 percent. "You fail fifteen percent, that's on the student," she told them. "You fail thirty? That's on you. Figure out a way to reduce that number." Some teachers were irate, interpreting this as a mandate to lower their standards.

Glynn also asked teachers to revamp their grading practices to make them more transparent and rational. When she had audited teachers' grade books, she found a haphazard mishmash of grading policies that teachers could not really explain or defend. Teachers were giving grades for participation but never articulated what constituted a strength or weakness in this area. They assigned mountains of worksheets that carried undue weight in final grades. They often failed to grade work in a timely fashion, so students did not know where they stood in the class. They handed out frequent zeros for missing or late work, which were statistically very difficult for students to overcome. Many Hancock students had been tripped up by the standard 0–100 grading scale. They failed because they racked up several zeros for missing assignments, which made it mathematically impossible for them to achieve a passing grade of 60 percent, no matter how well they performed on the rest of their assignments.

In short, the grade books did not reflect what students knew, what teachers were trying to teach, or how a kid might be improving. Glynn believed this mismatch was contributing to high rates of course failure. Some teachers started working to revamp their grade books. Others balked, particularly when she told them to eliminate zeros from their grade book. The harder Glynn pushed, the harder some teachers started pushing back. Even teachers like Castillo, who generally supported Glynn's efforts, thought the "no zero" policy was a bridge too far. "Let's say you are working at a factory. If I work half a day, I get half of my check. I don't think it's fair if you don't show up at all and still get half a day['s] pay. That's not how it is in the real world."

In fact, Glynn was running up against the same fierce opposition that administrators nationwide were facing when they tried to implement policies designed to reduce student failure. Public debate around the issue swirled after *USA Today* published an article entitled "At Some Schools, Failure Goes from Zero to 50," in May 2008. The article detailed efforts in a "handful" of districts, including the Dallas Independent School District, to limit or eliminate zeros. The article sparked a fierce debate in blogs, editorial pages, and online communities between those who believed that the policy helped fix the mathematical dilemma posed by a 100-point grading scale and those who argued that passing must signal some minimum level of competency. For the most part, the public seemed to oppose these measures, arguing that they represented a dangerous loosening of standards, a threat to teacher autonomy, and in some cases, outright fraud.

In Texas, the debate even made its way to the statehouse floor. Distressed by a number of "no zero" policies in districts across the state, state senator Jane Nelson, a former sixth-grade teacher, partnered with the Texas Classroom Teachers Association to draft a bill prohibiting such policies. In April 2009, the Texas House and Senate passed the law unanimously. As a result of the bill, "local administration of grading politics had to be micromanaged by the state education agency," which caused its own backlash. By November, several Houston-area districts had filed a lawsuit challenging the law.

The "no zero" policies had backfired spectacularly. Not only had they precipitated the legislative bans, they had also strengthened the teachers' and general public's commitment to the type of hard-line grading practices that the "no zero" policies were meant to curtail. Dallas, which began tracking on-track rates around the same time Chicago did, after its leaders attended a Gates-funded workshop at the Consortium on Freshman OnTrack, never managed to significantly reduce freshman course failure. In fact, Freshman OnTrack rates declined in Dallas during the 2009–10 school year after the law was implemented, and stayed relatively steady thereafter.

Martha Mac Iver, a professor at the Johns Hopkins School of Education who studied the initiative, observed that the impetus for the "no zero" policies was good, but administrators erred by introducing top-down mandates without a good-faith effort to get teachers on board. Glynn was determined to avoid making a similar mistake. She was bound and determined to get her staff behind her larger agenda to reduce freshman failure, and she was willing to force out teachers who could not or would not fall in line. She would cultivate the on-the-ground muscle that administrative decrees or policy decisions sometimes lack.

One of Hancock's counselors was among the most resistant people in the school to Glynn's agenda and one of Glynn's chief targets during that first year. Glynn believed the counselor had been ineffective and, in a word, lazy. She seemed to hide out in her fourth-floor office and rarely saw students. She was chronically late to school and meetings. She shuffled nearly all students who expressed an interest in college—even those with the grades and test scores to go to competitive four-year institutions—to the nearby community college, which required very little paperwork or effort on her part. In 2008, Hancock seniors were awarded a paltry $5,000 in college scholarships. Nearby schools with similar demographics were raising hundreds of thousands—even millions—of dollars in scholarships for their students.

Glynn targeted the counselor in particular because students' postsecondary success was such a critical component of her rebuilding plan. What was the point of doing well freshman year or graduating from high school if there was no payoff down the line? Freshman OnTrack was important—but only because it was in the service of other, greater things. "I wanted them to be on-track so that they could graduate in four years and whatever you decided to do, you would have choices," Glynn said.

"I *was* a Hancock kid. My family was blue-collar through and through, and I wanted to either go to college or be a carpenter. I was leaning toward the carpenter thing. My dad made things, and I used power tools from early on, and I thought that would be an honorable profession. And so I didn't want to send the message to Hancock kids that what your parents do is not good enough." She did, however, want to make it clear that graduating from high school could lead to better things than dropping out—whether it was college or trade school or a job. "When you are teaching other people's children, you have a deep responsibility. You are a signal—you are there to *inspire hope* in people, to listen to find out what they are hoping for and help them achieve it."

Glynn's first attempt to shake up the college counseling department was to physically move the counselor's office to the first floor, adjacent to the lunchroom and her own office. She believed the move would make the counselor more accessible to students and make it more difficult for her to come in late or make herself scarce. The counselor was livid. She complained to Central Office, arguing that the space did not have adequate room for private conversations with students. Central Office replied that space decisions were the prerogative of the principal. The counselor continued to write angry emails to Glynn and others about the space. She even appealed to the Local School Council. The LSC also sided with Glynn. The counselor soon became one of the ringleaders of a growing resistance against Glynn.

The resistance, a vocal minority, expressed itself in myriad subtle and unsubtle ways: Eye rolls and audible snickering when Glynn was speaking. Note-passing during meetings. Hallway tête-à-têtes that ceased abruptly when Glynn passed by. Much of it was adolescent and petty, but it was also effective at demoralizing the rest of the staff and impeding change. Glynn often had trouble making it through a meeting agenda because the resisters would slink in late, decline to do the assigned reading, or derail the conversation.

She countered the resistance with more meetings, more professional reading, and more data. She asked Harvard's Ronald Ferguson to administer the student survey he had created to measure a school's climate at Hancock. The survey asked students questions about how they perceived their teachers and their school. Research has linked students' responses to these questions to how much they learn. The results of the Hancock survey should have been eye-opening. Just 35 percent of the students believed teachers pushed for hard work and just 40 percent believed that teachers pushed for critical thinking. Nearly all the students reported that rigor was inadequate in math and science. Perhaps most damningly of all, the majority of Hancock students did not think their teachers cared about their future.

Somewhat predictably, members of the resistance criticized the survey. They argued that the questions were poorly designed, that the methodology was flawed. In short, they weren't buying it. Ferguson, an MIT-trained economist, had dealt with demoralized staff before. He was ready for the naysayers. After delivering the results, Glynn recalled, he said calmly, "Generally there are two responses when what I have to deliver isn't happy and joyous. One is, 'Holy shit! We have to change!' Then there are the other responses. Those people question the validity of the instrument. They say, 'This couldn't be accurate or true.' And those people are usually not open to change. But I'm here to tell you that this is your truth."

After Ferguson left, Glynn addressed her staff. She knew that not everyone was buying what Ferguson was selling. But she also sensed that some of the staff had been swayed by Ferguson and, more importantly, by the feedback from their students. She sensed an opening. "We are going to follow the Weight Watchers theory of change," Glynn said. She got a few eye rolls but also more than a few smiles. "Has anyone ever tried to lose weight?" she asked. "Generally where you start slipping is when you start making excuses. Like, 'I worked really hard today so I deserve a whole pizza.' Well, we could make a million excuses, but at the end of the day I'm inviting you all to get on the scale with me. The numbers aren't pretty. We can do better. We *have* to do better. They are closing schools down that aren't doing well, and by their definition we are not doing well. And I like my job, and I think all of you like having a job too. And I don't want anyone coming in and saying we can't do this job. So let's all get on the scale."

Glynn did a quick inventory of the room. Teachers were nodding at her, even some with whom she had spent much of the year butting heads. It seemed to Glynn like a step toward détente.

At the end of the year, most of the truly disaffected staff members began to depart. Some left of their own volition, others with a strong nudge from Glynn. The teachers' contract made it exceedingly difficult to fire a tenured teacher, but Glynn wasn't above making life difficult for those she thought were bad for the school and bad for kids. She wrote them up for failing to execute basic job duties—like turning in required paperwork or showing up on time. She showed up frequently in their classrooms to observe. She threatened to give them less desirable teaching assignments. And she had very frank conversations with those whose negativity was casting a dark shadow on the rest of the staff.

Over the next couple of years, about one-third of the Hancock staff turned over. The majority were people Glynn was happy to see go. She started recruiting top-rate talent from other schools, with an eye toward diversifying the mostly white staff. "Lots of kids noticed," Glynn said. "They were like, 'Wow, Ms. Glynn, we got Mexican teachers now!' When we were going through this change process, some teachers reported me to the law department and said I was hiring all brown people and all the white teachers were afraid." She let out one of her signature guffaws. "It was *insane*. I'm like, 'Look at me. Do you see our demographic?' I can't believe any place got away with having faculty like that. The law department said, 'You're doing the right thing.'"

In Glynn's otherwise difficult and often dispiriting first year, there was one clear bright spot. Hancock's Freshman OnTrack rate jumped from 58 percent to 72 percent. "I think they were really shocked," Glynn said of her staff. "In spite of all the backbiting and fighting behind the scenes, we still managed to make gains." The teachers who had survived that first year weren't yet the type of staff Glynn wanted or needed them to be, but now they had one clear, quantifiable success to build on. Glynn had spent the year forcing them to take a hard look at themselves. Now here was real proof of what Glynn had been saying all along—they were capable of doing better. The school was still far from high-performing, of course. Test scores remained dismal and college-going rates unacceptable. But neither was it the demoralized institution Glynn had inherited. It was a start.

CHAPTER 5

"David!"

Tania Dominguez, Tilden's attendance coordinator, was fuming. The previous day, David had sweet-talked her into giving him a bus pass, a reward for a few consecutive days of attendance, which was a rarity for him that fall. He had waxed poetic about how he had turned a corner and therefore deserved a pass, although they were technically reserved for students participating in a research study that the school was part of. Dominguez relented, fully aware he might well be playing her. Shortly thereafter, he and a friend flew out a back exit with jackets draped over their heads, though David wasn't as slick as he imagined he was. The disguises hadn't covered his signature enormous backpack, which he lugged everywhere on account of never having learned his locker combination. Dominguez was ready for him when he returned the next day.

"Oh, Ms. Dominguez . . ." David trailed off. At least he had the grace to look abashed.

"Don't talk to me. Don't even talk to me," she said, her hand up in the air, as if to block the pile of bullshit he was about to shovel her way.

"But Ms. Dominguez, I deserved a break! I deserved to be bad because I've been so good!"

"NO! You are supposed to reward yourself another way! What were you thinking?"

Mostly David had been thinking about how best to exit the building undetected. David didn't like to brag, but when pressed, he would admit with a sly smile that he did have a particular gift for ditching school. Indeed, despite ditching school throughout much of seventh, eighth, and ninth grades, he had never been formally reprimanded. "That's how you can tell you are a sneaky person," he said, and gave a wide grin.

As David described it, the whole enterprise involved a good bit of higher-order thinking: careful observation of where security personnel tended to congregate during specific periods; working knowledge of the various exits, including which doors had video cameras installed; and a cost-benefit analysis of leaving earlier versus later in the day. His classmates who on a whim flew out Door 8 and through the alley toward 47th Street were amateurs. If the security or police officers patrolling those areas didn't catch them, then the security cameras likely would.

His buddy Dominic, a friend from the neighborhood with reported gang ties, was his co-conspirator. Tilden teachers had identified him as a bad influence on David, but David called him a true friend, different from the acquaintances he had made so far at Tilden. David explained the distinction between Dominic and his other freshman friends. "They're just like kids I talk to at school. I'm not like going to talk to them about my life or anything, but friends like Dominic, I talk to them. They're the kinds of ones who help me out."

Usually David and Dominic would plan to ditch sometime after third period. Too early, and they were likely to be marked absent for the entire day; too late, and it wasn't worth the risk. They would meet in the hallway between periods, amble toward Door 3 (no video camera), linger unassumingly to test if anyone would order them back to class, and then, if no one seemed the wiser, bolt out the door, through the parking lot, and up to Emerald Street, laughing and panting, buzzing from the thrill of another successful escape.

Free and clear, they typically would slow their pace and make the twenty-five-minute walk back home to Bridgeport, a onetime Irish American enclave that now is home to a large Latino population. The bus pass they had wheedled out of Ms. Dominguez was an unexpected luxury. More often than not, they alighted on, of all places, the public library, where they would find an empty room to hang out in until their parents expected them home. David didn't see the irony in ditching school to go to the library. "We didn't ditch school to *go* to the library. We just ditched school because we didn't want to be here anymore."

From Dominguez's vantage point, it all seemed so illogical, the potential risks so great, and the payoff—a few unsupervised hours at the library—so modest. When it came down to it, this is what really infuriated her. It wasn't so much that David had betrayed her trust, though that was aggravating, but that he was making bad decisions that could permanently alter the course of his adult life before it even got started. She knew from experience the straight line from absences, to dropping out, to just barely scraping by. David maintained that he had no intention of dropping out of high school, but she knew how the decision to drop out, generally, was not really a decision at all, but rather a series of seemingly inconsequential, day-to-day choices that set students on a path they had never meant to travel, to a destination they had hoped to avoid.

The thing was, David absolutely knew better. Dominguez had seen this firsthand in one of the more painful exchanges she had witnessed between the school and a parent. In early October, Lyana Sun Han Chang, an AmeriCorps member from City Year (one of the nonprofits that partnered with Tilden), had placed a routine call to David's mom to inform her that he was, once again, not in school. City Year focused on reducing dropouts by supporting students during freshman year; their model was based in large part on the research from Chicago. City Year corps members were primarily recent college graduates who had committed to a year of service. They tutored freshmen in core academic subjects, monitored their attendance and behavior, and served as mentors. Each was assigned a small case-load of students to tutor, and many of them knew these students better than their teachers did.

At Tilden, City Year staff made calls to the home of every absent freshman every morning. Lyana, who tutored David in math, had tried reaching his mom on several occasions. Initially she had an incorrect number for David's home and so had never before managed to reach his mother. When Lyana explained that David was not at school that day, David's mom was at first disbelieving, then panicked. "Not my David!" she insisted. "My David would never lie to me." Lyana explained that they had an electronic system that allowed them to see who had swiped in that day and who hadn't—and David definitely hadn't. David's mother shouted at Lyana not to call her again, threatening to call the police and report her for harassment.

Half an hour later David's mom arrived at the office, blazing mad. David, who had shown up late that day, trailed meekly behind her. Swinney, the Tilden principal, met her in the hallway and ushered her into the attendance office. Again she threatened to call the police and sue the school for harassment.

"I'm sorry, can you explain to me why you are upset?" Swinney asked, his voice just-the-facts-ma'am neutral. Swinney had a gift for meeting hot with cool. He routinely brought students from a roiling boil down to a simmer just by speaking softly and maintaining steady eye contact. But Swinney seemed to be having the opposite effect on David's mom, who got even more agitated. She reiterated her threat to call the police if they continued to call her at home.

"We're not solicitors. We're calling because David is not here, and when he is here, he's tardy," Dominguez explained.

Swinney suggested that perhaps a group meeting with David and Dominic and his parents would be beneficial, since the two of them usually operated as a team.

"I don't want to hear about that!" she shouted. Then she turned to Dominguez and said, accusingly, "That's *your* job to make sure he doesn't walk out."

David, who had been making himself inconspicuous up to that point, spoke up. "Mom, *stop*," he begged. "This is what they're SUPPOSED to do. They're SUPPOSED to call home."

Everyone turned to stare at David.

"They're not wrong. I did cut. I messed up, Mom. And you knew I wasn't coming. *We* messed up."

It would have been a striking display of maturity for any teen, really, but it seemed especially so for David, who had just the other day explained to Dominguez that he *needed* to leave school early because he could not possibly go "number two" in a public restroom. Reflecting on the exchange months later, Swinney was still impressed. "I was like, *thank you*. Even though I'm not at the point in my career where I'm worrying about parents yelling at me, the kid got it. He is fourteen years old, and he got it."

After the run-in with David's mom, it would have been easy for Dominguez and Swinney to pathologize David. He was a kid who had missed more days than he had attended, with a mom who to date had been more of an adversary than a partner in the educational process. In so many ways, he fit right in with the dropouts profiled in the 1960 *Life* magazine photo-essay, whose decisions to leave school without a diploma were mapped onto glaring personal or familial failings.

To be sure, aspects of David's home life presented him with extra challenges. And yet this habit of pathologizing struggling students takes the onus off of educators and policymakers to examine how their own practices and systems might be contributing to that failure. It also ignores the fact that transitions generally, whether from middle school to high school or high school to college, present challenges to students from many different backgrounds and in many different settings. Roderick had found that ninth grade in particular posed a stumbling block for Fall River and Chicago students. It turns out that it poses a stumbling block for teenagers across the United States.

Ninth grade is the "place in the educational progression where students . . . are at increased risk of getting stuck." On average, ninth graders have lower grades and attendance and put less effort into their schoolwork than they did as eighth graders. This ninth-grade "bottleneck" has several causes, including students' inadequate preparation for more demanding academic work and the poor organization and climate of many high schools. But chief among them is the fact that many fourteen-year-olds simply are not developmentally ready for the responsibility thrust upon them when they enter high school.

During eighth and ninth grades, teachers decrease the amount of time they spend monitoring or supporting students. Chicago freshmen often talk about walking in lines from class to class in eighth grade but having the ability to "choose" whether to attend school in ninth grade. They talk about teachers who "made" them do work in eighth grade but barely noticed when they blew off assignments in ninth. As one student described the biggest difference between teachers in high school and in elementary school, "Teachers in eighth grade pushed us more to work and stuff like that. And they were always, like, on us to do our work, do our work, do our work. And then [in ninth grade], they're like, 'You know what, we try our best to tell you guys [to] do your work. You guys don't want to do it, then it's up to you guys.'"

Part of the change in the way that adults relate to students is due to the structure of high school itself. In Chicago's large, comprehensive high schools, where teachers teach 150 students per day, it is simply more difficult to forge personal relationships. But another factor is that teachers often think that freshmen need to start taking responsibility for their own academic successes or failures in order to prepare them for college. One Chicago teacher summarized his rationale for taking a more laissez-faire approach: "I give them time every day to do the [class]work. I don't accept if they come in the next day and say I didn't get it, because it's their choice. That's their part of the responsibility. They have twenty minutes to decide if they want to do their work and get a good grade or if they want to mess around. And that's okay, so you're going to take a zero, that's your choice." But this approach assumes that fourteen-year-old students, many of whom have never been given this level of freedom or responsibility, are ready to assume it. Scientifically speaking, that is a bad assumption.

Recent research on the teenage brain helps shed light both on David's behavior and on why ninth grade, in particular, presents a challenge for so many students. In the decades following Roderick's report, research on the teenage brain exploded due to advances in functional magnetic resonance imaging (fMRI), which allows scientists to track brain activity in exquisite detail. Prior to these advances, scientists generally assumed that the brain was fully mature by the teenage years, that it was essentially an adult brain with fewer miles on it. In recent years, scientists have come to understand that the brain remains a "work in progress" as youth move through their teenage years and even into their twenties.

The brain of a high school freshman differs fundamentally from an adult brain, or even from the brain of a high school junior, particularly in areas controlling self-regulation, organization, and planning. These differences have profound consequences for how students behave in different grade levels. During adolescence, development happens primarily in two regions of the brain: the limbic system and the prefrontal cortex. The limbic system's job is to create feelings (fear, lust, or rage, for example) that stimulate a response to our environment (to flee, to have sex, to punch someone, for example). Puberty brings about major changes to the limbic system, making it more easily aroused.

The prefrontal cortex is the region of the brain responsible for rational thought and for ensuring that we do not act on every whim of the limbic system. The prefrontal cortex controls many of the behaviors needed to succeed in work and school: planning ahead, reasoning, and regulating. The conundrum for teens and those who love them is that the prefrontal cortex "hooks up" to the rest of the brain a few years after puberty supercharges the limbic system, creating a biological mismatch that encourages young teens, in particular, to engage in risky, impulsive behavior that can have costly long-term effects.

One of the hallmarks of adolescence is sensation-seeking and risk-taking. Teens experience an outsized desire to drive fast, blast the radio loud, scream lustily through a horror movie, sob uncontrollably through a tearjerker—or ditch school even when it could cause them to fail a class. The payoff of these activities is far more intense during adolescence than it is at any other time before or after, due to the way the brain's reward system operates. As sex hormones trigger the proliferation of dopamine receptors, the teenage brain becomes particularly sensitive to rewards, from nicotine to a friend's smile. Dopamine is a brain chemical intimately tied to motivation; it's the "'I gotta have it' neurochemical." The proliferation of dopamine receptors between the prefrontal cortex and the limbic system explains why "things that feel good, feel better during adolescence." In early adolescence, in particular—when the prefrontal cortex is still too immature to block impulsive behavior—these cravings can be overwhelming, motivating young people to engage in activities that are unwise or even dangerous.

Adolescence lends itself to car metaphors. Laurence Steinberg, the Laura H. Carnell Professor of Psychology at Temple University and a leading expert on adolescence, has compared the onset of adolescence at puberty to "starting the engines," and the maturation of the prefrontal cortex to "developing a better braking system," a system which is not complete until around age sixteen or so—toward the end of sophomore year for most students. Even during late adolescence, connections between the limbic system and the prefrontal cortex continue to strengthen and mature.

Unfortunately, many adults—both parents and teachers—start affording teens more freedom around the time they transition to high school, well before the braking system has fully matured. One of the reasons that adults tend to overestimate the maturity of teens is that they *do* possess the ability to reason in complex ways.

"It's not that they don't have frontal lobes," explains Frances Jensen, a neurologist and expert on the teenage brain. "They can still do really well on their SATs and reason through things. But split-second decision making is a weakness." David, for instance, was able to show great emotional maturity in standing up to his mother. He was also perfectly capable of doing all of the academic work his teachers gave him. When Lyana from City Year got him to sit down and complete his math problems, "he would do them in five seconds. Like he could do them without even thinking," she recalled. And yet, he repeatedly ditched class, despite constant warnings from Dominguez and others of the long-term consequences. In the heat of the moment, Jensen explains, teens "don't involve their frontal lobes and that explains the 'Oh, I'll take a left into oncoming traffic because I think I can get past that truck barreling towards me.'"

Peers further exacerbate this tendency of teens to engage in risky behavior. Indeed, peer pressure helps explain why David behaved in ways that felt good in the moment but had the potential to permanently derail his academic career. The mere presence of peers can lead teens to engage in risky behavior, even if their peers are not actively egging them on. Steinberg and his colleagues designed an experiment to pinpoint why this is the case. They hooked up a group of teenagers and adults to fMRI technology to measure their brain activity as they participated in simulated driving tasks. The driving task required each participant to make a decision about whether or not to brake at an intersection as the traffic light was changing from green to yellow to red. Participants performed the task twice—once alone, and once as their friends watched from another room. When they were alone, the adolescents and adults performed similarly. However, when they knew their friends were watching, the teens were more likely to try to beat the red light. The fMRI scans showed greater activity among teens in the reward-related system of the brain when their friends were watching—but no comparable changes among adults. No wonder the mental calculus that David engaged in before ditching always seemed to tilt toward leaving school when Dominic was involved.

When peer pressure, dopamine, and other properties of the teenage brain are factored into the equation, it becomes more understandable why David could exhibit so much maturity in assuming responsibility for ditching school—and then, in the heat of the moment, bolt. It helps explain why a student like Malik, the "Little Malcom X" from Roderick's study, could be determined to do well in school—and yet end up in the cafeteria every day during math class playing cards.

Indeed, given what we know about the teenage brain, the wonder is not that half of all CPS students dropped out of school in the mid-1990s, but that half managed to stay in. At a time when prefrontal cortices are still developing, students were expected to navigate very large, chaotic schools and juggle the workload and expectations of several classes and teachers simultaneously. At a time when they were particularly sensitive to what their classmates were doing or thinking, they were thrown in with a new peer group that was generally much larger than their eighth-grade cohort had been. At a time when they were exceedingly vulnerable to peer pressure, they were expected to attend class even as a large percentage of their classmates were cutting. At a time when their brains were primed to respond to immediate rewards, they were expected day in and day out to eschew opportunities for instant gratification in exchange for long-off goals like high school graduation and college. And they were expected to do all of this without much coaching, monitoring, or support from teachers or administrators, who assumed that freshmen should already know how to behave as high school students. In short, they were expected to act as if, at fourteen years old, they already had fully functioning braking systems and knew how to use them.

Teens need careful monitoring and support to shepherd them through this perilous time, but historically the job of high schools has been to impart as much knowledge as possible to those most willing and able to receive it, to separate "the sheep and the goats," to borrow a biblical term. This approach assumes that freshmen have the intellectual and emotional maturity to consistently behave in ways that benefit their own long-term interests. But brain research suggests that a large percentage of high school students are simply not ready to take responsibility for their own learning when they enter high school, and sorting them by the maturity level they exhibit as freshmen is likely to permanently disqualify large swaths of students who might otherwise grow into the role of student. High school students need adults who conceptualize their role more broadly. They need adults who don't see themselves simply as instructors or arbiters, but also as something of prefrontal cortex proxies while the teens' brains are still developing. As a result of the Freshman On-Track movement in the last decade, teachers across Chicago—and particularly at Tilden—have begun to do just that. It's been a fundamental, district-wide shift that has significantly improved students' chances of graduating.

The freshman teachers gathered on a Wednesday in mid-November 2015 in a third-floor classroom for their monthly team meeting, run by Ms. Holmes. Before the other teachers arrived, Holmes had arranged the desks into a tight semicircle. Seating had been a bone of contention in past meetings. The previous year, a small clique of teachers had positioned themselves a few feet behind the rest of the group during every meeting. Holmes had interpreted this as a not-so-subtle rejection of all that the meeting stood for. She hoped the semicircle would preempt any symbolic opting out this year.

These monthly Freshman Success Team meetings were a core part of the work designed to keep freshmen on track to graduate at Tilden. During the meetings, Holmes would lead the team through exercises to parse the data on freshman grades and absences. The group would consider broad trends, such as which courses the freshmen tended to fail most frequently, as well as specific cases of students who were struggling. The goal was to use the data to pinpoint who needed help and how best to get it to them. An English teacher, Holmes knew her Salinger. She thought the job of a freshman teacher should be to serve as their "catcher in the rye."

Holmes believed that many of the students who arrived at Tilden had simply never learned how to be students, and it was her job to help them get there, rather than bemoan the fact that they weren't there yet. Freshmen, she believed, needed to be protected from the biological forces that had been unleashed on them, not punished for behaving like the fourteen-year-olds they were.

Most Tilden teachers agreed—to a point. They were willing to give makeup work, let the occasional absence slide, or offer extra tutoring for struggling students, but most stopped short of believing that it was their *job* to prevent students from failing. They believed it was a student's job to come to class, learn, and demonstrate that learning, and that it was a teacher's job to teach the material and evaluate whether learning had taken place. Some hard-liners even believed that a healthy dose of failure was necessary to motivate students and prevent the students from walking all over them. "I don't think it's necessarily the worst thing in the world," said Richard Persaud, a Tilden math teacher. "I think sometimes it can also wake a child up."

Holmes vehemently disagreed with this view. She had started referring sardonically to the Tilden hard-liners as "grade-book gangsters." The "grade-book gangsters" were the teachers who pushed their chairs away from the table at the freshmen pod meetings, and who signaled with crossed arms or monosyllabic answers that they were simply going through the motions to keep freshmen on-track to graduate. "That's what I call them," she explained. "It's like, 'Oh yeah, you can be really hard because you control the grade book. You just a gangsta!'"

Holmes figured there were better ways to maintain order. "I've said this in my class," she explained. "'I'm not going to get into a power struggle with you because I have all the power because all I have to do is fail you. I can make it so hard that you will never pass my class, but I'm not going to do that.'" She continued, "'In the end you will lose if I want you to lose, but that's not the point. The point is we are trying to negotiate, and figure out how to help you learn the things you need to know, and it's not just about school but about life and whether you are going to be successful or not successful, depending on the choices you make for yourself.'"

Holmes may have been particularly sensitive to power plays in the classroom because she was on the receiving end of one in high school. Holmes was a bookish loner as a teen. She read voraciously to escape the tedium and isolation she felt living in rural Alabama. She rarely caused trouble in class. She quietly did whatever work her teacher assigned and then quietly pulled out whatever book she was reading in order to pass the rest of the period. One day in history class, she got into an uncharacteristic fight with her teacher. The teacher insisted on a particular fact that Holmes, an avid connoisseur of historical fiction, was certain was wrong. The two debated for a bit. The teacher told Holmes she didn't want to hear another word about it. Holmes stopped arguing. The class turned the page in the textbook. The very first paragraph on the next page proved Holmes's point.

"Told you," the teenage Holmes couldn't resist saying.

"If you're so smart, I guess you don't need this class," the teacher shot back. She kicked her out of class for the rest of the semester, only allowing her to attend on Fridays when the class took their weekly quizzes. For the rest of the semester, Holmes wandered the halls during third period, Monday through Thursday. "It was just a power thing," Holmes recalled. "I mean, I wasn't the best, because I should have shut up. But I was also the kid."

Holmes's academic career hadn't been derailed by that one incident. She ended up with an A in the class despite only attending once a week. And other than that one history class, she had perfect attendance. "Because my Mama didn't play that," she said. "I got suspended one day, my Mama didn't know because I still got on the bus. . . . When the bus arrived, I walked downtown and went to the library and sat there until it was time to come home, and then I got back on the bus."

But she knew that many of her Tilden freshmen were much more vulnerable than she had been as an adolescent. Many of the freshmen she taught were on the brink, trying to decide whether to "break good or break bad," as she put it. Persaud agreed with her about that. "Every year I have surprises that go one way or the other," he said. "It's not like the movies at all," he explained, laughing. "All of the teacher movies, it's great, they go into the crazy setting, and then everybody makes it out, and they all go to college. It doesn't happen like that here. There are successes all the time. But you will see on the converse side, you see a lot of people who *don't* make it out—smart kids too."

Xavier was one of those students who was very much on the brink. Now a Tilden senior, he had forged a relationship with Holmes during his freshman year. His Facebook profile consisted mostly of posts about his gang: photos of him flashing gang signs or pointing a gun at the camera, and tributes to friends who were locked up or dead. There was one post, however, that stood out. It proudly announced that he was just five months away from earning his high school diploma. Holmes was at least in part responsible for the fact that he was within spitting distance of that milestone.

During his freshman year, Xavier's good friend Endia Martin was killed. At the time of her death in April 2014, Endia was also a Tilden freshman, a sweet, popular cheerleader whose death rocked the entire school community. It hit Xavier especially hard, both because he was so close to Endia and because he felt partially responsible for her death. Endia was shot and killed by another fourteen-year-old girl, a tragic end to a feud that had been simmering for months on social media between the shooter and Endia's best friend, Lanekia Reynolds. The girls had been exchanging increasingly heated messages on Facebook about a boy the shooter had dated in seventh grade. One day in April, Lanekia and the shooter agreed over Facebook to meet for a fight after school to settle the matter.

According to testimony that Lanekia later gave in court, she and Endia were sitting on a front porch at a home in Back of the Yards on the day of the proposed fight, still dressed in their school uniforms and talking about a friend's birthday party. The shooter approached, carrying a loaded gun in the waistband of her school khakis and flanked by a few dozen friends. The shooter pulled out her gun, and Endia tried to flee. Reynolds was shot in the arm and survived. Endia was fatally shot in the back as she scrambled to get back inside the house. Xavier witnessed the whole thing. He had tried to stop Endia from going to the scene of the fight that day, and he figured he would regret for the rest of his life that he had not tried harder.

When Xavier returned to school after the shooting, he appeared barely sentient. He stared blankly out the window or placed his head on his desk for entire class periods. He didn't say a word to anyone. But he came. Every day. And Holmes figured that counted for quite a lot. Other teachers disagreed. They argued that Xavier had barely been passing their classes before the shooting, and now he wasn't doing any work at all. If he couldn't pull it together, he deserved to fail. One teacher, who has since left the school, even stated that Tilden kids should be able to bounce back quickly because they should be used to their friends dying at this point.

Holmes was livid. Endia's death was the ultimate example of the tragic consequences of teenage recklessness. She refused to let Xavier become more collateral damage. Here was a student who had just lost his best friend, who already had one foot in school and one foot on the streets. A couple of failing grades, she believed, would permanently tip the scales in favor of the streets. She made a passionate appeal to his math teacher. "I was like, 'First of all, he's really into his gang but he comes to school every single day. Only missed one day and that was for her funeral. And on top of that, they were really close friends. You just can't fail him. I refuse to let you him fail him.'"

Two years later, she still gets emotional thinking about Xavier's plight that year. She said, with feeling, "I check up on him, and everything that comes out of his mouth on his Facebook and his Twitter is about his gang, about his Moes or his block or whatever, but that boy is in school *every day*. He's working. He's trying. He's putting so much effort in, and he's one of those kids, I don't know if he's going to college, I don't know, *but* he does want something better. He wants something different, and he's here trying to get it, and you've decided because he's grieving the loss of a friend that he needs to fail because he didn't turn in a couple of worksheets for you?"

Ultimately, the math teacher gave Xavier a mercy D. In June 2017, Xavier walked down the aisle at Tilden's graduation wearing a blue cap and gown and a triumphant smile. He posted photos on Facebook of himself and his mom embracing. "As Long As She Happy I'm Happy I Did This All For You Ma Love u Foreva," he wrote. He hopes to attend college someday to be a computer technician. "I always planned to go to college," he said. "I always promised Endia I would graduate, even before we came to this school." His final Facebook post from graduation day indicated that he, like Holmes, also saw his struggle to graduate from high school in life-and-death terms: "All I Can Say Is I'm #Blessed Made it All The Way Through HighSchool In Didn't Look Back in Still Was Outhere Everyday in This Shit Fight For My Life Day By Day But I Made It Just For Yall." The post included a broken heart emoji and a praying emoji. Then he tagged Endia's memorial page and the pages of two other deceased friends.

Holmes has dozens of similar anecdotes, stories of students at a crossroads and of teachers who made all the difference. And so here she was at a Wednesday afternoon meeting in November, determined to tip the scales in favor of as many students as she could. She started by handing out a list of freshmen who were failing at least one class but in the building at least 85 percent of the time. These were the lower-hanging fruit, the ones most likely to respond to the types of interventions that the success team was able to devise.

"I want to make sure we talk about these kids," Holmes said to the group, which consisted of seven teachers and seven City Year corps members in their early twenties, wearing their signature red jackets. City Year was one of several nonprofits that provided Tilden with services and manpower that it otherwise could not have afforded to provide. Some partners supplemented work that went on in the classroom by providing tutoring or enrichment programs in non-core subject areas like art or digital media. Others worked with students in more of a mentoring capacity, providing social and emotional support and skill training. These partnerships were a lifeline for Tilden, which was not large enough to support a big staff or offer a varied curriculum. Principal Swinney relied heavily on these partnerships, but he also resented that dependence. Managing them—Tilden had more than half a dozen external partners at any given time—took substantial time, energy, and patience. The natures of the partnerships were often in flux, as staff from the partner agencies turned over, or a partner organization adjusted its focus or mission, or as funding for the partnerships came and went. Swinney fantasized about having a permanent staff that could provide the services which partners provided.

"I sent out the agenda early. It was intentional to make sure people had time to look at these kids, think about them, really meditate on them," Holmes continued. All of the teachers seemed reasonably engaged. And the semicircle appeared to have worked— no one seemed more or less a part of the group.

"We have seven kids with eighty-five percent attendance rates. That means these kids are in this building. They are here but they are failing." She gave the group three minutes to discuss each student— first Mateo, who was always late, then Alyssa, who frequently fell asleep in class, and then Cristina, an honors students who had given up in math after a failing grade. "Sierra Smith," Holmes said, with an eye roll that was a mix of fondness and exasperation. "She has an F in

Algebra. She has a B, a C, an F, and perfect attendance. *So*, what is her deal besides trying to look cute all the time?"

"All. The. Time," chorused Vincent Gray, an English teacher who team-taught with Holmes, providing extra support for students with learning disabilities.

"She literally doesn't do anything," said Persaud, her math teacher. "Today I pulled a group together of students who were all struggling. She literally just held the book and let the other students do the work. She always has something to say about how she shouldn't be failing. And her tests and quizzes are terrible," he said bluntly.

Holmes mentioned that Sierra had told her that she tended to get distracted by her friends in class.

"I think that's somewhat true," said Evan Merryman, one of two male City Year volunteers. Unflaggingly good-natured, he almost always had a smile on his face. The students often tried to work out whether Mr. Evan was really as agreeable as he seemed. So far the answer seemed to be yes. "When I pull her out, about two-thirds of the time it's great," he said. "About one-third of the time, she won't do anything. She'll just comb her hair and try to look cute."

"Has anyone called her guardian?" asked Darrell Jenkins, Tilden's Junior ROTC instructor. "I mean, she's doing good in other classes. It's not like she's doing that in all her classes."

Before anyone could answer, the school's gym teacher jumped in with an observation. "Something interesting about her—her sister is extremely smart. She's at Whitney Young maybe? Isn't that the smart school?"

Holmes confirmed that Whitney Young was indeed one of the city's "smart schools," reserved for students across the city with the top test scores and grades. "Anyway," the gym teacher continued, "I said, 'Why aren't you there?' And she said, 'I'm not smart. I can't do that.' I just thought that was interesting."

This was a common refrain among Tilden students. Many of them had been told—by their peers, but also by their elementary school teachers—that Tilden was populated with dumb kids. Most of them believed it, both about themselves and about their classmates.

"She's actually pretty bright," Holmes said. "She has a B in my class and she wants an A."

Foster, the gym teacher, interrupted, "I think she's just distracted a lot. She's dating Timothy and there is always drama—"

"There is *always* drama there," Holmes agreed emphatically, setting off a round of laughter. "So our action step is *break up with drama*."

"Could we put her on some sort of plan where she comes twice a week for thirty minutes of tutoring?" asked Jenny Siegel, refocusing the group. After serving as a City Year corps member at Tilden last year, Jenny had been selected to act as team leader this year. "I feel like she's just really struggled in math, and she's really self-conscious about it and she doesn't know where to go at this point."

"Sure," Evan agreed. "I don't know if she would come after school, though."

"Maybe we could try a bribe?" Jenny suggested. "Like maybe if she comes after school she gets some lipstick or something? I've literally heard her say, 'I'll do anything for lipstick!'"

Holmes turned to Persaud. "Do you have a vague idea of what percentage she has?"

Persaud furrowed his brow. "Forty percent–ish? Maybe a little lower?" he ventured.

"So, it's possible to pass," Holmes clarified.

"I mean, it's *possible*," Persaud said skeptically, as if he were weighing the odds of Sierra going to the moon.

"My other concern with math is that it's just so foundational. If she doesn't get it this semester, what will she do next semester?" Holmes wondered, as much to herself as to the group. Glancing at the clock, she realized she had exceeded the three-minute time limit she had set for each student. "Okay, let's start with the plan, see if we can get her to buy in. And, seriously, I will buy her some lipstick if that's what it takes."

If Sierra had overheard the discussion about her, she would likely have engaged in her signature expression of disdain: side eye, lip curl, dismissive tongue click. In her opinion, the problem she was facing had nothing to do with her schoolwork or her teachers, and it couldn't be fixed with lipstick. The problem, in a nutshell, was her classmates. She had hoped that high school would offer her a reprieve from all of the social drama that had swirled around her in elementary school, but after a brief honeymoon period during the first month of school, she was again at the center of the storm.

"When I got into high school, I wanted to be a changed person," Sierra said during an interview at Tilden. She was wearing diamond heart-shaped earrings, tight-fitting tan jeans, and her blue Tilden shirt. She carried a ruby red purse that matched her ruby red lipstick. "I know I get into a lot of stuff, but it's not even because of me. It just be other people. They just be feeling some type of way, and I don't know why."

During the first couple of months of school the trouble was with Amber, one of the first girlfriends she had made at Tilden. For reasons that Sierra could not quite identify, things had soured between the two of them. They came to a head one day that fall in Biology class. Amber and Jalen, a lanky, popular freshman who played basketball, were sitting at the back of class, loudly "rating" the girls in the class. Jalen said Sierra was a 10. Amber disagreed loudly enough for her ex-friend to hear, which was intentional as far as Sierra was concerned. Amber and Jalen proceeded to fight about it in a way that the whole class could hear, leaving Sierra "very, very irritated."

Not one to let a slight slide, Sierra confronted Amber. She suggested, politely in her retelling of it, that if Amber didn't have something nice to say, she should refrain from saying anything at all. "I'm like, 'Okay, for one, you don't have to rate me. Why you walkin' around putting your opinions on people anyway? You gonna call someone a three and it's gonna make somebody mad. It's *rude.*'"

Reflecting on how the argument had affected her, Sierra's indignation gave way to jaded weariness. "So this drama kept on going on for like a week. I was so tired of school because people just kept on asking me stuff. Kept on saying stuff about me and Amber. It's just like you into all this drama. Your friends just drift away. It's just hard trying to keep friends, stay out of drama, keep your grades up, remember what class to go to. And this is all at the beginning of the school year. And all the teachers are like, 'Remember, this is high school now and you can't do this and you can't do that.' It's just, like—it's REAL hard. And when stuff starts getting hard, I don't know. I feel like I don't want to go back," she concluded sadly.

Over the course of several interviews, it became clear that Sierra's high school experience was largely defined by how well she was getting along with her peers at any given time, which is entirely typical for teenagers but easy for adults to miss, especially when they are trained to focus more on students' academic skills than on their emotional health.

As an adult, it's not difficult to recall intellectually the leading role that your friends played in your teenage years, but it's nearly impossible to conjure up the intensity of those relationships, the flame of new friendship, the prickly burn of rejection, how your very survival seemed to hinge on whether you were invited to sit with your peers at the lunch table. In fact there are biological underpinnings to the social drama that teens experience.

Steinberg calls adolescence "the perfect neurobiological storm, at least if you'd like to make someone painfully self-conscious." He explains that brains become more adept at decoding what people are thinking or feeling at the very same time that they become acutely sensitive to rejection or acceptance, to the point where the experience of rejection actually resembles that of physical pain on neuroimaging scans. Psychologists have posited that there might be an evolutionary reason why the teenage brain is wired to respond to peers in this way. This sensitivity serves to push young people away from their family unit and into the wider world. And yet these changes can also make it especially difficult for teens to cope with the social pressures of high school, because they are so attuned and sensitive to what their peers think and do.

As a result of these developmental changes, Sierra and many of her classmates needed as much help navigating peer relationships as they did figuring out algebraic equations. As Chicago's high schools became increasingly adept at supporting freshmen, they devoted more resources and attention to helping students maintain healthy peer relationships. Indeed, one of the main functions that Tilden's many partner organizations provided was to support students' social and emotional growth.

At Tilden that help came in the form of Laird Walker, who ran the school's Peace Room, a place students could go to decompress, process trauma, seek advice, or mediate conflicts with peers or teachers. The Peace Room was, in a word, peaceful, with denim beanbag chairs, a cozy gray shag rug, and posters emblazoned with helpful tips for de-escalating conflict, such as "Hear me out before you shout." White Christmas-tree lights were strung along the walls and a punching bag and boxing gloves occupied one corner. A large poster hanging next to the punching bag read, "The True self in everyone is good, wise, and powerful."

Walker, thirty, had attended Chicago's public schools in the early 2000s and now worked for Umoja Student Development Corporation, which, like City Year, was a key partner at Tilden. Umoja's goal was to increase student engagement, attendance, and achievement by building strong peer-to-peer and peer-to-adult relationships. Walker wore a lot of hats, including mentor, counselor, and de facto therapist for Tilden's students. A former basketball standout who had played hoops at Lake Forest College and then professionally in Turkey, he was something of a gentle giant. Soft-spoken and contemplative, he listened to students intently and without judgment as they talked to him about their personal lives, classmates, and teachers. Like Swinney, who every year had a student or two who asked to call him "Dad," Walker met a need for a lot of fatherless students who were hungry for a black male role model.

Sierra and Amber spent a lot of time in the Peace Room that fall. "If there is drama or I feel threatened, I can go to him and tell him and we will pull the people that I feel are bothering me, and he'll put us in the circle and we'll work it out," Sierra said. Walker was trained in restorative justice techniques, a set of practices that allows victims and perpetrators of crimes or other wrongdoing to work together to reach a resolution that is mutually acceptable. The goal of restorative justice is to avoid more punitive measures—like prison for crimes, or suspensions or expulsions for school-based infractions. Umoja used restorative justice to address conflicts from the community that spilled into school and to teach the social and emotional skills that students needed to be able to resolve conflicts peacefully. The organization understood that conflicts between students, and between students and staff, often disrupted the learning environment for students and contributed to burnout and turnover among teachers.

For Sierra, who liked most of the adults at Tilden but could not seem to extricate herself from conflict with her peers, Walker was a lifeline. "Usually every time I go in there, I'll be able to work it out," she said. On several occasions that fall, Walker managed to mend the relationship between Sierra and Amber. Before long, though, the drama between the two of them would flare up again. "He helped us. And we became friends *AGAIN*. Like a dummy, I took her back *AGAIN*. But then we stopped talking *AGAIN*. I just don't know if she don't like me and she pretends to be my friend. I don't know what about her upsets me," Sierra said. "We put all that drama in the past to be friends. But then she was telling some girl I was saying something about her, and I didn't say that," Sierra asserted, her voice rising. "So, I was like, 'What's your problem? Why would you say that?'" She concluded, "I don't think she knows how to be a friend."

According to Walker, Sierra's assessment was pretty accurate. Amber, who was struggling with personal issues at home, including a stepdad she had accused of flirting with her, had not really learned yet how to be a good friend. Sierra had. "She really values healthy interactions and relationships," Walker said of Sierra. Walker thought Sierra would fit in seamlessly with some of the kids in the honors classes who came from more stable homes and tended to stick together. Instead, she opted to befriend everyone. "She chooses to love her peers in a way that they are not used to. She listens to them, she doesn't curse them out, she's not showing any outward signs of trauma," Walker observed. "Because of that," he hypothesized, "she's been a target. Like some of the girls think she thinks she's better than them."

Walker wished he had enough time to do more proactive coaching and mentoring with students and teachers alike. In particular, he wanted to work with teachers to help them better understand that a student who was defiant or disruptive during class was often processing some sort of trauma. Teachers sometimes took these disruptions personally or tried to suppress them through punishments or threats. Too often, Walker believed, their first impulse was to throw the book at students, rather than trying to get at the root of their behaviors. "They feel like they shouldn't *have* to do that, and I can see why they would feel that way," Walker said of his colleagues. "But I always think, if I were teaching, I would want to be the best teacher for the population and do whatever works to keep them on track. But I'm not a teacher."

As Walker was finishing up his reflections, Marcus sauntered into the Peace Room like he belonged there, which at this point he did. During the fall quarter, Marcus spent even more time in the Peace Room than Sierra did, though for different reasons. He had begun frequenting the room ever since he nearly came to blows with Mr. Persaud, his math teacher, during the first month of school.

An ex-jock who could often be found lifting weights after school with students, Persaud exuded a tough, no-nonsense air. "This is a classroom. We're going to learn. This is *not* playtime," he said of his classroom management philosophy. He wasn't afraid to go toe-to-toe with students, especially if their antics were preventing other students from learning. "I've argued with a lot of students over the years," he said. "If I don't have two or three standoffs a year, something's wrong."

Persaud acknowledged that some students had trouble adjusting to his approach. "I take a firm stance," he said. "Not every kid is going to react to that in the best way." Marcus was one of those kids. He and Persaud butted heads almost immediately. Marcus recalled Persaud snapping at him on the first day for something he did not do. Marcus snapped back. They got into a verbal altercation. From that point on, Marcus was convinced Persaud was singling him out for scrutiny, just waiting for him to mess up. This made Marcus want to act even worse.

One day a few weeks into school, Persaud kicked Marcus out of class for causing some type of disruption. Marcus lingered by the door, waiting to be allowed back inside and growing increasingly frustrated as the minutes ticked by. When Persaud came to the door to admit another student, Marcus followed, ducking beneath Persaud's arm when he tried to block the way. Persaud grabbed Marcus's book bag to prevent his reentry, which caused Marcus to stumble. He flipped to fight mode, popping up off the floor with his teeth clenched and fists balled, coiled and ready to strike. "I'm gonna fuck your ass up," he shouted. He managed to get a shove in before security staff hauled him away to the dean's office.

Marcus was enraged that a teacher had placed his hands on him. Persaud was livid that Marcus had disrupted class; directly disregarded his order not to return to class, thereby further disrupting the class; and threatened him physically. Neither was about to back down. Walker had decided to try to mediate a truce between the two of them by staging a "peace circle," where they could both express their feelings about the incident.

Walker conducted pre-meetings with both of them, hoping to lay the groundwork for a resolution. First, he met with Marcus, who explained that he had been in trouble in his old school and wasn't trying to get kicked out of this one. At the same time, he was fixated on being grabbed by a teacher and not at all ready to apologize for his role in the altercation. Walker advised him to focus on feelings, not on Persaud's actions, during the peace circle, "since feelings are not debatable." Marcus identified a few adjectives that described how he felt when Persaud grabbed his book bag: "angry," "frustrated," "surprised." Walker then went to check in with Persaud, who insisted there wasn't much to talk about. Marcus had walked into the room when he had asked him not to. He had already disrespected him, and then he disrupted the class a second time by trying to return. So he grabbed his book bag. End of story.

The mediation didn't go well. Walker started the meeting by recapping the incident. Walker wanted to make it clear that Persaud had not intended to harm Marcus, but that the action nevertheless had really shaken Marcus. He wrapped up his introduction. "Now, what we're trying to figure out is how do we set healthy boundaries and find healthy ways to coexist and work through this frustration."

Things deteriorated from there. "You should never have put your hands on me" was Marcus's opening gambit.

"You're a kid," Persaud responded. "You're a student. You gotta do what you gotta do."

When a solution failed to materialize, the dean ended up spoon-feeding them one. They agreed that if Marcus started to feel too angry to sit in class, he could come to the Peace Room to work through his feelings with Walker. Meanwhile, Walker kept working with Persaud behind the scenes to introduce techniques that he might use to help Marcus better manage his anger during class.

"It was clear that his interactions with Persaud were being triggered by things that really had nothing to do with Persaud. And Persaud struggled to really connect in a way that he wanted to with Marcus. But Persaud did try. He did try," Walker said. He may have tried, but Marcus still felt like he was being singled out and picked on in math class. Soon, Marcus was coming to the Peace Room at least three or four times a week during math class, every time he felt like he was ready to fight Persaud.

It was a tremendous amount of time and energy to invest in a single student, but Walker believed Marcus was absolutely worth the effort. He was a natural leader—and fiercely loyal to those he loved and cared about. Many of the skirmishes he got into at school were the result of him protecting someone, often his older sister, who was a sophomore at Tilden. Walker said that if you created a relationship diagram for Tilden students, with arrows indicating who was getting what out of a relationship, all of the arrows would be pointing away from Marcus and toward other kids. He gave and gave and gave, and often he did not expect or get much in return.

He was also "one of the brightest kids in the building," Walker said. When he wasn't getting kicked out of math class, he was often being asked to demonstrate how to solve particularly tricky problems to the rest of the class. He was patient with the students who didn't get it and commanded the attention of kids who generally drifted off in class. He was critical of the workload at Tilden, often complaining that teachers expected too little of students. He was able to clearly articulate the type of instruction that would be more engaging to him. "I want something that I don't know how to do, so once someone teaches it to me, I can understand and then teach it to someone else," Marcus said.

Walker believed that if Marcus could only get a handle on his anger, he could sail through this academic year and perhaps on to college and one of the hopeful futures that Walker liked to envision for him. When insiders talk about Freshman OnTrack in Chicago, they talk about it as a policy, a set of practices, or a research finding. Walker liked to think of it as a talent-loss strategy. He figured if there was a kid in the building whose talents the city of Chicago could not afford to lose, it was Marcus Clark.

CHAPTER 6

Seven years before Marcus and his classmates began their freshman year, as nascent efforts to improve on-track rates were just getting under way at Hancock and other schools, Chicago Public Schools experienced a major shakeup. Midway through the 2008–09 school year, newly elected President Barack Obama nominated his pickup basketball pal Arne Duncan to serve as U.S. Secretary of Education, and Ron Huberman took over as CEO of the district. Duncan had been at the helm of CPS for more than seven years, from June 2001 through December 2008, providing an unusually long stretch of stability for an urban school district. His departure threatened to upend the work he had championed, including the fledgling Freshman OnTrack movement. After Duncan's departure, Freshman OnTrack might have faded away, as education initiatives often do when their champions move on. Instead, Freshman OnTrack became central to Huberman's plan to overhaul the system through a relentless focus on data-driven decision making. The question became, would teachers get on board with Huberman's approach? And would it work?

When Chicago mayor Richard Daley appointed thirty-seven-year-old Huberman to succeed Duncan, Huberman was depicted by the Chicago media as a savvy technocrat and something of a wunderkind, having already served as the mayor's chief of staff, the head of the city's Emergency Management Department, and the head of the Chicago Transit Authority. Good-looking and personable, an openly gay ex-cop, the immigrant son of Israeli Holocaust survivors, and a University of Chicago graduate with advanced degrees in both business *and* social work, Huberman seemed destined for political greatness. He was an insider and an outsider, an intellect with street cred, a no-nonsense numbers guy with a heart.

What he lacked, however, was education experience. Huberman's tenure would be "the purest test" of Mayor Daley's theory that management expertise should trump education experience when it came to running a large school system. And it would be the "ultimate trial" of a corporate brand of reform that assumed that a well-run system of data analysis and measurement could turn around a school system still seen as faltering.

Huberman was a disciple of performance management, an approach to improvement that was borrowed from the corporate world. Performance management involves setting detailed, measurable performance goals; creating plans to meet those goals; and regularly reviewing and analyzing data to determine whether the goals have been met or whether plans need adjusting. GE used the system to evaluate its managers and weed out the lowest 10 percent of performers. It was similar to the work that some high schools had already begun to embark on around Freshman OnTrack, but formalized and expanded to more metrics. Indeed, Huberman would publicly promote Freshman OnTrack as the example of what performance management could accomplish.

Huberman was determined to implement performance management strategies at every level of CPS, from Central Office departments like IT and Procurement down to the school level. He charged each department with identifying their key work processes and creating metrics to measure whether they were working efficiently. The Procurement Department, for example, agreed upon metrics such as "percent of contracts signed under seventy days." Eventually high schools were held accountable for twenty-nine metrics, including the percentage of juniors meeting college readiness standards on the ACT, attendance, expulsions, teacher attendance, and percentage of freshmen who were on-track to graduate.

Each metric was tracked monthly. Results were color-coded (red for below target, yellow for nearing target, and green for meeting or exceeding the target). Schools and departments were expected to create plans for improving each metric, particularly those "in the red."

Many Chicago educators balked at Huberman's performance management approach. At the Chicago Transit Authority, performance management was credited with producing cleaner buses, faster trains, and fiscal solvency. But Huberman's critics pointed out that children were not trains or buses, nor were they products to be rolled off an assembly line. Each brought a unique mix of strengths, challenges, and experiences to school. A system that held every student and every school to the same set of standards was fundamentally flawed. He "has to understand we are working with children with emotional and social issues coming into the classrooms. You can't manage something you don't understand," Chicago Teachers Union president Marilyn Stewart argued.

Huberman acknowledged that his approach had "never been attempted in a large urban school district," but he insisted that the fact that no one had tried to systematically analyze data or measure progress in schools was one of the central problems plaguing the American education system. There was no way to gauge how "we are doing school by school and student by student," Huberman told a crowd of the city's civic leaders at the City Club of Chicago, where he unveiled his education plan.

He explained that the current method for judging success in education primarily rested on a single annual standardized test—a point-in-time measurement that shed little light on how students were learning or teachers were teaching. He provided an analogy from the corporate world. "Let's pretend CPS was McDonald's, and in 680 restaurants, once a year, at 2 p.m., we took cash out of drawer and decided to make decisions based on that."

Huberman was at the vanguard of a national movement to use data to spur improvement in schools. The No Child Left Behind Act had ushered in a new era of data use and accountability in education, as it held all public schools accountable for ensuring that all students were meeting standards on state tests. But by the late 2000s, districts and schools were beginning to use data for more than just holding themselves to a minimum standard. For the first time, sophisticated new data systems were providing schools with granular data on students, teachers, schools, and programs. These longitudinal systems tracked attendance, grades, course-taking patterns, test scores, disciplinary infractions, and other key pieces of data over the course of students' entire academic careers. Schools, once criticized as data deserts, were drowning in data about their students.

But these new data systems were being used for two different, sometimes contradictory, purposes: to hold schools, teachers, and students accountable for meeting external standards, and to help teachers and school leaders improve their craft. There were difficulties imbedded in using data for accountability and improvement simultaneously. So-called "high-stakes accountability" could in some cases ramp up pressure on schools and individuals to the point that it became counterproductive. In extreme cases, high-stakes accountability led to cheating—both in Chicago and across the country. And critics charged for every clear-cut case of cheating, there were likely to have been dozens of examples of subtle data manipulation or of activity more in the interest of data improvement than genuine learning, such as "teaching to the test."

Huberman had one notable supporter: Melissa Roderick. Huberman had been one of her students when he was earning a master's degree at UChicago, and she believed he had the capacity to strike the right balance between data and the human side of education. "The best and the brightest public administrators should be running large public agencies," Roderick said at the time. "When he was in my class he was a cop on the street and he would come in and talk about his experience with such caring and such empathy that I think the people will be surprised at how much he cares and respects the families of Chicago."

But the public would rarely see that side of him. Instead, he would become known for the bruising nature of his performance management (PM) sessions, during which data were flashed up on a screen and administrators were forced to answer for poor performance or negative trends. The sessions had a theatrical air—or, his critics charged, the air of a Roman carnival. They took place on the fifteenth floor of district headquarters and were open to anyone, from principals to administrative staff to the district's top executives. Tables were arrayed in a U-formation, with the school or department under review seated on the left side of the room, support departments seated on the right, and Huberman's executive staff (which he called the "C-Suite") seated front and center. Three oversized screens were located at the front of the room. They depicted the department's organization chart, its PM matrix, and a running list of next steps formulated over the course of the meeting.

"To make PM effective you have to be willing to make decisions at the meetings. . . . On one side you want the department that's up for review to be the folks that are driving the meeting, with the C-Suite asking the tough questions," Huberman explained. Huberman added that the emphasis of the meeting was always on fostering improvement. "We don't care if your spreadsheet's all red. We want to know that you're going to go from red to yellow and yellow to green and you have a plan to get there."

But many principals did not experience the performance management sessions as a growth opportunity. Jackie Lemon still shudders when she remembers her time on the hot seat. She was a principal first at Walter H. Dyett High School, a neighborhood high school, and then at Talent Development High School, a charter school run by Johns Hopkins. Both Dyett and Talent Development served very high-poverty, high-crime areas. And both schools served a high percentage of students who came in with very low performance. At Dyett, Lemon greatly improved the school's climate and reduced suspensions and other disciplinary actions, but she never could get a handle on attendance or Freshman OnTrack rates, both of which were always extremely low. At Talent Development, she had more resources at her disposal, including a full-time staff member whose job was to track attendance and grades, and her Freshman OnTrack rates were higher. Still, maintaining numbers that were acceptable to Central Office was a constant challenge.

Her performance management session at district headquarters was brutal. She was given a date to appear and an empty slide deck to populate. She entered the conference room to find a room full of people she didn't know. "I felt like I was on display. Like people said, 'Oh! Jackie's there today? I'm going to go watch this,'" Lemon recalled. Immediately she was put on the defensive, as the C-Suite demanded she defend her enrollment numbers, her attendance, and some other data points that she already knew were on the low side. They homed in on the periodic attendance dips her school experienced. She explained that attendance tended to drop temporarily when someone in the neighborhood was killed. Sometimes it was one of her students who had been shot, and then parents were particularly reluctant to send their kids to school. She felt the disapproval of the room. One administrator—she didn't even know what department he was from—observed that other schools in crime-ridden areas managed to get their kids to school every day, even after a shooting.

She felt her blood pressure start to rise as her mind flashed to the many funerals—now in the double digits—that she had attended for murdered students. She pictured the hallways after yet another shooting had ravaged her school community. Teachers openly weeping. Kids sobbing. Staff catching students in embraces as they stumbled through the door. And now this pencil-pushing asshole was claiming that there was a magic formula for getting her kids to school after a classmate or friend or family member was murdered? "I genuinely do not know what you want me to do when a parent says, 'I'm not sending my kid to school today for safety reasons,'" Lemon said as evenly as she could manage. "I called extra security. I reached out. Tell me, what should I do?" Her supervisor, wanting to protect her, signaled for her to keep cool. Lemon couldn't help herself. "*Look*, you've emailed me to tell me my numbers are low. You've sent me a fax. In principals' meetings, you have showed me reports with red all over. You have repeated the same information to me in so many ways. I *know* it's low, *all right?*"

The session hadn't accomplished a thing in Lemon's estimation. Before the session, she didn't know how to do what they were asking her to do—and she certainly didn't have a better handle on how to do it afterward. "If I don't learn something new, I'm not going to change my behavior. Folks were just leaving those sessions in tears or furious," Lemon recalled. "Your beating me up is *not* motivating. It's like giving a student an F and assuming they are suddenly going to be motivated."

In Chicago, frustrated teachers and principals like Lemon began to fight back against the data-driven corporate reform agenda. The insurgency reached a crescendo in Huberman's second year at the helm of CPS, when Karen Lewis was elected the president of the Chicago Teachers Union in a hotly contested election that centered more on education policy and practice than on the bread-and-butter union issues of wages and benefits.

Lewis, a high school chemistry teacher, had campaigned primarily on the claim that the previous administration had failed to put up a fight against mayoral control and the corporate agenda that had dominated the past fifteen years of reform in Chicago. She said she had not been looking to leave the classroom when she formed her Caucus of Rank and File Educators (CORE), but she was fed up with the direction of school reform both locally and nationally. "Chicago's the incubator for a whole bunch of madness, so we decided that we had to do something about it," she said. A firebrand leader and orator, Lewis in June 2010 won 59 percent of the vote to become CTU's next president, galvanizing what had become a divided and dispirited rank and file.

In an impassioned acceptance speech before a roomful of delegates, Lewis thundered, "This election shows the unity of 30,000 educators standing strong to put business in its place—out of our schools. . . . This so-called school reform is not an education plan. It's a business plan." She went on to blast Huberman and previous administrations for their reliance on standardized tests that "labeled our students, families, and educators failures" and for using those failing test scores to "whip up public support for charters and contract schools."

Lewis was suspicious not just of test scores but of all metrics used to judge the success or failure of schools and teachers, arguing that they put undue pressure on teachers. Shortly after the election that brought Lewis to power, the *Chicago Sun-Times* and the CTU administered a survey to teachers asking them whether they had ever been pressured to change grades. Nearly one-third of high school teachers admitted they had experienced pressure to inflate grades and one in five acknowledged changing a grade under duress.

Some teachers blamed pressure from coaches and parents. Others blamed pressure from the Freshman OnTrack initiative. One teacher said she felt compelled to offer last-minute makeup opportunities to help students avoid failure. Another said that the grading scale at the school had been lowered, and still there was pressure to change grades. "That's all this district cares about," a math teacher complained. "How many kids are failing. Not how many kids are learning."

In a press release responding to the charges of grade inflation and tampering, Lewis decried the pressure that teachers and principals were under to raise Freshman OnTrack and high school graduation rates. Mayor Daley responded that Huberman would never have asked principals or teachers to change grades. Jackson Potter, part of CORE's leadership team, replied that Daley's defense was disingenuous. "The Mayor should know CEO Huberman's singular focus on data to close or turn around schools and to withhold funding is in part to blame for school staff possibly gaming the system." Freshman OnTrack, which had begun as a metric to help to pinpoint the factors that led to dropout, was in danger of morphing into something else entirely—another flashpoint in the school reform wars.

Huberman stepped down in November 2010, a few months into the 2010–11 school year. His departure had been expected ever since Daley announced his intention not to run for another term as mayor, but the timing of Huberman's announcement caught many by surprise. "The principals have been left high and dry," Clarice Berry, president of the Chicago Principals and Administrators Association, complained at the time. Huberman's critics sensed an opportunity to swing away from Huberman's data-driven strategy and Daley's corporate reform agenda. "I'd like a real superintendent who understands teaching and students," Lewis said, conspicuously avoiding the term "CEO" that Daley had adopted for the head of schools.

Daley subsequently appointed an interim CEO, Terry Mazany, president of the Chicago Community Trust, who vowed to temper the more punishing aspects of performance management. Mazany was blunt about the state of CPS after Huberman's departure. "The system was in free fall," he said. "And there was a loss in a unifying vision for education."

One of the primary obstacles to maintaining sustainable change in large urban districts is the revolving door of superintendents. The average tenure of an urban superintendent is just three years. "I think the challenge in CPS as in all big systems is focus," Huberman said, reflecting on the turnover the district experienced before and after his tenure. "Arne [Duncan] had his strategy; I had mine; Terry [Mazany] for his short tenure had his, so I think it's very easy for people doing the work at the school level to drown it out because they kind of have to."

And yet amid all of the churn, shifting priorities, and deteriorating relationships between teachers and CPS administrators, the system did remain focused on Freshman OnTrack. Citywide, freshmen's on-track rates climbed before and after Huberman's tenure, from 60 percent the year before the Freshman OnTrack initiative was launched; to 64 percent during the 2008–09 school year, when Duncan left and Huberman was named CEO; to 69 percent during the 2009–10 school year, Huberman's only full year at the helm of CPS; to 73 percent in 2010–11, the year Huberman resigned and Mazany took temporary custody of the district; to 75 percent in 2011–12, the first full school year in which the system was under the control of newly elected mayor Rahm Emanuel and his hand-picked school chief, Jean-Claude Brizard, who had previously served as the superintendent of the Rochester City School District.

When he arrived from Rochester in spring 2011, Brizard embarked on a citywide listening tour to hear from teachers, students, parents, and community groups. His takeaway from the tour was that nearly two decades of continuous reform under mayoral control had created a palimpsest of disconnected, half-realized reforms and policies. "CPS was not short on strategy," Brizard said. "It was short on execution. I called the system Frankenstein's monster because I saw a lot of amazing parts, but the whole was incoherent."

Freshman OnTrack was the clear outlier. "When I talked to principals—I don't think there was one exception," Brizard recalled. "They all talked about the ninth-grade metric. Principals didn't just care about it, they believed in it, and they believed in the results they were getting." Brizard marveled that people from across the education reform spectrum all seemed to converge around Freshman OnTrack. "I know Huberman was often accused of being just a metrics monitor. But even people who were not obsessed with metrics—the ones who were interested in really deep, esoteric pedagogical discussions, the folks who were the quintessential educators, bought into it. . . . It had become a fundamental barometer for the system. It was everywhere. I've *never* seen that before. Ever."

One of the key forces working to sustain and deepen the Freshman OnTrack work across the district amidst the administrative churn of the previous decade was a group of high school

principals that Roderick had begun convening in 2005, which
would eventually evolve into a supportive nonprofit, the Network
for College Success (NCS). Like Huberman, the group was focused
on using data to improve schools. Unlike Huberman, however,
they were less focused on accountability and more focused on
giving teachers and principals the tools and know-how they
needed to respond to what the data revealed about their schools
and students. They managed to strike a balance between the data
detractors and the data hawks.

The main requirement for entry into the fledgling group was that
the principal was not planning on retiring in the next couple of years.
Drawn mostly from Roderick's personal connections, the group was
small and eclectic, a mix of young and veteran principals from a
cross-section of the city's schools. They included Elizabeth Kirby of
Kenwood High School, which was located near the University of
Chicago; Beryl Shingles from Morgan Park, a high school on the far
South Side; Don Fraynd, the founding principal of Jones College
Prep, a selective enrollment school located amidst the skyscrapers of
downtown; John Horan, one of the founders of North Lawndale College Prep, a small charter high school on the South Side; and Asuncion Ayala, the principal at North-Grand, a mid-sized neighborhood
school on the West Side.

Roderick also recruited two school reform veterans, Sarah Duncan and Mary Ann Pitcher, to help facilitate the group. Eventually
they would become its full-time co-directors, along with Jackie
Lemon, the principal who had been so cowed by Huberman's performance management session. Both Duncan and Pitcher came out of
Chicago's charter and small schools movements—Pitcher had helped
found Young Women's Leadership Charter School, a charter high
school for girls, and Duncan, along with her brother Arne, had helped
run Ariel Community Academy.

"We were all searching for system change," Pitcher says, "but
then the system never put in place any mechanisms with which to
share innovation. . . . It became very competitive. We were kind of

creating parallel systems, and it was dangerous for people to share. It still is because they're competing for dollars out there."

Much of the proceedings of the early NCS meetings were focused on how to build trust and communication among people who were not accustomed to working together, a crucial step that Huberman's PM approach had omitted. The group devoted part of its second meeting to developing a list of norms designed to create a safe, supportive environment that challenged principals to reflect and improve. The initial list they generated reflected both their hopes and their fears around cross-school collaboration. It included:

> Don't look for excuses to say, "This doesn't apply to me."
> Be patient helping to problem solve (even when it doesn't directly apply).
> Avoid lecturing, "showing off."
> If you think you're talking too much, look around and ask.

And the eminently practical:

> No stealing (staff) from others' schools.

Initially, the group focused primarily on the instructional challenges they were facing in their buildings. It wasn't until the spring of their first year together that Roderick presented information on Freshman OnTrack to the group, introducing the work that would come to define NCS. When Roderick first introduced the group to the research on the freshman year, Arne Duncan had already put Freshman OnTrack on the accountability framework, but most principals knew little about the metric or how to move it. Roderick defined Freshman OnTrack to the group and explained why it was important.

Next, Roderick shared the attendance and on-track rates of every school in the network and asked them to reflect on them together. Recognizing that such public displays of data were likely to put the group on the defensive, Pitcher immediately worked to defuse any anxiety the group might have. She emphasized the importance of confidentiality. She said they were disseminating all of the schools'

data not in the spirit of competition, but with the "hope of collaboration." She said that reviewing each other's data could help the
principals identify common problems as well as pockets of success
that the entire group could learn from.

"It was amazing, it was really a light bulb moment," Sarah Duncan recalled. There was one data point that stood out from the
others. During the 2004–05 school year, North-Grand High
School, a brand-new neighborhood high school on the city's West
Side, had posted a 91 percent Freshman OnTrack rate. This was at a
time when the district-wide rate was just 59 percent. The only schools
in the city with a higher percentage of passing freshmen were the
selective enrollment schools that consistently graduate most of their
students. The brand-new school was led by Asuncion (Sunny) Ayala,
who had moved to the mainland from Puerto Rico when she was a
child and was the first person in her family to attend college.

"Everyone kind of looked at that, and looked at Sunny, and they
were like, 'What are you doing?'" Duncan recalled. Fraynd of Jones
College Prep was particularly eager to pick her brain. His Freshman
OnTrack rate was 82 percent, decent but not spectacular given the
students he was serving. Fraynd was drawing students with the very
highest grades and test scores in the city. Every last one of the freshmen at Jones had excelled in elementary school. Now nearly one in five
of them was ending the year off-track. How was North-Grand, serving students with much lower skills and much higher needs, outper-
forming one of the district's showcase schools on this critical metric?

"She saw her students in a beautiful way," Duncan recalled. "Her
approach was very direct." Indeed, Ayala, who in heels barely
topped five feet, could often be found in the North-Grand hallway,
physically dragging hulking teenagers to class. "Her attendance was
very good and, I don't know if she had read the research or not, but
she believed it did not make sense to fail a kid unless you had worked
hard to make sure they succeeded. If there was an F, and you couldn't
show you had tried multiple times to help, that's not acceptable.
That means you are failing the child."

Ayala explained to the group that if a student was late or didn't show up during first period, someone from her staff made a call home. To every missing kid. Every single day.

"Who makes those calls? What budget line do you pay for that out of?" Fraynd asked.

"This is a family. We all make those calls," insisted Ayala, "My clerks make the calls, my counselors make the calls, my teachers make the calls, *I* make the calls."

"That was a moment," Duncan said. "Because the group realized she doesn't have any extra resources, but she has just organized the building to get this result, and when kids show up, they do a lot better."

Over the years, cross-school comparisons would spark some of the most powerful insights around how to drive Freshman OnTrack rates. According to Bryk, networks allow for the identification of "bright spots" or "positive deviants"—places where unusually positive outcomes are occurring—and for discerning what it is that these places have actually done. Within the trusting, focused context of a network, comparative data can "create a sense of moral urgency—if others can accomplish this, we can and should be able to do better too. This positive response stands in sharp contrast to the defensiveness that comparative data tend to generate in high-stakes accountability contexts. In the latter cases, the knee-jerk reaction is to discount the data, question their credibility, and explain away differences as others having better students or more support or better conditions, and so on." Roderick and the NCS staff weren't doing anything radically different than Huberman—whose approach had led to so much discounting, questioning, and explaining away—had, but they were doing it within a context of trust and learning, among educators and school leaders who were all grappling with similar challenges, which made all the difference.

One of Huberman's first major actions as CEO had been to reorganize the district's sub-regions, a move that ultimately led to the formalization of NCS as an official district network. District reorganizations, particularly those involving the sub-districts that CPS was divided into, were something of a rite of passage for CPS CEOs and also a major contributor to the policy whiplash that educators on the ground experienced with each change in management. When Huberman followed suit and announced his particular reorganization plan, NCS principals sensed an opportunity.

"Principals were just really struggling with the areas under Arne," Roderick recalled. "And somebody came up with the idea of being our own area," the subdistrict units Huberman had created (building on previous Vallas and Duncan reorganizations). "And then they said 'we can only do it if one of us takes the head role.'" Sean Stalling, a principal at Manley high school and a member of NCS, threw his hat in the ring. Roderick petitioned Huberman, her former student, to fold the network into the area structure he was developing. He agreed. NCS became Area 21, which included fourteen high schools.

Area 21 principals defined themselves in opposition to the type of old-school administrators who believed that their primary job was to keep the hallways clear and the lights on. Area 21 principals were comfortable with data, viewed education through a social justice lens, and were more concerned with fostering a strong climate and engaging instruction than in simply maintaining order or operating efficiency.

This shared sensibility made it easier to trust one another and to learn from one another. "Without the safe space with people that I *knew* were smart and cynical and embittered in the *right* way, we wouldn't have become what we have become," reflected Karen Boran, who became the principal at Hancock in 2012. "There was none of this, 'These little kids are shiny little apples and we're going to save them.' It was always, 'No, *goddammit*, these kids deserve a spot in the middle class, and how are we going to wrestle the system to make it happen?'"

By the time NCS became Area 21, it had adopted Freshman OnTrack as a major focus of its work. Stalling, the NCS head from

Manley, was a huge proponent of both Freshman OnTrack and Huberman's performance management structures. He melded the two, making Freshman OnTrack one of the key metrics he held his team accountable for. The fact that Stalling, their boss, was focused on the metric, provided extra incentive to get better at Freshman OnTrack. Principals began clamoring for more information about how to move the metric.

Unlike high school reform under Vallas, in which every high school in the system was forced to implement advisories and freshmen academies, the approach to keeping freshmen on-track evolved over time, with input from every school in the network. The work to improve freshman performance evolved through trial and error and the swapping of information in various venues.

"It's not like we sat down in a corner, came up with something, and brought it to people," said Sarah Howard, an NCS coach who worked with both Tilden and Hancock. "It was more like, 'My boss keeps putting that f—— data on the screen. I better figure out how to work on this.' It created a demand for help. And that set the stage for some problem solving around how *do* we work on this?" NCS and Area 21 began putting coaches (independent, full-time staffers) in schools to help facilitate Freshman OnTrack. They also regularly convened principals, district staff, researchers, and school counselors to swap ideas.

One thing that became clear to Roderick was that many NCS principals needed help thinking about how to use the metric to spur school-wide improvement. Some of them were not data savvy at all. Others understood how to analyze data but wanted different data than what the district was providing. The reports disseminated by the district were excellent for tracking individual students throughout the year, but they were less effective for detecting school-wide trends that would allow principals to craft classroom and school-wide prevention strategies that would hopefully cut down on the number of students who were showing up on the district's watch lists.

Roderick and the Consortium began producing individualized Freshman OnTrack school reports for every high school in the district. They showed the school's historic on-track rates, attendance, and grades, and whether they were improving or declining over time. Each of these metrics was also broken down by students' gender and incoming test scores, allowing schools to determine which groups of students needed more support in those areas.

This segmentation allowed schools to detect trends they otherwise would have missed. Stalling, for example, could look at his report and see the toll that the 2006–07 school year—his first as a principal at Manley—had taken on his female students. That year, the school had received an influx of students from different neighborhoods due to a district boundary change. The report showed Stalling that the on-track rates of his freshman girls had dipped 15 percentage points, from 66 percent in 2005–06, to 51 percent. Meanwhile, the FOT rate of his boys had actually improved one point. Stalling had spent the school year trying to maintain peace among warring gangs. He had worried continuously about maintaining order among his boys, who were the most likely to act out. The report showed that his girls were waving their hands for help, too, albeit more quietly than the boys had. The report told a crucial story about that year, one he would have otherwise missed.

Though NCS's approach to Freshman OnTrack evolved and deepened over time, it was always rooted in the belief that robust systems, structures, and shared leadership were the path to scaling innovation and bringing about system change. NCS leaders often quoted Atul Gawande, the surgeon and bestselling author, who argues that the single greatest challenge facing the medical system is its extreme complexity, and that the surest way to improve it is to reduce its complexity through systems and structures that promote reliable delivery of care. He cites a surgical safety checklist as one elegant solution to this complexity. When critical-care doctors and nurses at Johns Hopkins University began creating and following checklists for all their routine procedures, care was revolutionized. Infection rates plummeted, hospital stays shortened, and survival rates improved.

Gawande acknowledges that his approach goes against the grain in surgery and emergency care, which fetishizes the brilliant, lone-wolf surgeon. Likewise, NCS's approach ran counter to some popular currents in education reform that were more focused on recruiting and holding on to "superstar" teachers than on fostering the conditions that lead to effective teaching. The national push to revamp teacher evaluation, for instance, focused primarily on improving teacher quality by identifying and rewarding top talent and weeding out low-performers. NCS took a different approach, based on the theory that since there were only so many superstar teachers available, the best way to achieve system-wide improvement was to make it easier for teachers to be effective by creating effective systems and structures for them to work within.

"There's this idea that a school can find a Michael Jordan and it'll be fine. But Michael didn't win championships until he had a team around him and Phil Jackson worked out the triangle offense. We're obsessed at the network with systems and structures because that's how you build something that will last," Roderick said.

The most effective structures that NCS helped to establish were Freshman Success Teams, the groups of teachers, counselors, and other staff from each school who worked with freshmen in some way (Holmes's group at Tilden was one such team). These teams met regularly to discuss individual students and to review data on school-wide absence, grade, and failure trends. The ninth-grade team approach proved to be a major breakthrough. In the early years of Freshman OnTrack, most NCS schools still relied on a single coordinator to do most of the heavy lifting around supporting ninth graders.

Over time, principals in Area 21 began seeing Freshman OnTrack not just as a strategy for supporting freshmen, but as an overall strategy for using data and teacher teams to drive school-wide improvement. "I'm not just being rose colored. That was a good network for me to be in. And I was, let's say, a hard person to have in a network because I challenged everything," said Janice Jackson, who was a principal at George Westinghouse College Prep when she joined NCS. "But I felt like Sean really created a learning network. He was the person who really taught me as a principal this notion that you get further with teacher teams. And I started pulling data every two weeks. . . . I would not have started implementing those practices if I had not been in Area 21."

Jackson was exactly the type of leader Roderick was hoping to develop when she started the network. Growing up as one of five children in a working-class family that lived on the city's South Side, Jackson had attended Chicago's public schools and Chicago State University for college. She had hoped to be a college professor, but found her calling as a social studies teacher at South Shore High School, then one of the lowest-performing schools in the state. At age twenty-seven, she became the founding principal of Al Raby School for Community and Environment, a neighborhood high school on the city's West Side that she helped design. Arne Duncan later named her the founding principal of Westinghouse College Prep, a newly opened selective school. Like Roderick, Jackson had aspirations to transform not just a single school, but the entire system. On her admissions essay to her doctorate program at the University of Illinois–Chicago, Jackson stated that she hoped someday to lead Chicago Public Schools (something she did, indeed, achieve).

As more and more Area 21 schools adopted a team approach and began to regularly review data on school-wide course failures, its principals became increasingly aware that inconsistent, and sometimes arbitrary, grading practices were contributing to the high rates of freshman failure. NCS and Stalling, in turn, began working to build principals' capacity to create fair, consistent grading systems. "When I started having those discussions as a principal with my teachers, I started to see that people had different philosophies that drove their behaviors," Jackson observed. Her best teacher had one of the highest Advanced Placement pass rates in the city.

He also had a very high failure rate. He thought of those two things as opposite sides of the same coin. Jackson pushed him to think about them as diametrically opposed.

"I think a lot of people still think rigor means things being hard as opposed to rigor being meeting students where they are and taking each student individually to the next edge of growth," Jackson reflected. As Glynn had done at Hancock, she started auditing her teachers' grade books. She asked tough questions of teachers who were failing large percentages of students, but also of teachers with zero failures. She wanted to know how they were assessing students, what type of work they were assigning, and the purpose of each assignment. She urged teachers to move away from grade book entries that described the content they had covered—such as "Chapter 1 test" or "Article on Columbus"—and to instead emphasize the skill they expected each student to learn and demonstrate. "That was a heavy lift," she recalled, one she would not have embarked upon without the help of NCS. "I think Freshman OnTrack has been transformational for this district. I truly believe that," Jackson reflected. "And one thing I would say that has really been key, is it started the conversation around grades."

The fact that Freshman OnTrack became a conversation about grades at all was a testament to the power of networks. The Freshman OnTrack handbook, which the district created to share best practices gleaned from the pilot lab schools, could describe the type of work and interventions that might support a Freshman OnTrack strategy, but without the ongoing opportunities to learn from other schools, it's unlikely that a handbook alone would have translated into the type of deep adaptive work that flourished in Area 21.

"We needed the Network to make this happen," said Karen Boran of Hancock. "We could not have done it on our own because we did not have the knowledge or access to data to build a model in our head about what success was supposed to be. Most of us never worked in a school that was successful as a CPS educator. I'm a reading teacher, I never taught a kid at grade level. So I needed M.A. [Pitcher] and Sarah

[Duncan]. I needed Jackie Lemon. I needed Elaine [Allensworth]. I needed other principals like Maurice Swinney and Juan Carlos Ocon across the table from me saying, 'We're doing this but we're not doing this and how might this look in your school?'"

In recent years, networks have gained attention as a key mechanism for school improvement. Education authority Michael Fullan is one of the foremost advocates for using networks to catalyze education reform. Fullan, the former dean of the Ontario Institute for Studies in Education at the University of Toronto, studies how improvement happens across large systems. He argues, "For system change to occur on a larger scale, we need schools learning from each other and districts learning from each other. My colleagues and I call this 'lateral capacity building' and see it as absolutely crucial for system reform." Fullan argues that "most theories of change are weak on capacity building and that is one of the key reasons why they fall short."

In addition to capacity building, NCS provided participants with a sense of community and camaraderie, a sort of "us against the world" mentality. When his area was up for review during one of Huberman's performance management sessions, Stalling spent the first part of the meeting outlining his strategy for improving attendance and Freshman OnTrack numbers. The strategy centered on building professional learning communities at each school.

"We learn from each other," Stalling explained.

"But what if it's the blind leading the blind?" Huberman challenged.

As Stalling expounded on how professional learning communities worked in Area 21, Huberman abruptly cut him off. "Enough with the 'Kumbaya moment,'" he snapped. Ultimately, "Kumbaya moment" became a running joke in Area 21. Stalling used it as a motivator. "We were like, You don't think this works? We're gonna show you," Stalling said.

The principals in Area 21 were by and large a competitive group—Stalling was a former baseball coach, Roderick enjoyed nothing more than playing the role of triumphant underdog, and Liz Kirby of Kenwood and Jackson were hotshot principals accustomed to being the smartest people in the room. Before long, they turned that competitiveness outward. The reports the district began to send out comparing Freshman OnTrack rates among the various areas provided all the motivation they needed.

"You would see Area 21, Area 19, and you would see where we all ranked," Stalling recalled. "Then you got some friendly competition. Akeshia Craven was another chief. She was bought in. Then you had Rick Mills. I'm going to say he was bought in, but I also think he was super competitive. We caught wind that Rick told his principals in a meeting that they *better* not lose to Area 21. And at that point, we rolled up our sleeves, and we said, 'We're gonna kick his ass.' So you had that dynamic in play."

This competitive dynamic is actually a common phenomenon among cross-school networks, Fullan argues. "As schools learn from each other, their sense of identity and allegiance expands, spurring an even greater commitment to improvement. Along the way we have discovered an interesting twist, which we call 'collaborative competition,' in which networks of schools compete with each other to do better—all in a spirit of pursuing important moral goals."

Freshman OnTrack lent itself to this type of cross-school learning and friendly competition because it was a metric that people could move in a relatively short period of time. So many of the metrics that schools were held accountable for weren't particularly malleable, at least in the short term. A competition to improve ACT scores? Most schools hadn't figured out how to move high school standardized test scores by much—and even if they had, they certainly weren't going to see improvement from one month to the next.

Craven, who ran Area 19, recalled how the metric made the principals in her network feel successful, often for the very first time. "So much of what we were looking at—graduation rates, ACT outcomes, grade-level proficiency on end of grade testing—all of those things were proving to be so much more difficult to move. So when people saw Freshman OnTrack moving relatively quickly, it created a lot of momentum and excitement of being able to see the fruits of your labor." There were also tangible benefits in the form of improved student lives. Your Freshman OnTrack rate went up 10 points? That could represent twenty or thirty kids whose lives were demonstrably better than they would have been otherwise. Your average ACT scores went up a quarter point? It was a lot harder to draw a direct line between that quarter point and a better quality of life for kids, now or in the future.

At the end of its first year as an area, Area 21 (the NCS schools) led the district's other areas in growth on most available metrics, including, not surprisingly, Freshman OnTrack. Area 21's FOT rate improved to 72 percent, an increase of nearly 8 percentage points. The network ended with the highest Freshman OnTrack rate of any traditional (not charter, selective enrollment, or turnaround) high school area. They also showed the largest improvement over the previous year among traditional networks. At the end of the year, Roderick sent out a congratulatory email to NCS principals and staff. The subject line read: "Kumbaya Kicks Ass."

Of course, this being CPS, kumbaya—in this iteration, at least—proved short-lived. Brizard, following in the footsteps of his predecessors, reorganized the district's area structure again, thereby creating another episode of the instability that practitioners regularly experienced during that period of rapid turnover at CPS. He cut the number of areas, rechristened them "networks," and redrew boundaries to "keep communities and neighborhoods whole." The goal struck many working in the system as odd, since CPS's policy for years had been pushing the district away from a neighborhood school model.

Under the new structure, Area 21 high schools were dispersed among four of the five high school areas, and NCS went back to being a voluntary group rather than an official CPS network. Pitcher from NCS saw a silver lining. "This way allows our schools to share what they've learned with the schools in their new networks."

This prediction proved to be accurate. The Freshman OnTrack work spread, as teacher leaders and assistant principals who had participated in Success Teams at NCS schools became principals at other schools. For instance, Mike Boraz had been Kirby's assistant principal at Kenwood. He became principal at Lincoln Park High School and brought his Freshman OnTrack expertise along with him. The school's FOT rates improved from 77 percent the year before he arrived to 90 percent in 2017. Janice Wells, the one-time assistant at Manley, became principal at South Shore International High School. That school's FOT rates improved from 77 percent in her first year to 98 percent in 2017. Many other teachers and assistant principals fanned out across the district, spreading the Freshman OnTrack gospel too.

Likewise, as principals who had participated in some of the early NCS activities were promoted or moved on to other schools, they brought Freshman OnTrack with them. Donald Fraynd, the Jones College Prep principal, became the city's high school improvement officer, and then the chief school improvement officer. Kenyatta Stansberry Starks participated in the Network when she was principal at Harper High School. She went on to lead Marshall High School and briefly serve as the district's deputy of student transitions, before taking the helm of a Chicago charter high school. Ernesto Matias, principal at William H. Wells Community Academy High School, which participated in some of the earliest iterations of NCS, became a network chief, responsible for thirty-seven elementary and high schools. Kirby, the Kenwood principal who had taped a copy of the graph showing the relationship between freshman absence and dropout to her computer, became one of the chief transmitters of the work after Brizard appointed her chief of the Southwest Side High School Network. She later became the chief of school strategy and planning. And Janice Jackson, who started with NCS as principal of the Al Raby high school and then became principal at Westinghouse College Prep, moved on to serve as a network chief. In July 2015 she was named the district's chief education officer, CPS's number two administrative role. And in December 2017, she was named CEO of Chicago Public Schools. She became the first CEO since mayoral control began to have once served as a CPS teacher or principal. She had been both.

Between 2006 and 2017, thirty-four CPS high schools were part of NCS, some for a year or two and some for the duration. During that period, its format shifted several times, but it maintained its focus on shared leadership, freshman success, principal leadership, and college readiness. That focus provided crucial continuity for NCS schools when the district underwent yet another upheaval in the fall of 2012.

That September, the Chicago Teachers Union went on strike for the first time in twenty-five years. Mayor Rahm Emanuel labeled it a "strike of choice," arguing that the two sides were not very far apart on terms when the teachers voted to strike. But the strike was never really about bread-and-butter issues such as pay and health care, or about air conditioning or the use of test scores in teacher evaluations—two sticking points, according to the union. It was, above all, a protest against the way teachers were being treated in Chicago and nationally. "Let's be clear—this fight is for the very soul of public education, not just only Chicago but everywhere," Karen Lewis said at the time.

Lewis and Emanuel, who was elected mayor in February 2011, had clashed almost from the start. "His agenda is the same agenda that we have seen throughout the country, which is an agenda of blaming teachers for everything that's wrong with public education systems, not looking at any of the systemic issues," Lewis said.

Emanuel, President Obama's former chief of staff, had been determined to be known as the "education mayor" when he was elected. He had pushed a string of reforms that were anathema to the union: a longer school day, teacher evaluation systems linked to student test scores, merit-pay programs, the expansion of the city's charter school network, and the shuttering of low-performing, underutilized schools. With teachers walking the picket line, Chicago was the national epicenter of reform—but not in the way Emanuel had envisioned. The national media and national education-reform community closely followed the strike, perhaps the most high-profile revolt against the national education reform agenda to date.

Wrote University of Illinois labor professors Steven K. Ashby and Robert Bruno,

> A labor conflict focused solely on compensation at the start developed into a challenge to a national education reform movement that, teachers charged, was systematically destroying public education and using Chicago as its test case. Unlike in past strikes, tens of thousands of teachers, clinicians, and paraprofessionals marched repeatedly in Chicago's neighborhoods and downtown. Thousands of community members and parents joined the demonstrations. Crowds swelled, shutting down streets in the city's Loop district. Instead of accepting the loss of classroom control and corporate style-management of schools, which teachers had been told for decades was "inevitable," the CTU reinvigorated a national teachers movement by fighting back.

After seven missed school days, the strike ended. The deal called for average teacher raises of 17.6 percent over four years. It established a teacher evaluation system that was based partially on student test scores, though test scores would count for less than what Emanuel had initially called for. The deal scrapped Emanuel's plan to base pay raises on merit rather than on longevity, and gave more protection to laid-off teachers with strong ratings. In exchange, Emanuel got a longer school day and more leeway for principals to hire the teachers they wanted.

The strike effectively ended Brizard's career in Chicago. Three weeks after the teachers returned to work, Brizard tendered his resignation. He was replaced by Barbara Byrd-Bennett, the system's chief education officer, who had previously served as the school chief in Cleveland, Ohio. Byrd-Bennett had played a more visible role in negotiations than Brizard had and was publicly credited with brokering an end to the strike. Brizard's tenure had lasted just seventeen months.

Reflecting later on the strike, Brizard argued, "We severely underestimated the ability of the Chicago Teachers Union to lead a massive grassroots campaign against our administration. It's a lesson for all of us in the reform community. The 'how' is at times more important than the 'what.'"

Other observers gleaned similar lessons. In a postmortem of the strike, Alex Kotlowitz, the author of *There Are No Children Here: The Story of Two Boys Growing Up in the Other America* and a contributor to a Peabody Award–winning documentary about the toll of gun violence on Chicago's students, argued that the strike was about something even more essential than the merits of one reform agenda over another. Kotlowitz argued that it was, ultimately, a referendum on whether we as a nation expect too much of education generally and teachers in particular. In the course of the preceding decade, it had become a common refrain to call education "The Civil Rights Issue of Our Time." George H.W. Bush said it when he passed the No Child Left Behind Act. Obama and Duncan frequently repeated the mantra. Kotlowitz argued that reformers might have taken that belief too far, not because education is not a crucial civil rights issue, but because singling out education as *the* civil rights issue of our time absolves many other institutions and sectors of society from their responsibility for addressing other systemic inequalities, from health care to housing, that ultimately play out in the classroom.

The nation has always put considerable faith in education as a great equalizer. But as social and economic inequality grew, as living-wage blue-collar jobs disappeared and the cognitive demands required for jobs that paid a living wage increased, the complexity of that task increased exponentially. Schools were being asked to do something that had never been asked of them before: to graduate all students college- and career-ready. Perhaps the ask had become too great. Kotlowitz wrote:

> It's been too easy to see this dispute as one between two hotheaded personalities—Mr. Emanuel and Ms. Lewis, or as a play for respect. . . . In Chicago, 87 percent of public school students come from low-income families—and as if to underscore the precarious nature of their lives, on the first day of the strike, the city announced locations where students could continue to receive free breakfast and lunch. We need to demand the highest performances from our teachers while we also grapple with the forces that bear down on the lives of their students, from families that have collapsed under the stress of unemployment to neighborhoods that have deteriorated because of violence and disinvestment. And we can do that both inside and outside the schools—but teachers can't do it alone.

Kotlowitz's cry that "teachers can't do it alone" was meant to be a call to arms, but it was also a good encapsulation of why Freshman OnTrack became so embedded in the culture of the district. At a time when teachers felt isolated and under fire, Freshman OnTrack was spreading through networks of peers who supported one another. And at a time when teachers were struggling to meet the nation's growing expectations for what schools and teachers could accomplish—particularly schools and teachers working with children living in poverty—Freshman OnTrack made teachers feel empowered and successful.

"As a principal, I was always trying to put in front of my teachers things that were within our sphere of influence because working in a neighborhood school, working in a tough community, there are so many things that are outside of our control. When you find something you really can control and impact, as a principal you have to really double down on that," Jackson said.

The fact that Jackson and her peers conceptualized Freshman OnTrack and, by extension, the dropout problem as something within the control of schools was a testament to how far the district had come from the mid-1990s, when Roderick was conducting her research on dropouts. It was a testament to the research, which got the ball rolling, and also to the networks that gave people working in schools the tools and skills to make the work feel manageable.

Which is not say that the work of Freshman OnTrack felt manageable in every context. At Hancock, where the student population was relatively more advantaged than at Tilden, Freshman OnTrack rates in the nineties became routine. At Tilden, it was a constant struggle to maintain Freshman OnTrack rates above 70 percent. Freshman OnTrack at Tilden was an affirmation of Kotlowitz's admonition: "Quality schools and quality teaching clearly can make a difference in children's lives, sometimes a huge difference[,] but we too often attempt to impute to teachers impossible powers." Indeed, the second semester of the 2015–16 school year at Tilden would provide a powerful test of where teachers' abilities to prevent failure started and ended.

CHAPTER 7

The students lounging on beanbag chairs in Tilden's Peace Room on an icy day in mid-February each had a story to tell about how a change of scenery, coupled with the right supports from teachers, could alter the course of one's academic career. They were the Tilden freshmen who had ended first semester on-track, despite having eighth-grade academic records that put them at high risk for course failure. Mr. Swinney, the principal, had wanted to get them into a room together to discuss how they had beaten the odds, information that he hoped to use to continue to refine the school's approach to freshmen. He asked Mr. Walker, the Peace Room facilitator, and Kelvin Chung, Tilden's counselor, to facilitate the discussion. He hoped the freshmen would be more honest without a classroom teacher, who might be seen to be judging what they were saying, in the room. On the appointed day, though, one of the daily crises that seemed to chew up Mr. Walker's time kept him from the meeting. Ms. Holmes agreed to pinch hit.

Though the room itself was spacious, the group's post-lunch exuberance made it feel like a crowded postgame locker room. It also smelled like one. "Someone *stink*," one of the freshmen loudly observed. A loud chorus of denials followed.

"It smells like straight poo," confirmed Marcus, one of the ten students in attendance. He was wearing his signature diamond studs in both ears, baggy khakis, and a black T-shirt that said "BAM," which stood for Becoming a Man, the name of the mentoring program he participated in. Despite conflicts with Mr. Persaud, his math teacher, and other teachers, he had ended the semester without any failures. When Roderick was doing her study, before the Freshman OnTrack movement, the odds of someone like Marcus ending his first semester on-track were virtually nil. Sierra had also finished the semester on-track, though she was not in attendance this day. David, who had failed all of his courses first semester, had been invited to a separate meeting Swinney had organized to help off-track students get back on-track.

"*People!*" Ms. Holmes yelled above the commotion. "*People!*" she tried again. When the chatter eased slightly, she began her spiel. "If you read your invitation to this group, you would have seen that, um . . ." Holmes searched for the right words to tactfully convey the purpose of the meeting. As usual, she settled for the direct approach. "We are going to be open and transparent with you. All of you came into this high school with a big red flag on you."

"'Cause we're slow," came a voice from the back of the room.

"No. *No*, not because you were slow. Because you were at risk," Holmes clarified.

"Because we bad," yelled another.

"No, not because you were bad, because you were at risk," Holmes repeated. "They said that you were at risk of failing ninth grade—"

"Who said?"

Holmes persisted, "—probably due to either one or a combination of three things: One, your attendance in junior high. B, your grades. Or you had multiple behavior issues during your eighth-grade year. But—"

The teens resumed talking at full volume. Nobody relished a rundown on how they had struggled in the past.

"*SHUSH!*" Holmes said, fixing the room with a stare. "*But* despite coming to high school with this big red flag over your head, all of you finished the first semester on-track, which means you passed all of your core classes. Which means you're doing really well, and—"

Holmes did a quick scan of the room, and then said, "One, two, three, four, five, Marcus, six. Six of you are actually taking honors classes right now. So for people who, quote unquote, 'were supposed to fail,' you're doing really well." This turned a few heads.

"Who told you that?" demanded one girl.

"Who told us that?" Holmes asked rhetorically. "We looked at the dataset." She continued, "The quote unquote 'statistics' told us that, but you guys defied those statistics. So what we want to know [is] what made you more successful as a high school student than you were in junior high, and what can we do to support other ninth graders to make them more successful, and what can we do to continue to support you."

Side conversations ceased. It was a pleasant change of pace to be interviewed about their successes rather than lectured on their failures. Jakiyah, a self-possessed, often sharp-tongued student, volunteered to go first. "I didn't like eighth grade," she said.

"Why didn't you like it?" Holmes probed.

"It's just in a very dangerous neighborhood. The students was very irritating. I couldn't learn because they were always talking and distracting me." Holmes raised an eyebrow. Jakiyah had earned a reputation at Tilden for both talking and distracting.

"I didn't like eighth grade either," said Javion, who was seated next to Jakiyah. "I went to Dulles. I was fighting with everyone. My grades were low."

"Okay, so you had issues with people who were getting in fights," Mr. Chung clarified.

"I have anger management problems," Javion admitted.

"And how is Tilden better for you?" Mr. Chung asked.

"Here I'm cool with everybody," Javion said simply. "Ain't nobody make me mad here."

Holmes looked inquiringly at Javion. "Are you in an anger management program here?" she asked. "Because I find it very surprising that you said you had anger problems. Because you're really pleasant. Like, I've never seen you mad."

"I just don't show it," Javion explained.

"I'm not mad either!" Jakiyah interjected.

"I'm just *saying*," Holmes enunciated, fixing Jakiyah with a look, "that he said he has an anger problem, and I've never seen that side of him. He's always really pleasant in the hall. I see him speaking to everyone, so maybe there's something about Tilden—"

"Me too! I'm pleasant!" Jakiyah interrupted again.

"Okay! I'm not saying you're not!" Holmes said with exasperation. Jakiyah and Holmes had a complicated relationship. Holmes knew Jakiyah was smart and charismatic. For better or for worse, she held a lot of sway over her peers. Holmes often told Jakiyah she could "use her powers for good or evil." Sometimes Jakiyah called friends who were skipping school and ordered them to get themselves to class. Sometimes they actually listened. But she could also be disruptive in class and occasionally cruel to classmates who demonstrated any sort of weakness. Holmes believed it was a ploy to deflect attention from her own problems and insecurities. Jakiyah fought frequently with her mother, whom she had accused of abuse, and often ran away from home to stay with friends. Still, she had done well this semester, playing on Tilden athletic teams and ending the semester on-track with an A, two B's and a C. She also had near-perfect attendance. She had many dreams about the future and wanted to attend college out of state, maybe in California.

"I always wanted to be a police officer," she said during an interview later that year. "I like helping, I like to help." Some of the recent shootings of unarmed black men had soured her on that career, though. "I don't like the police no more. They ain't ever there on time, but that used to be my dream job, but I would like to be a nurse or a teacher. I'd like to teach younger children. I like kids."

Incongruously, Jakiyah was part of a group of girls who routinely talked about dropping out of school to work as strippers. Details the girls had rattled off about pay and working conditions were alarmingly specific, enough so to convince Holmes that they were seriously weighing the option. Holmes spent a lot of time talking with Jakiyah, hoping to tilt the scales away from the pole and toward the classroom. Jakiyah appreciated it. "Without Ms. Holmes, I'd probably drop out," she said. "Ms. Holmes is the kind of teacher who wants to help you."

"Okay. Okay, okay, okay. About eighth grade," interjected Makayla, a chatty and exuberant teen. Makayla had ended first semester on-track—barely. For much of the semester she had had F's in math and biology. "Stop interrupting me!" she remonstrated. "Okay, so about eighth grade. There was lots of girl drama. A *lot* of *drama*. Drama every day. We got suspended. We had to go to counseling. There were fights every day. We never got to be in class or getting work done. Then my math teacher transferred out to go work at a college, and we got a new teacher and we had to do different stuff for her and then she failed me. That's why I had to go to summer school because she failed me."

Often, when Tilden students talked about failure, they talked about "being failed" in the passive voice, as if they had played no part in the transaction. It was more than a rhetorical tic. Many students believed grades were awarded haphazardly and unfairly, and in many cases they were right. These grading practices, in turn, caused students to stop trying, convinced that their efforts wouldn't pay off.

Holmes tried hard to make the connection between effort and grades. She constantly corrected students when they claimed that a teacher had "given them" an F, though privately she agreed that Tilden did need to implement a more uniform and fair grading system that emphasized mastery of specific skills over compliance and effort. Today, however, Holmes focused on Makayla's reference to the "drama" she had experienced in eighth grade.

"So, do any of you use the Peace Room this year to avoid drama?" Holmes asked.

"No," Makayla explained, "because he don't keep it, uh . . . con-ah . . . ? con-fa . . . ? Uh, what's the word?"

"Confidential?" Holmes supplied.

"Yeah, he snitch."

Holmes explained that Mr. Walker had an obligation to report instances of abuse or threats against other students.

"Okay, so how is Tilden better for you?" Chung asked, trying to refocus the conversation.

"It's kinder. Not as much girl drama, more mature. Tilden kids in here don't like to fight. They are quiet and friendly and stuff—"

"That's a lie," opined one of the males in the group, drawing laughs.

"There aren't really a lot of fights in here," Makayla insisted. "They're just arguments. People don't really fight, they talk. They just go to the Peace Room."

"You talk a *lot*," Marcus observed.

"Thank you! I know!" Makayla chirped.

Makayla had hit upon one of the key determinants of whether students stay in school: their sense of belonging. Research has found a clear link between students' feelings of belonging (the quality of their relationships with peers and teachers) and their willingness to work hard in school. "Our kids are *so* relational," Holmes observed. Many Tilden students picked and chose where to exert effort based on whether or not they liked the teacher of the class.

Nicole, a talented student who earned top grades first semester despite occasionally missing full days of school to care for her younger brother when everyone else in the family had to work, offered her take on the difference between eighth grade and Tilden.

"In eighth grade, there was a lot of drama that involved girls," she explained. "I focused more on that and started missing school. I didn't want to be a part of it. My grades started going down."

Nicole had attended one of the district's top-rated K–8 schools. It had a fine-arts and performing-arts magnet program and a gifted program that drew students from outside of its boundaries. Many of the Tilden students who attended the school said that the work had been harder there than in high school.

"They would teach us high-school-level-type stuff, and I was out of school so I wouldn't be able to catch up," Nicole explained. "I knew I would have to go to summer school so I stopped trying."

"And now?" Chung inquired.

"The teachers are nicer. I stay out of drama. The teachers are more supportive," she said.

Chung asked Nicole what teachers could do to better support the students who had failed a course or two first semester. Her answer revealed the critical role that teacher-student relationships play in students' efforts.

"Some teachers, they'll teach you something and right away assume everyone in class knows how to do it. They don't really teach you how to do it fully where all the kids understand it. There are some kids who do really understand it, but there are some who don't."

"So, teachers should check in with students," Chung summarized. "Things that are basic to a teacher might not be basic to students."

Makayla interjected, "The teacher should already *know* if kids aren't caught up. They should know 'cause they are the teacher. They know the level students read at." Students' determinations of whether or not a teacher was supportive often hinged on whether or not they noticed when they were struggling and offered the proper help.

"If they see children are failing, they should ask, 'Is something going on?'" Nicole added. When she had missed school to take care of her little brother, she had taken note of which teachers had inquired after her and which had not. Holmes was one of the teachers who had asked. She had proudly produced a photo of her baby brother to explain the situation. Holmes had been suitably admiring of the baby's cuteness, Nicole had noted approvingly.

"So, teachers should research if something is going on with a student?" Chung asked the group.

"Not research," Marcus snapped. "Just *ask*."

As more students offered up their turnaround stories, it became clear that the primary obstacles that had tripped them up in eighth grade were absenteeism, behavioral issues, and interpersonal conflicts. Not one student cited an inability to do the work as the primary reason for their previous failure. Now that they were attending school regularly and doing the work consistently, they were passing. Some, like Nicole, who had earned all A's first semester, were truly thriving. The students' self-reports were consistent with the Freshman OnTrack research showing that attendance and studying—not test scores or background factors—were the strongest predictors of both ninth-grade course failure and grades, which in turn were the strongest predictors of graduation.

It was also clear that one of the main reasons their academic behavior had improved was that Tilden's teachers were providing more individualized support for social and academic issues than most of the students had received in eighth grade. This was a dramatic departure from what Roderick had found in the mid-1990s, or what Allensworth had found in the mid-2000s. Back then, students overwhelmingly reported receiving less support in ninth grade than they had in eighth grade. But Freshman OnTrack efforts seemed to be reversing that trend in district schools generally and in Tilden in particular.

Daniela, a diminutive student who rarely caused any trouble in class, was one of the students who had made a particularly dramatic turnaround in high school, and she credited it to the increase in support she had received at Tilden. "When I was in Libby, I got caught with a weapon," Daniela admitted.

"She got caught with knives!" Marcus supplied.

Daniela giggled.

"You all are telling me things I just did not know," Holmes said, shaking her head. Often when students talked about their struggles and misdeeds in elementary school, Holmes expressed surprise. In some cases, she was genuinely surprised. In others, she was not particularly surprised but managed to fake it. She wanted to send a clear message that whatever failures or struggles they had experienced in elementary school, those events no longer defined them.

"So, anyway, I didn't do good in math. I didn't pay attention in math," Daniela said.

"Math is my favorite subject," Marcus interrupted.

"So how is Tilden different from Libby?" Chung asked.

"I think Tilden is much better. There are more people here to help you, understand you, help you know the things you don't know."

"So, Tilden is more caring, more supportive of you," Chung clarified.

Daniela nodded.

Elementary school teachers may have counseled their students to avoid Tilden, but Tilden's students and teachers alike recognized that their low-rated (according to the district's metrics) school offered a kind of personalization that was rare in American high schools. Ironically, Tilden's past failures had contributed to this strength. Because so many students opted out of this neighborhood high school, Tilden's freshman class numbered just seventy-two students during the 2015–16 school year, making it easy for teachers to know every student in the building.

"Everyone here has someone," observed Jenny, the City Year team leader. "Every kid has a connection with someone. It's easy at the end of the year to break it up and say who is connected to whom because everyone is connected to someone."

Holmes, who sometimes wished her colleagues would do even more to support Tilden students, nevertheless agreed with Jenny's assessment. "One thing that Tilden does really well is help kids who struggled in junior high, who are at risk," she observed one day at a Freshman OnTrack meeting. "We do a phenomenal job at that. We had a kid who transferred to Phillips a while back. He came back, and I asked why he had returned. He said, 'Because you guys loved me and they didn't.' All the teachers at this school do *care*, and they want you to be successful."

Tilden's teachers and staff worked to ensure that success by offering an array of supports for freshmen that would have been unheard of at Tilden or at most other district schools just a decade prior. Each Tilden student was assigned a mentor who regularly reviewed the student's grades and attendance and helped set goals for the future. Freshmen also attended intervention sessions twice a week. These were essentially advisory periods (the type that Vallas had tried to institute district-wide without much success) during which students reviewed their homework and worked on academic skills and interpersonal relationships. Every Tuesday at intervention, students received a "BAG" report—an update on their behavior, attendance, and grades. The reports consistently reinforced the importance of these measures while ensuring that no student was caught unaware of his or her academic standing at the end of the semester.

The constellation of supports for freshmen also included the monthly Freshman Success Team meetings, during which teachers discussed students like Sierra, who had required a good deal of extra attention (and some nontraditional support in the form of lipstick bribes) in order for her to finish first semester (just barely) on-track. She had avoided an F in Persaud's math class by the skin of her teeth. In the old days, before the district's push around Freshman OnTrack, students like Sierra who were struggling in math would have been shuffled into some one-size-fits-all program, likely tutoring of some sort. The success team meetings helped teachers realize that academic struggles could have an array of causes. Some students struggling in math might require tutoring, but many others, like Sierra, needed more help with motivation, self-esteem, and relationships, which was what she received.

Over the course of the first semester, Walker met with Sierra and her friends in the Peace Room. City Year staff bribed her with candy and lipstick and other small rewards so that she would stay after school and work with them. Persaud conferenced with Sierra's grandmother, imploring her to get her granddaughter to school on time. He also gave Sierra loads of chances to make up missed work. Sierra ended the semester with a D. It wasn't exactly an academic triumph, but she did manage to avoid failure and finish the semester on-track, which meant her odds of graduating increased more than threefold.

It took an array of staff and nonprofit organizations to address all the specific needs of Tilden's students. One thing that stood out about most of these programs was that they were not strictly—or even primarily—focused on teaching content or building academic skills. Rather, they were focused on ensuring that students exhibited the type of academic behavior that was likely to make them successful in school. Those behaviors included attending class regularly, completing homework and classroom assignments, asking for help when needed, working respectfully with peers and teachers, and persisting at tasks even when they were complex or taxing.

Ms. Dominguez monitored attendance and called home whenever a student was absent. A Knock at Midnight, a truancy intervention program, tracked students down when Dominguez couldn't reach them. "They could find a kid under a rock," Dominguez observed. Mr. Walker from Umoja and others worked to defuse conflicts between students, and between students and teachers, and to build students' social and emotional skills. City Year corps members offered tutoring to any Tilden freshman who needed it but, as important, they worked to create a sense of community, greeting students by name every morning as they filed into school and hosting regular events and celebrations for freshmen. When Tilden freshmen weren't in class, they could often be found in the City Year room, chatting with mentors like Jess Enriquez and Anthony Bryant, who had grown up in Chicago.

All of these efforts were consistent with the growing national focus on so-called non-cognitive factors. Researchers define non-cognitive factors as "the sets of behaviors, skills, attitudes, and strategies that are crucial to academic performance" but are not necessarily captured by aptitude tests: perseverance, study skills, conscientiousness, and social acumen, to name a few. Students' grades are generally a reflection of both their academic skills and their ability to employ these non-cognitive factors.

Part of the impetus for the growing focus on non-cognitive skills is the substantial body of research that shows that grades—far more than test scores—best predict how well students will fare later in life. Allensworth and Easton demonstrated that students' freshman-year course performance matters more for high school graduation than test scores do. Other researchers have found that grades also matter much more than test scores do for college-going, college graduation, and other life outcomes. Though the public often views standardized tests as a fairer, unbiased way to measure students' skills, grades clearly capture something important that test scores miss: both students' academic ability *and* their non-cognitive skills.

One focus of efforts to improve students' non-cognitive skills—both in Chicago and nationally—has been on improving students' academic perseverance, the ability to keep working at tasks over a long period of time. One of the most oft-cited psychological studies justifying these efforts is by psychologists Angela Duckworth and Martin Seligman, who found that self-discipline was actually more important for predicting academic performance than IQ. They argue that a failure to exercise self-discipline is "a major reason for students falling short of their intellectual potential." When Sierra refused to do her math work because it was hard for her, when David cut school, when Marcus got kicked out of class, all were struggling with self-discipline in one form or another.

It can be easy to misinterpret the literature on non-cognitive factors and equate a lack of academic perseverance with laziness or some other individual character flaw. However, as Roderick has often observed, "No kid is gritty and perseverant enough to thrive in the crappy high schools some Chicago kids were forced to attend." In fact, the evidence is clear that many of the behaviors and attitudes that students display are not simply intrinsic to them but are highly influenced by the schools and classrooms they attend. That is, there are features of certain classrooms and schools that make it much more likely that students will attend class regularly, complete assignments to the best of their ability, and persist when the going gets tough—in short, do all of the things it takes to earn top grades.

One way that educators can influence how hard students try is by influencing their academic mindsets, or the beliefs they hold about themselves as learners. Stanford University professor Carol Dweck was one of the first researchers to recognize the role mindsets could play in academic success. She found that students' mindsets about intelligence play a leading role in whether or not they persist in the face of difficulty. Students who believe that intelligence is a finite quantity that they either have or don't have ("fixed mindset") tend to withdraw in the face of challenge because they worry they might appear dumb or incompetent if they fail. Students who believe that the brain is like a muscle that can be strengthened with learning and effort ("growth mindset") tend to seek out challenges because they see them as an opportunity to improve.

Dweck and her colleagues have focused in particular on one-off interventions that can promote positive mindsets, but classroom and school contexts—grading policies, trust between teachers and students, teacher support for student work, teacher expectations, to name a few—also play a significant role in determining students' academic mindsets, which in turn help determine whether or not students work hard and display strong academic behaviors.

Indeed, Roderick and her UChicago Consortium colleagues identified mindsets as a key piece in understanding *why* students who do well freshman year might continue to do well throughout high school. In a comprehensive review of the literature on noncognitive factors, they found:

> Positive academic mindsets motivate students to persist at schoolwork (i.e., they give rise to academic perseverance), which manifests itself through better academic behaviors, which lead to improved

performance. There is also a reciprocal relationship among mindsets, perseverance, behaviors, and performance. Strong academic performance "validates" positive mindsets, increases perseverance, and reinforces strong academic behaviors.

This reciprocal relationship between academic mindsets and academic success is likely to be one reason that such a strong relationship exists between freshman year failure and dropout and, conversely, freshman year success and graduation. Indeed, the Consortium identified four specific mindsets that were tied to students' academic performance.

1. I belong in this academic community.
2. My ability and competence grow with my effort.
3. I can succeed at this.
4. This work has value for me.

To summarize, students are far more likely to persevere academically when they believe they are a part of a community of learners; when they believe hard work, rather than innate ability, is the secret to success; when they believe they are capable of learning the material presented to them and doing the work assigned to them; and when they believe the work is worthwhile, either because it is inherently interesting or because it will be useful for some later goal.

The students who were gathered in the Peace Room to discuss their first semester turnarounds were clearly displaying some of these positive academic mindsets. One recurring theme was that the students felt they belonged at Tilden, more so than they had in elementary school. "In eighth grade, I was the new kid," said one teen who had spent much of the period chatting with another teen who shared a beanbag with him. "So, I didn't know nobody, and I didn't get along with nobody. When I came to Tilden, it was like, City Year and teachers and other kids, they were like, cool."

Many explicitly discussed how they were succeeding this year because they were thinking differently—about themselves and school. Taylor, who had attended a charter elementary school, was one of those who talked about how he had changed his mindsets when he got to high school, though he didn't use the term "mindset."

"In elementary school I was always getting in trouble and trouble," he said. "But I'm more mature than I was back then. When I came to Tilden, I realized I could do better, and that's what I did," he explained succinctly. When he came to Tilden, he came to believe he *could* be successful, which made it more likely that he *would* be successful, or able to muster the academic mindset "I can succeed at this." There is clear evidence linking students' self-efficacy (the belief that they can succeed) with effort. Simply put, people (teens and adults alike) try to do things they think they are good at and avoid things they think they are not good at, particularly if they have a fixed mindset. And like other mindsets, self-efficacy can be a self-fulfilling prophecy. When students think they will fail, they resist trying, which leads to failure, which reinforces the original belief about their competency.

This is why Holmes was so very determined that Sierra pass math first semester. It wasn't just about ensuring that she did not experience failure in that one class; rather, it was about disrupting her negative mindset around math. "I had to have it out with Persaud over her math grade," Holmes noted. "It wasn't even about her lack of skill or work. It was her attitude. I was like, 'Fine, but if you're going to grade on attitude, make it just a small percentage of her grade.'"

Holmes acknowledged that Sierra was occasionally prone to displays of poor attitude, particularly in math. But she believed that the attitude was really just a shield she put up—the dis-identification that Claude Steele writes about. She believed Sierra didn't try hard in math because she expected to fail at it. Holmes had noticed that she freaked out whenever she got below an A on any English project that had involved any amount of effort on her part. She seemed to think it confirmed what she secretly suspected, which was that she was dumb.

Persaud had a harsher interpretation of her behavior, believing Sierra expected to have everything handed to her. He said he passed her in the end because "she did step up her game." Though he was willing to work with any student who was willing to put in the effort, Persaud also resented the implication that the onus was on him to ensure that students received a passing grade.

"The whole system has changed. You're stigmatized if you fail a kid. It's a teacher's fault, which makes no sense," he lamented. "The pressure comes down on you for failing kids. But at the end of the day, what's the purpose of it? If you pass an algebra class, you are expected to be able to do X, Y, and Z."

Holmes agreed that demonstrating basic skills should be a requisite of passing classes. But she also believed that helping students develop the belief that they belonged to an academic community and were capable of success was even more important. She didn't believe failing a kid could possibly serve that purpose. Holmes hoped this small success in math might inoculate Sierra against future failure by changing her mindset. She hoped that seeing her effort at the end of the semester pay off would be enough to engender that shift. Truthfully, though, she feared it wouldn't be.

Marcus, sitting at the far end of the peace circle, was the last to share his experiences with the group. As usual, his classmates listened when he spoke.

"In elementary school I was fighting my teachers. I used to bring weapons to school. I used to get put out of class every day. I used to bring weed to school. I got kicked out of Libby—"

His peers hooted at his matter-of-fact itemization of past transgressions.

"Then when I transferred to Graham, I didn't really know nobody. That's when I had trouble, really, with the students. I didn't know nobody so I got into it a lot. Since I came here, I had to slow down. I be getting older. I started thinking that it ain't worth it to keep on getting kicked out, keep on having to transfer, move, so I said, 'Forget it, I'm just going to do right.'" He paused. "Like, I know I'm smart. I used to be a straight-A student—"

"I remember that," Daniela confirmed.

Mr. Chung summarized, "So, you're saying you matured, you got older, you made a personal decision to act right. Thank you."

Chung's pithy summary of Marcus's trajectory over the year was a vast oversimplification of the daily war the teen was fighting with his own demons—and that Tilden teachers and staff were fighting on his behalf. The battle was best illustrated by the emoji Marcus often posted on his Facebook page: a devilish, leering face with horns. He posted the horned emoji whenever he was up to—or considering being up to—no good. Often it was accompanied by a pistol emoji (representing his gang) or a fluttering leaf emoji (representing weed), as in: "If ion squeeze that trigger where im from they'll end up Killing me," followed by emojis including the devil face and pistol. Sometimes he followed those posts with regretful laments about how lonely or misunderstood he felt. "Can somebody be proud of me? Like, fuck I'm trying, I'm trying so hard."

Indeed, his teachers confirmed, he was trying admirably to be the best version of himself and to reconnect with the boy he had been before—as he put it—"I really jumped off the porch." In the first few weeks after his run-in with Persaud, Marcus could hardly stand to be in math class, despite the fact that math was his favorite subject.

Marcus began coming to the Peace Room to visit Mr. Walker whenever he felt like his anger was going to get him into trouble. That in and of itself was a breakthrough. Prior to his work with Mr. Walker, Marcus hadn't really recognized the extent to which his emotions were controlling his life. "I mean, I knew that angry feeling was there. I just didn't pay it no mind," Marcus said. "[Mr. Walker] pointed it out to me. He was like, 'Marcus, from my point of view, you get angry too quick. The littlest thing will enrage you.'" Marcus started thinking maybe he was right. He recalled that before he worked with Mr. Walker, he had seen signs of disrespect everywhere. Even something as simple as a person calling to him without using his name could set him off.

Walker began to fill a hole in Marcus's life. There were plenty of black male teachers at Tilden, but Walker was different. He wasn't a classroom teacher, so he didn't need to worry about maintaining classroom order or authority. He never got in power struggles with kids, and he never tried to exert any authority over Marcus. He simply listened to what he had to say without judgment. "I ain't got no father figure in my life," Marcus explained, "so before Mr. Walker, I ain't really got no guides. Now I do."

But Walker did more than just listen. He also introduced Marcus to a variety of techniques he could use to keep himself on a more even keel. Every time Marcus lost his temper, Walker would ask him to recall how he felt just before the blowup, hoping he would start to recognize the physical signals by himself before he blew his lid.

Marcus had never spent so much time reflecting on his feelings or differentiating among them. "I really didn't show no emotion but anger," Marcus said. Mr. Walker helped him realize that there was a whole rainbow of emotions—sadness, fear, frustration, anxiety, jealousy—that he had experienced as one single, throbbing hue. He learned what calmed him down (bright colors, deep breathing techniques, music) and what didn't (dark colors, counting backward from ten—"Not enough numbers," Marcus observed).

Whenever he entered the Peace Room, Walker would ask him to rate his anger level, which usually was at a 10. They would talk a little bit, trying to get at the root cause of the blowup. Often Marcus ended up talking about his complicated relationship with his mom. After a few minutes, Walker would check in again. "How are you feeling now?" Marcus would generally report that he had cooled to a 5 or 6. When he got down to 3, he would go back to math class. There were times first semester when Marcus would come to the Peace Room every thirty minutes, for five minutes at a time.

Occasionally, when he was having a particularly bad day, he started the day in the Peace Room rather than risk a blowup in math class. He'd feel the old familiar pit in his stomach, the tension in his neck, the dull ache of his nails digging into his palm, and he would know how the day was likely to end up if he didn't get help first. "I'd know he'd just say something to me, and then I would just pop off, and then he would put me out, and I'd probably have to go to the dean's office," Marcus recalled. "So I'd just say, 'Can I sit in here, Mr. Walker?' And he'd say sure. And we'd have a conversation and he'd eventually try to get me to go back in there."

Walker thought Marcus's growing ability to recognize his anger ahead of time and do something to preempt it was a remarkable breakthrough. Some Tilden teachers disagreed, concerned that Walker was "coddling" Marcus. Emanuel Smith, Tilden's dean in charge of discipline, was one of those who worried about Marcus's dependence on Mr. Walker. He believed that some of Walker's tactics—and some aspects of Freshman OnTrack in general—wouldn't translate well beyond the walls of Tilden.

It wasn't that Smith wasn't dedicated to serving his students or to Freshman OnTrack. Letters from grateful students he had mentored lined his office wall. "Thank you for putting up with my ignorance," one student wrote. "You are like a father to me," wrote another. And there was this heartbreaking note from one ninth grader: "I would like to give thanks to you Dean Smith for pushing me to succeed and go someplace in life but to be honest with you I think I am going to drop out because I don't think I am going to pass freshman year. But thanks for being their [sic]."

But Smith's approach differed from Walker's. He was a proponent of "tough love" and wondered whether Walker's approach would adequately prepare students for "the real world." He said of Marcus: "He's one of those where restorative practices and peace circles have become a crutch. Has there been progress? Okay, yes, but at the same time, every time something happens, you can't go to the peace circle to talk about it. Children are most effective when they can handle things on their own, without an adult needed to guide them. In the real world, there's not going to be a conversation every time you get into trouble."

Debates about Freshman OnTrack often came down to precisely this argument. What, exactly, was expected of people in "the real world," and what tactics were most likely to prepare students to face that eventuality? Not every school working on Freshman OnTrack offered peace circles or restorative practices, but most schools with strong on-track rates offered students multiple chances—whether it was to make up a grade, learn a new skill, or redo an assignment. Smith had been the Freshman OnTrack coordinator at Wells, a school on the Near North Side, before he came to Tilden. He loved that job and was good at it. He managed to spur a whopping 17.4 percentage-point increase in Wells's on-track rate between the school years that ended in 2008 and 2009. But Smith's work at Wells focused more on extra tutoring and careful monitoring of students, rather than on peace circles and restorative justice techniques. It was a reminder that FOT looked different at every school, and that FOT was often less about a specific intervention than about the process of monitoring and discussing what was in the best interest of students.

Indeed, Walker and Smith often engaged in lively debates about Marcus and other "frequent fliers" in the dean's office. During one Freshman Success Team meeting toward the end of first semester, Smith expressed concern about the number of chances Tilden's staff were providing to students. Holmes, Walker, and Sarah Howard, the Network for College Success coach, had spent part of the meeting pushing Swinney to reconsider how the school graded makeup work.

Howard asked the group, "Can we focus recovery on, Do they know what they need to know from that class? Rather than on, Did they *do* all the assignments, and did they show me due respect by coming back with everything I asked?"

Smith responded skeptically. "The only issue I have with that is, when you do that, you set the kids up for failure, in a sense," he said.

"You allow them to think it's okay to play around and then take an exit exam. It just sends out the wrong message."

"This requires a much longer conversation," Howard replied. "But I think we can do both without punishing them for being fourteen."

Walker nodded his agreement. "Some kids missed huge chunks because of crazy circumstances. It might make sense to have more opportunities for makeup when things are just really jacked up like that."

Howard observed that sometimes "the real world" wasn't as unforgiving as people made it out to be. "If you counted the number of papers that I turned in late in college you would be stunned," Howard said. "I think there is a false narrative out there that you have to hold them *hard*, that you have to put the 'dead' in deadline."

Smith and Walker continued the debate after the meeting wrapped up. Smith said he thought there was altogether too much coddling taking place at the school, and that students, particularly the boys, were starting to take advantage of it. He cited Anthony, a habitual truant, as one of the chief offenders. Walker disagreed with the term "coddling" and pushed back on his characterization of Anthony.

"We can't expect kids to change overnight," Walker argued, using the same even tone he used to talk with students. "Shit. Anthony? He's a lot of work, he's more work than ninety percent of kids in this building. I don't see it as coddling. Everybody has different styles. Anthony, man, if he shows up to school and stays in school the entire day, that's a reason to celebrate."

Smith broke in. "That's just a reasonable expectation."

"It's a reasonable expectation for someone who has a place to sleep," Walker rejoined.

"See, see, this is what gets me," Smith replied excitedly, gathering speed as he warmed to the topic. "I was adopted. Not only was I adopted, I've had to sleep in a house with no lights. I took showers in winter in freezing cold. We had candlelight dinners because my mom was embarrassed and didn't want to tell us the lights were out. We had rats. We had roaches. I've slept on pallets. So don't *come* to me with this bullshit ass story about, you know, life is so hard. I get it. I get it. I understand, and *that's* why I share these things with you to let you know, 'Hey, this is not the end, but in order to get where I'm at or surpass where I'm at, You. Have. To. Stop.'"

He plowed ahead, barely coming up for air. "I've had my fair share of struggles, but I made up in my mind that I didn't want my kids to see what I saw. And in spite of all the crazy stuff that was going on—being adopted, losing my grandmother, being tossed around. A lot of stuff happened. I just made up in my mind like, no matter how bad it is, if you have someone trying to help you, you can get through."

Walker, who had been listening intently to Smith, interjected. "Yeah, those are some moments, man," he said sincerely. "I think your story has so much value, and kids can draw from that. And I also know humans are complex. We are all very different. And I wish, I *wish*, they fucking had like half of the resilience you had when you were their age, but everyone is just a little bit different."

Marcus's performance toward the end of first semester lent credence to Walker's approach. "Mr. Walker, he really got through to me," Marcus said gratefully. "I've started being able to control my anger. I've started learning how to hold things in, but also learning that if I hold things in too long, I'm just going to pop off." Other teachers noticed the improvement. Marcus recalled the day Persaud complimented him on his turnaround. "He was like, 'Mr. Clark, I really see you've been improving and I thank you for that.' So, we cool now."

As he learned to control his anger, his academic performance began to improve in all his classes. Over the course of first semester, he became increasingly engaged in class discussions. More and more, Holmes noted, he participated in class rather than spending the entire period with his head on his desk. One day in December, Holmes's class was reading the classic Holocaust memoir *Night* by Elie Wiesel. One section of the book talked about how Wiesel and his family were marched out from their home, in front of their neighbors, to be deported to the notorious concentration camp Auschwitz.

Some of the boys in Holmes's class started posturing. "Man, they weak," one declared. "I'd break out of line," claimed another. Marcus, who hadn't appeared to be listening to the discussion at all, swiveled in his seat and fixed them both with a withering stare. "No," he said emphatically, "you need to think about the situation they were in. They didn't have guns. They were outnumbered. They would have died more quickly by going ahead right then. You have to plan. You have to strategize. They weren't being weak. They were being smart."

Holmes and Vincent Gray, her team teacher, exchanged a brief grin. Marcus was sharp, no doubt about it.

"Y'all dumb as hell," Marcus concluded, and then resumed staring off into space.

Two steps forward, one step back.

Holmes began making a point of giving Marcus opportunities to shine. He enjoyed reading aloud in class and at some point had designated himself the official arbiter of who would read which passages in her class. "He wanted to dictate who could read, so I let him," Holmes said. If it was a longer part and someone couldn't read that well, he would explain, not unkindly, that he might do better with a different part. "He'd be like, 'You stutter, but here's a good part for you.' He was actually really diplomatic," she said.

As the second semester began, there was another reason teachers had hope for Marcus. He had started dating a girl they all very much approved of. She was smart and funny and kind and she didn't put up with any of his "ignorance," as she called it.

The student who had not managed to pull off a first-semester turnaround was David. Despite a Hail Mary attempt during the last few weeks of school to complete missing assignments, he had ended up failing multiple courses. Toward the end of first semester, he had approached both Holmes and Persaud and asked them for makeup work, which they had provided. He had worked furiously to complete missing assignments—going to the City Year room or to Ms. Holmes's classroom during lunch for the last month of the semester. In the end, though, it wasn't enough. Though he was proficient in all of the math concepts—he had learned most of them already in elementary school Algebra—he couldn't make up a semester's worth of work in two weeks.

Still, unlike Sierra, he never attributed his struggles to a lack of ability. He knew he could do the work, and his teachers constantly conveyed that message too. "He knew. We reiterated what he knew, that the only reason he was failing was because he was never here," said Ms. Lyana, one of the City Year corps members who worked closely with David.

Though his last-minute sprint came up short, it had imbued David with a certain level of confidence. He saw his class averages rise precipitously as he turned in missing assignment after missing assignment. And as he did the work, he received lots of positive feedback from teachers. He was particularly grateful to Ms. Holmes, who failed him but had also spent a lot of time with him making up work and encouraging him to get back on-track the next semester. "She is pretty an amazing teacher," David said. "She's the one who helped me return to school, focus on my work, improve on what I did. She basically put it to me how I needed to do it for the second semester, and that's what I'm doing," he said, during an interview a month into second semester.

David also had another revelation during that period—namely, that listening in class was actually more interesting than staring into space, which was how he had previously occupied himself in class. "Classes are an hour and thirty minutes. It can be pretty boring. But if I'm on task, then I don't have to worry about just sitting there and waiting until the bell for the next class, because you're doing something. You can focus on something else," he explained with sincere enthusiasm.

David also had some new motivation to pull his grades up, though it wasn't the type of motivation he liked to talk about. Over Christmas break, he had been arrested for driving in a stolen vehicle. He claimed he was just joyriding and didn't know it was stolen. The juvenile court judge had agreed to drop the charges if he could bring in a strong report card the next semester. Persaud had also offered to write him a letter of support if he earned good grades second semester.

The arrest had set off some changes in his home life. After he was arrested, his father insisted David come live with him, his girlfriend, and their baby son on the Southwest Side. His father, who had recently bought a house, was a steadying influence. He made sure David was awake every morning before he left for his construction job. His father's girlfriend dropped him off at school every morning and picked him up every afternoon. In the evenings they played soccer together in the park. The opportunities to ditch had diminished considerably.

"He's kind of a strict parent," David explained, "and it's kind of good for me. It's starting to help me out to do better." David admitted that he actually liked being held accountable by his dad. Truth be told, his behavior last semester had come to frustrate even him. "Like, every day I would think to myself, 'I'll just leave today and do better tomorrow,' but then I would do the same stuff over and over and over. It just became a habit." It was a relief to no longer have to rely on his own still-developing self-control. "It's more better how my behavior changed living over here from over there, because over there I had lots of opportunities." By opportunities, he meant opportunities to get in trouble. "That's why I felt like it was okay, because if I left school I wouldn't get in trouble with my mom like I do with my dad, so I had more opportunities. He's more strict. If he found out I ditched he'd probably just yell at me or give me a big lecture of what I have to do better."

His goal for second semester was to earn all A's and B's and have the grades to transfer to Curie Metropolitan High School, which was closer to his dad's house. "In five years I'll be really happy knowing that I tried my best in school starting this semester," he said. "I want to say, 'Yeah, I started coming, I made a big turnaround.' I just want to say that I got good grades and everything."

CHAPTER 8

At the end of Glynn's first year at Hancock, the 2008–09 school year, the Freshman OnTrack rate had jumped 14 percentage points. The following year, on-track numbers jumped again, from 72 to 80 percent, a stunning 22-point increase in just two years. Still, there was considerable work to do to turn Hancock into the type of school that reliably propelled students to their "rightful place in America," a goal Glynn often exhorted for.

In her third year, Glynn had a new partner in this work: Karen Boran, whom she had recruited from Central Office to be her assistant principal. Like Glynn, Boran was a fierce believer in education as an engine of upward mobility. "Middle class, baby," was her mantra for all her students. Boran had grown up as one of ten children on a Wisconsin farm. Neither of her parents had attended college. "There wasn't a day that went by that I didn't know that school was my ticket out if I didn't want to get up at four a.m. every morning to milk the cows," she said.

Before coming to CPS, Boran had chaired the Department of Developmental Studies at National Louis University. Her job there was to help underprepared students adjust to college. Reviewing the scores of CPS graduates, she found that many were reading at a third- or fourth-grade level. She found it unconscionable that these mostly low-income students were being charged hundreds and sometimes thousands of dollars to take remedial courses to get them up to speed. "I realized grade thirteen was too late," Boran said. She went back to school to get her teaching credential and become a reading specialist. She then served as the director of high school curriculum at CPS from 2007 to 2009, first under Duncan and then briefly under Huberman, but it was a bad fit. "I was going to work in Central Office. I was going to stop people from doing stupid things like insisting that everyone follow one reading program or 'We're all going to do vocabulary of the day.' I really thought I could do this. For a while I could, and then I couldn't." When Glynn offered her a job, she leaped at the chance. Better to make a difference on a small scale than to be ineffectual on a large scale, she concluded.

When Boran arrived at Hancock in September 2010, the start of Glynn's third year, many of the truly disgruntled teachers had left or were on their way out. Glynn had spent the first two years weeding out those she didn't believe had the will or capacity to change. Now came the even greater challenge—developing those who remained.

One early Friday morning before school, about a month into the 2015–16 school year, a dozen Hancock teachers, all of whom taught or worked with freshmen in some capacity, gathered for the school's semimonthly Freshman Success Team meeting. Their schedule did not provide enough time during the school day to meet, but the teachers had voted as a group to convene every other Friday before school hours because they believed these meetings were crucial to their mission of keeping every freshman on-track to graduate.

Today's meeting began with an update on the school's year-to-date on-track figures for the school's freshmen. "We're at 96 percent core passing rate, and 60 percent of our freshmen have a 3.0 or better," announced Erin Neidt, the school's Freshman OnTrack coordinator and a Freshman Physics teacher. "Give it up!" The teachers gave out a collective whoop. Hancock's Freshman OnTrack rate had topped 90 percent for three years running. The teachers were determined to hit or surpass that mark again this year.

Neidt's meetings were a lesson in efficiency. Like any good science teacher, she appreciated procedures and protocols, and her graphs were impeccable. As she did at the start of every meeting, Neidt reminded the teachers of their "agreements," which she projected onto the screen:

Start/End On Time

Confidentiality

Step/Speak Up

Be Present

Listen/Appreciate Diversity/Learn From Each Other

Solution/Support Oriented

Assume Positive Intent

She also reminded them of the purpose of the meeting. Several years earlier, teachers and other support staff had crammed into the Hancock library to craft a mission statement for Freshman Success Team meetings. Neidt included that statement in every presentation she gave to the group. It read: "Our mission is to maintain a student-centered environment where clear expectations, supported by a reflective, data-based approach to prevention, intervention, and recovery, motivates all students to successfully graduate and be prepared for college within four years."

The mission statement was a repudiation of the culture that Glynn had inherited. Neidt recalled that the whole school was there at the library to create that mission statement. "We wanted to define or refine what the Success Team would be," Neidt said. "We wanted to say, 'This is how we are going to use that time.' Because some people wanted to use that platform to complain about students."

One way the group fulfilled that mission was by discussing two struggling freshmen at every meeting. Neidt selected the students the group would discuss and disseminated their names along with the agenda prior to the meeting, giving teachers ample time to reflect on the students before they were asked to discuss them publicly.

The goal was to never allow staff to forget that behind the impersonal numbers there were real kids with unique hopes, fears, strengths, and challenges.

The first student on today's agenda was Lucas, one of just a handful of Hancock freshmen who were failing multiple classes one month into the first semester. Neidt projected Lucas's school ID photograph onto the screen. She figured it was easier to maintain a "student-centered" environment when the student's sweet face was staring back at the group. Lucas's photo revealed a serious-looking teen with a collared shirt buttoned up to the top and hair combed with a neat side part. Below the photograph was a list of Lucas's grades in each class, his attendance, and a note that Mr. Mirek had emailed Lucas's father to inform him about his low English grade. The email had bounced back.

For the next twenty minutes (one teacher set a timer), Lucas's failure was a mystery the group was charged with unraveling. The clues were contradictory. He had perfect attendance, suggesting some level of motivation, but also a bad habit of showing up late to class. He had rock-bottom grades in three classes (F's in English, Health, and World Studies), which raised the possibility of a learning disability or emotional problems. But he also had A's in Computer Science and in Mr. Castillo's notoriously demanding Algebra class, proof he was capable of high levels of rigor. What was going on with Lucas?

"Okay, what are the worries?" Neidt asked the group. The discussions about individual students followed a protocol that Neidt and others had devised and modified over time. Teacher concerns came first. Student strengths came second. Concrete goals and action items came third.

"He's doing some work but he's missing quite a few assignments," supplied Paul Mirek, Lucas's English teacher. Lucas had a 37 percent average in Mirek's class.

"I would echo that," said James Michaels, who taught World Studies. Lucas's average in that class was a 48, better than his English grade but not by much. "He's had to have many reminders about turning in homework on time and completed."

"I have him in first block, and he's been late three times to my class," Neidt said.

"He's also chronically late to fifth block," Mirek added. "I tried emailing his dad regarding his performance but it bounced back." He continued, "He does participate to a degree, but when it comes to individually turning in his assignments, he's just not producing."

"For science, he did not pass his first assignment, but he did attend office hours," Neidt said. "We went through the quiz. He seemed like he got it when we reviewed it the second time. He was really concerned about his grade. He said, 'Let me show you I know this.' He is missing a couple of assignments. He turned them in exceptionally late after a number of reminders."

When no one else offered any more concerns, Neidt shifted gears. "Okay, what are the positives?" She prompted, "It looks like he's good at math and computers!"

"I'm curious about that math grade," Mirek said. "I know Castillo's class is a lot of work. If he's completing it and his grade is truly a 100, I want to know why he's completing that work."

Mirek's question was a crucial one—and precisely the type of question these meetings were designed to prompt. Often the variation from one class to another in how students performed was the key to figuring out how to reach them. A student who was failing one class might be passing or even excelling in others. Teachers often had very different impressions of these students, proof that any one teacher's perception of a student could be incomplete, biased, or just plain wrong. Comparing and contrasting information from different classes could sometimes alter a teacher's perspective on a student and provide an important reminder that the context of the classroom—the subject matter, the other students in the class, the teacher, the classroom environment—played a defining role in how a student performed.

Castillo responded to Mirek's query. "One thing I'm doing now, which is really paying off, is to make a phone call to parents if they miss a single assignment. He missed only one, and after the phone call, he did all the work. So that's been working. It's something you should try."

Mirek nodded. "The email to his dad didn't work, but he did willingly give me his mom's phone number."

"He's really positive, really friendly," Neidt offered. "Even if you have been reminding him about his work, he doesn't shy away from being reprimanded. He's like, 'Yeah, yeah,' big smile on his face. I don't think he's doing it to be non-conforming."

"And speaking of what he's been doing," Mirek said, "he has a low grade because he didn't do his first major writing assignment. But he has one where the rough draft is due next week, and he has that document now, so maybe he has turned that corner."

"Another note," Neidt chimed in. "Even though he's late every day, he does *come* every day."

One of the teachers in the group who did not have Lucas in class asked whether he worked better in groups or alone.

"In groups he does get a little bit distracted," Neidt said. "He's great with his team. They respect him. He's respectful. But a few times I've caught him just looking out the window. I think he just gets easily distracted."

"Socially it depends on who he is grouped with," Mirek said. "I grouped him with Ignazio for a moment and then said, 'Okay, this will not work.' But when he's grouped with someone who is a stronger reader or writer, he works up to their level."

Mr. Schmidt, Lucas's Computer Science instructor, concurred. "Right now Computer Science is all group work. I did have to move him from sitting far away. But now that he's up close, things are much improved."

"That sounds like a potential suggestion in class," Neidt said. "Do we want to set some behavior goals for Lucas?"

"I want him to find a system where he figures out what he needs to complete and when he needs to complete it by," Mirek said. "It's true that he's not unwilling to do the work. Maybe it is a matter of forgetting."

"I do think organization is part of his issue, which most fourteen-year-olds also have a problem with. I have a pretty clear plan for how students are supposed to organize their binders," Heather Pavona, who coordinated the Success Teams across grades, offered.

Neidt pulled out Lucas's binder for her class. "There are a few things out of place," she said, flipping through it.

"I think engagement is a problem for him," Mirek said. "If he's not engaged, it's going to be harder for him to do his work. He told me he was not a fan of most of the books he is handed."

"Yeah, there is a lot of reading in science," Neidt said.

"Maybe that's why he's doing so well in Computer Science. It's all hands-on," Mirek said.

"Okay, targeted goals," Neidt said. "Completion and organization of assignments seems like a really good starting place for Lucas. If he is starting out with these kinds of grades, he's going to get really discouraged really quickly."

Neidt transcribed a "SMART" goal for Lucas: "By the end of two weeks, Lucas will have one or less late assignment." Underneath the smart goal, she wrote, "Teachers will assist him with reminders, organization and continue to monitor progress."

Neidt promised to communicate the goal to Lucas and work with him on his organizational skills. They all agreed to revisit Lucas's progress at the next meeting in two weeks.

Of course, these meetings, which the Network for College Success began videotaping as an exemplar for other schools, had not always been such models of efficiency and cooperation. It was NCS that introduced the freshman team concept at Hancock and then helped create the meeting structures and protocols to make them work. The meetings were crucial to Freshman OnTrack at Hancock and other schools across the district, in part because they allowed teachers to problem solve together and in part because working together on a common problem had a way of changing teachers' mindsets toward their students, their colleagues, and their job.

NCS coach Sarah Howard had been working with Glynn since the 2008–09 school year to improve Hancock's instructional leadership teams—groups of teachers who came together to improve curriculum and instruction (not to work on Freshman OnTrack). In subsequent years Hancock's teachers would take what they had learned about teacher teams and apply it to Freshman OnTrack meetings. Glynn recalled that in her first year, meetings tended to go one of two ways: either they were themed parties with snacks and costumes, or they devolved into gripe sessions about kids, families, and Glynn herself. But that changed.

Howard helped Glynn institute meeting structures that kept the group focused on the work. To break up cliques, she started putting colored dots in meeting packets and having people sit with those who had the same color. "The haters always sat together and passed notes, so that kept them from doing that," Glynn said.

She asked her staff to adhere to certain agreements, such as arriving and ending on time, and then assigned a "process monitor" to make sure that everyone was sticking to the agreements. At the start of each meeting, the process monitor would note the percentage of staff that had arrived on time. Though the process monitor never called out anyone by name, no one wanted to be the laggard responsible for bringing down the average. People started arriving on time. Glynn also made the process monitor responsible for keeping people on task. When the group veered off topic, the monitor would ask staff to table the conversation for another time or vote to continue it and extend the length of the meeting. People started staying on topic.

Glynn also started rotating the meeting facilitator role. The facilitator was responsible for developing the agenda and getting it out to staff ahead of time. When people struggled with the facilitation, she helped coach them. "People stopped bitching about the facilitator," Glynn recalled. "Then it became all about the work and less about the bitching. People said, 'Okay, this is hard work and I'm learning to become a leader.' That's when we really started rocking and rolling."

The most significant undertaking of the pre–Freshman OnTrack leadership teams was the move to standards-based grading, a process that took five years to implement fully. Traditional grading systems generally include a mix of the results of tests, quizzes, and homework assignments, as well as measures of behavior, attendance, and participation. Points are assigned to each of these categories and count toward a student's final grade, which can be wrecked by a single missed assignment or blown test. Students and teachers alike become fixated on point accumulation rather than on mastery, promoting the type of "fixed mindset" that Duckworth and Seligman warned about. What is the advantage to seeking out challenge when point accumulation is the goal?

In standards-based grading systems, the focus is on whether students are able to demonstrate proficiency on specific agreed-upon standards (for example, the ability to use textual evidence to support an argument in English, or the ability to solve a two-step equation in math). The emphasis is on what a student knows and can do rather than on accumulating points. Students receive multiple opportunities to practice and improve their skills and to demonstrate what they have learned. Students are more likely to display a growth mindset because their grade is based on where they end up, not on how they got there.

Standards-based grading became a crucial component of Freshman OnTrack at Hancock. It reduced the overall number of failures by giving students multiple chances to succeed and eliminating some of the more problematic grading practices that were contributing to student failure when Glynn first arrived (arbitrarily assigning participation points, over-weighting homework assignments, and administering tests that were not good reflections of what had been taught, to name a few common ones). It also shifted the focus of remediation away from compliance-oriented makeup work. Getting struggling students back on-track was no longer about completing a flurry of missing assignments, but about ensuring students could demonstrate particular skills.

Glynn believed the shift to standards-based grading was a natural outgrowth of the Freshman OnTrack work at Hancock, which had been designed to uncover the root causes of student failure. "Before the grades were standards-referenced, you could look at the grade book, and it would tell a story, and it wasn't a good one. There wouldn't be any formative assessments, and then suddenly there is a summative assessment, and fifty percent would fail, and then there would be another topic that they would move on to," Glynn observed. "And as I said from the beginning, Freshman OnTrack really doesn't mean anything if we're not clear on what grades mean, and so that sent us on a journey of what does a standards-based grading system look like? What do we mean when we say this is standards-based? What do our grade books look like? How do we determine success? What does excellence look like and how do the kids know it? And it was all about being fair and equitable for kids."

Boran explained why standards-based grading, and especially its emphasis on multiple opportunities to demonstrate mastery, was essential for ensuring an equitable experience for all Hancock students, particularly English language learners or those with learning differences. "I was a crappy swimmer as a kid," Boran said. "They made me jump in the pool on the first day, and I nearly drowned. Eventually I learned to swim. But should I be graded on that initial failure? Should I have to carry that failure to the very end of my swimming career?" The point was to teach her how to swim, not to grade her on her ability to swim when she started learning. Boran firmly believed the same should apply to freshmen. They should be graded on where they ended up, not on whether they entered high school with the skills and knowledge to succeed immediately.

After the instructional leadership team became established, NCS began working to help Hancock apply similar structures to a meeting dedicated to Freshman OnTrack. Up to that point, Freshman OnTrack had been more about working around classroom teachers, as they were not particularly invested in that topic. Gayle Neely, Hancock's first Freshman OnTrack coordinator, spent much of her time engaging students, not teachers. "She was really tracking kids who were failing, and she would have them reach out to teachers to find out why they hadn't received a grade for an assignment or makeup work," recalled Letty Hernandez, who eventually took over for Neely and was later named the assistant principal. "So she really pushed kids to take on that responsibility." The approach had its benefits, but it placed much of the responsibility for preventing failure on Neely and the students while absolving teachers from engaging meaningfully in the process of preventing failure. "Teachers were like, 'Let me just give kids a packet of work and we will be done and everyone will be happy.' Yeah, I was guilty of that," Hernandez admitted.

The Freshman OnTrack meetings changed that. John Ambrose, an assistant principal, had attended some NCS meetings and became inspired to start a freshman-focused team at Hancock. He took the idea to Glynn, who agreed to set some time aside for the meetings. Ambrose then recruited an assortment of interested teachers and staff to attend the meeting. Krystal Muldrow, who was charged with helping NCS schools develop freshman teams, helped Ambrose develop the agenda for the first meeting. "I called them 'the motley crew,'" Muldrow recalled. "I don't know how he gathered them, but he did. There was some of everybody. . . . I was like, 'Who are all these people?' And he was like, 'You know, I just asked some people if they were interested or they teach freshmen.' So this motley crew came together, and they were really into the research and they were talking about kids from the beginning."

The Freshman OnTrack coordinators—first Letty Hernandez, then Erin Neidt—set the tone for how the meetings would proceed.

They stipulated what the meetings *would* be about (ensuring success for all students), and as important, what they would *not* be about (venting). The coordinators assumed responsibility for ensuring that freshman teachers had the right mindsets. No longer was it just Glynn and Boran exhorting teachers to support kids. Now it was the teachers' colleagues too.

Each of the coordinators believed fiercely in Freshman OnTrack and in using the meetings to ensure that everyone was working together toward the same outcomes. "It has to be about beliefs and about the structures to make sure it's happening," Hernandez said. "It has to be, 'We are going to do this, and we are going to monitor you, and'—I hate to say it this way—'we will break you. We will influence you to believe this.' It sounds awful but [it was] necessary," Hernandez concluded.

Pavona, who took over as the on-track coordinator when Hernandez was made assistant principal, said that her role as a teacher sometimes made the message more palatable. "I'm still teaching, so I have a lot of cred as a teacher," Pavona said. "I work super hard as a teacher and I work really hard at my job. I try to make myself useful to other teachers. And I *try* to be supportive. But I kind of really don't care. I don't care if people feel negatively about me. I don't really feel like I'm there to be BFF for people, especially people I don't think are doing the right thing for kids."

Teachers proved adept at getting their peers on board, and soon teachers began spearheading an effort that many of them had initially resisted. Muldrow, the NCS coach, recalled one early meeting in which an art teacher was struggling with his role in preventing failure. "He felt they were just giving kids a grade, and the kids were not even trying. He said, 'They don't even show up. They won't come after school.' And before I could open my mouth, another teacher and team lead were like, 'Well, wait a minute. You're talking about ways that kids are *not* engaging, but we're not talking about the ways we are pushing kids away. What are the structures, what are the ways of doing, the ways of being, that are actually hindering students from fully engaging with us?'

"And the way they did it was very professional, it was an invitation to shift. . . . And I saw that [art] teacher after that meeting change the way he talked about kids. Because the teacher wasn't anti-kid, he was just frustrated because he was like, 'I'm trying, I'm giving these opportunities, I'm staying after school or coming before school to provide extra time and space for support and the kids are not taking advantage of it.'

"And other people were like, 'Well, can we think of it this way? Does that child have a responsibility immediately after school that hinders him from being able to take advantage of that? How did you invite the student? What were the words you used?' I do remember them just probing, and he was really upset at the time, but I think what happened was they really took on a supportive stance. 'We understand that you are frustrated. We are just trying to get at the root cause of this so you can better support students.'"

As teachers' mindsets began to shift, the systems and structures around Freshman OnTrack began to evolve at Hancock, this time led by teachers rather than just Glynn and Boran. One of those teacher-leaders was Pavona, whom Glynn had recruited from Kelvyn Park High School, the site of one of the original Freshman OnTrack labs.

When Pavona arrived at Hancock at the beginning of the 2011–12 school year, the school had just received a federal School Improvement Grant (SIG), worth $5.6 million over three years. The grants, distributed by the Illinois State Board of Education, were earmarked to help turn around the lowest-performing schools in the state. Schools that received SIG grants were given the option of firing and replacing the majority of their staff, handing over management duties to an outside group, or partnering with an outside organization to implement new reform strategies. Hancock chose the third model and selected the Network for College Success as its lead partner organization.

The SIG money, which Hancock received beginning in the 2011–12 school year, allowed Glynn to recruit new teachers like Pavona, and to implement an on-track strategy at every grade level. Glynn had glimpsed the potential of having teachers use data to develop plans to prevent freshman course failure. The semimonthly meetings were starting to pay dividends. The Freshman OnTrack rate had risen to 87 percent in the 2010–11 school year, the year before the school received a SIG grant. Now she wanted to extend that work.

She put Pavona, who had led the Freshmen Academy at Kelvyn Park High School, in charge of coordinating and monitoring student progress at all grade levels. Immediately, Pavona felt overwhelmed. "I would have people come to me about kids with seven failures and kids with one failure, or Letty [Hernandez, the former Freshman OnTrack coordinator who had become the assistant principal] would be like, 'Is this kid on your radar?' and it was *just so many kids*," Pavona emphasized. "At any given moment it could be two hundred kids who had one failure or more failures, and I was like, 'How in the *world* am I going to handle this? I can't meet with all these kids individually.'"

At the time, struggling students were generally sent to lunchtime tutoring or to Saturday school. And there was little differentiation between the services given to students who were failing one course versus failing all their courses. "I am a systems and structures person," Pavona explained. "I needed some sort of framework."

Adelric McCain, who goes by Dell, a transition success coach with the Network for College Success, helped Pavona develop one. Later, NCS would help codify the approach and spread it to other schools. It was another example of how Freshman OnTrack differed from so many other off-the-shelf programs and tools. It evolved over time based on the needs and expertise of those working in the trenches, and then spread through networked communities of professionals in similar circumstances who could help build the capacity of the staff in each building to implement it. When Pam Glynn became principal in 2008, the school did not have the capacity to implement the sophisticated systems of supports that Freshman OnTrack eventually became at Hancock. Freshman OnTrack worked at Hancock because practitioners who were committed to solving the problem of freshman course failure worked over time to develop and refine a complicated web of interlocking systems and structures. They also required coaching to get there.

"I couldn't say more amazing things about NCS or Dell," Pavona said. "He's the best. When we had the SIG grant, he coached me for an hour every other week. It was such a luxury," she effused. "At no other point in my career have I been able to problem solve, reflect, and share ideas in that way. Unfortunately, it's just not a part of teaching."

Together, Hancock and NCS staff created a plan for how to structure meetings and create systems that would ensure that students were reliably provided with the right level of intervention. McCain gave Pavona reading on Response to Intervention (RTI), a framework that originated in the special education field. The theory behind RTI is that the majority of students (Tier I) can be reached through strong classroom instruction and school-wide policies, while a smaller group of students (Tier II) require some sort of group intervention, and a third group (Tier III) requires intensive one-on-one support. RTI encouraged schools to use data to diagnose students' needs and monitor whether interventions were working. Hancock fit a typical RTI model, in which 80 percent of students responded well to run-of-the-mill interventions (Tier I), 15 percent required extra support (Tier II), and 5 percent required intensive support (Tier III).

Pavona and McCain decided to structure the Success Team meetings (the meetings intended to ensure that students in every grade were on-track, one team per grade) to reach Tier I and Tier II students, whom they defined as failing fewer than three courses. Tier III students, those with four or more failures, would be handled by a different group, which they called the Care Team, made up of counselors, administrators, special education teachers, and staff from the nonprofits working at Hancock that specialized in social and emotional issues. The Care Team would figure out how to deliver wraparound services to students, from counseling to health services. The theory was that students failing multiple courses were probably struggling with issues that went beyond what classroom teachers could reasonably be expected to address.

Pavona sat on both the Care Team meetings and the Success Team meetings, serving as a bridge between the two. "The primary purpose of the Care Team was to share information and make sure resources were not being duplicated without the right hand talking to the left, and not repeating the same intervention without any result, over and over, which at the time was happening *a lot*," Pavona noted.

One purpose of securing the SIG grant had been to obtain extra resources to help students struggling with social and emotional issues. When Glynn became principal in 2008, the United States was in the midst of the "Great Recession" caused in part by the collapse of the housing market. Hancock families were hit hard, Glynn recalled. "The emotional health of our kids *really* concerned me at that time," Glynn said. "The economy was shit, and people in that neighborhood were struggling. People's houses were being foreclosed. Many of their parents are paid under the table and so if there wasn't work for them, they were just stuck. I remember this one family worked at a banquet hall, and people stopped spending money on weddings and stuff, and they were really struggling. Kids just had all sorts of issues, and we had a counselor who was there one day a week for nine hundred kids. We had suicidal ideation, and I was like, This is *crazy*. I was screaming and hollering." The SIG grant allowed Hancock to hire a full-time counselor and others who eventually made up the core of the Care Team. Freshman OnTrack is often billed as a cost-free intervention. And indeed, it can be done by rearranging systems and structures already in the building. But it is important to note that Hancock, the exemplar of how to run a successful on-track program, benefited greatly from the SIG grant and its temporary infusion of extra resources.

The first part of Success Team meetings generally involved looking at overall trends in data in order to craft policies and interventions that might benefit all students. For example, after reviewing school-wide attendance data, the team was able to see that tardiness was a major contributor to poor grades. They decided to switch to block scheduling, which gave them ninety minutes with students on alternate days, rather than forty minutes with them every day. Now, even if students were thirty minutes late to class, they still received an hour of instruction. Teachers found the shift reduced the amount of chaos in the hallways by cutting down on the number of passing periods. Even better, it allowed them to build some instructional momentum and delve into topics in greater depth.

The second part of Success Team meetings was set aside to discuss Tier II students like Lucas. The purpose of these discussions was twofold: first, to develop a plan to help that struggling student in particular; and second, to take any strategies developed for that student and apply them to other students who might be facing similar struggles.

The focus on Tier II students made the Success Team meetings far more palatable to Hancock's teachers. "Creating a system where we were really talking about the right kids at the grade-level team meetings, I think that really changed teacher perception," Pavona said. "Because they no longer felt like they were being blamed for a child's failure, or somehow compromising their moral and belief system[s] by passing a kid who is always absent, or has lots of behavioral problems, and is just struggling universally. Because now we are looking at kids with very good attendance, no misconducts, who are doing well the rest of the day, and we can really focus in on kids' strengths to figure out how to help them succeed."

Of course, such a system was better suited for Hancock, where there were only a small percentage of Tier III students, than it was for

Tilden, where the majority of students fell into the Tier III category. These differences help explain why Freshman OnTrack looks so different in a school like Tilden than in a school like Hancock—and why any program or tool that fails to take into account the diverse contexts of different schools is bound to fail.

One of the Tier II interventions that Hancock teachers honed over time was "Scholar Hour," an after-school tutoring program. When Pavona arrived, tutoring happened during lunch, on Saturdays, or on a catch-as-catch-can basis. Kids were never quite sure where they were supposed to be, and teachers and students alike resented having to give up their lunch periods for tutoring.

Over time, Scholar Hour evolved into a period called Academic Lab, a non-credit-bearing course at the end of the school day when counselors hosted student groups and teachers provided tutoring. Students who were doing well could use the time to socialize, play board games, apply to college, listen to music, or complete homework. "The idea was to create more of a collegiate atmosphere," Pavona said. It was also a time when students could seek out help from teachers and learn to advocate for themselves, a crucial skill for college. Like many aspects of Freshman OnTrack, the idea for Academic Lab was borrowed from another school. "Basically we stole the idea from Jones [College Prep]," Pavona said.

By 2015–16, when the teachers were discussing Lucas, nearly all the Hancock staff had adopted the mindset that it was their job to help prevent student failure. Pavona observed, "It is our moral imperative to make sure kids graduate from high school now, because what other options do they have if they don't graduate from high school? And I do think that shift in belief is nearly complete at Hancock. People get that. There's not a lot of pushback anymore. . . . People are willing to work with kids and willing to support them."

Which is not to say that the work ever became easy or clear-cut. Freshman OnTrack was always a delicate negotiation. How much support was too much? How many chances too many? Where did teacher responsibility end and student responsibility begin? Not everyone was going to agree on where to draw the line, but the meetings provided a venue for calibrating staff's responses collectively and cooperatively. It didn't work for every kid every time—but eventually it worked for most of them.

Two weeks after the Success Team first discussed his case, Lucas was back on the docket again. If a student continued to struggle, the Success Team might review his case multiple times throughout the year. This process of circling back ensured that plans could be recalibrated if they were not working and that teachers were held accountable for following through on whatever action steps they had devised.

Lucas, it seemed, hadn't made much progress since the last meeting. As she had at the previous meeting, Neidt projected his photo and updated grades, which remained inconsistent. He still had A's in math and Computer Science, and F's in English, Health, and World Studies. Neidt also projected the goals and action steps that the group had agreed on for Lucas during the last meeting. The goal was one or fewer late assignments in the next two weeks. The action steps included planning ahead for group work to avoid distractions, assisting with reminders and organization, and looking into his bilingual profile to see if his issues were related to his English language skills.

"I need to set up a meeting with Lucas to figure out what's going on with him," said Dolores Lagunas, the English language learner (ELL) coordinator. "His scores are just so inconsistent." She promised to get to it in the next week.

"I don't know if it's my classroom policy that's keeping it low?" Mirek wondered. "After two weeks, he didn't get in his major assignment so he got a zero. I don't know about that kind of policy? Is that really going to doom him?"

It was a self-reflective question, the type of question that Hancock teachers now routinely asked of themselves. It wasn't the type of question that many people had been asking when Glynn first arrived at Hancock.

A math teacher who had transferred from a neighboring high school that also worked intensively on Freshman OnTrack asked whether Mirek should just forgive the missing assignment. "Maybe if he has a come-to-Jesus moment, you could let him start fresh come December?" she ventured.

"So, just excuse the missing assignments?" Mirek's tone was questioning, not combative.

"No," said Michaels, the World Studies teacher, "if it's two weeks late, it's a zero. You can't coddle them."

"If he got his stuff together, started handing in B's, would he still be able to pass?" asked the math teacher.

"I think so," replied Mirek. "There are still a couple of weeks left. There is still the possibility of doing well."

"Did he turn in his narrative?" asked Pavona.

"No, and that is a huge thing," Mirek replied.

"It sounds like he hasn't met expectations," replied Aidan Phillips, the other Freshman Physics teacher who worked alongside Neidt.

"It's tough. This is freshman year. There is where we set expectations," observed Michaels.

"But they are also still making the transition from elementary," Pavona rejoined. "We need to figure out what he knows. Is this about organization or skills?"

"I did a home visit two weeks ago," Castillo, the math teacher, offered. He had also offered this suggestion at the previous meeting. "After that he changed a lot. A lot of time kids are just assuming things are fine. He lives really close to here! Four minutes!"

"There wasn't a working email," Mirek said. It was a fact he had already raised in the last conversation about the family.

"I think that should be written down as a next step," Pavona said. "If he didn't turn in his narrative, that's really huge. That's seventy percent of his grade."

"Another thing I noticed," Castillo said, "He's *really* smart. He is just super lazy. If you need help translating, I can do it."

The first time Mr. Castillo came to his house, Lucas peeked out the window, saw who it was, and hid. At the time, Lucas was the only one at home. He watched Mr. Castillo knock on the door. He watched him wait on his doorstep. And he watched him walk away after a few minutes of no one answering.

The next day, Mr. Castillo approached him in class. "Where were you yesterday? I stopped by your house. I told you to tell your mom I was coming."

"Oh, I guess I forgot," Lucas lied. "I thought I had dodged a bullet," he recalled later.

Castillo was not deterred. A week later, he showed up at Lucas's door unannounced. His mother was on her way to the gym. Lucas was upstairs playing video games. He heard a knock. His mom opened the door. He heard Mr. Castillo introducing himself. "I'm your son's teacher," he said. "I asked him to tell you I had stopped by."

"Lucas!" he heard his mom yell. His stomach flip-flopped. He slunk into the living room and attempted to avoid eye contact with his mother, who was giving him the stink eye. He greeted Mr. Castillo formally, then sat uncomfortably on the living room couch as Castillo addressed his mother.

"He's doing pretty good in math class. He's just not turning in his homework," Castillo explained.

Lucas breathed a little sigh of relief. He had expected Castillo to really ream him out.

Then Castillo took out his laptop. He showed Lucas's mom the gradebook application that allowed parents to track all of their students' assignments, absences, and tardies. Lucas despaired. He had hoped she would never figure out that she had that type of access to his actions at school.

"I didn't want her to know," Lucas recalled. "Now, *now* she knows what period I'm going to, what period I'm going to be late to, if I'm behind in anything. She checks like every day. She gets messages like every day. Now she says, 'What happened in this class? What happened in that class?' Every day." Lucas shook his head regretfully.

After Castillo left, Lucas's mom read him the riot act. "She wasn't mad about doing bad in math. She was mad I hadn't told her he had come," he recalled. "She gave me like five lectures about it."

Lucas did intend to do better after that house call, but follow-through was an issue. He liked to hang out with friends or play video games after school. Often, he wouldn't even open his backpack until one or two o'clock in the morning, and sometimes he wouldn't open it at all. Also, he was overwhelmed by the volume of assignments. He had never had to work very hard to do well in school. He figured he could skate by on natural ability in high school as well. By the time he figured out he couldn't, he had dug himself into a hole he didn't know how to climb out of.

"In the beginning all I wanted to do was school, school, school. I thought it would be so much fun," Lucas recalled. "But slowly by slowly, the assignments started piling up. They gave us a lot more assignments than I was used to. . . . I was kind of stressed because I was falling behind really bad. It got to a point where I was like, 'You know what? I'm going to leave all the assignments in the past and focus on what I'm doing right now.'"

Lucas estimated that every single one of his teachers had at one time or another sat him down, lectured him about his potential, and offered to help catch him up. Lucas couldn't decide if he appreciated or resented all their attention. "I don't know how they know this, but they would be saying, 'You shouldn't be this type of kid, I see you have potential' or something like that. So they started talking to me about schoolwork and schoolwork, and I got kind of fed up with it. So, I just started ignoring them a little bit. They told me what to do, and I mean I did take their advice but sometimes I was having a rough start to the day, and I'd be like, 'Okay, okay, okay,' but I wasn't really listening to them."

He may not have always been listening, but he did acknowledge that their support mattered. "It did give me a little push to have all those teachers by my side," Lucas said. He was particularly appreciative of Neidt, who spent countless hours working with him. "She really helped me," Lucas said. "She gave me SO many opportunities to do better. She would say, 'Stay after school this day.' She would test me again. That really motivated me to do better in school."

Over the course of the year, Hancock teachers met with Lucas's parents frequently. Lucas's mom told them that Lucas's older brother, whom Lucas worshiped, was struggling. He had been a gifted student, "a total nerd," whose plaques and certificates lined their shared bedroom, according to Lucas. During his senior year, he started making big plans for college. That was when his parents broke the news. He had not been born in the United States, as he had believed, but had been brought to the country illegally when he was an infant. The future he had imagined for himself now seemed out of reach. He would not be eligible for federal loans. His family would not be able to afford college. And even if they could afford it, what was the point if he couldn't find legal work upon graduation? He sank into a deep depression. Lucas's mom worried it was affecting Lucas as well, making him think hard work was pointless, though Lucas had been born in the United States and would have all the opportunities his brother didn't have.

Lucas knew his mom blamed his brother's struggles for his lack of motivation freshman year. Lucas wasn't letting himself off the hook that easily. "My mom thinks it was that, that [it] impacted my grades, but really it was me," he said. "She tried to get me in so many after-school programs, so much church stuff, because she thought that was affecting me, but she still doesn't understand. It wasn't that. I just didn't want to do school."

Whatever the root of Lucas's troubles was—trouble at home, lack of organization, immaturity, or just plain teenage laziness—Hancock's teachers were determined not to let it permanently derail his academic career. They created an action plan for him. They enlisted the help of Youth Guidance, the school's mentoring program. They sent him to lunchtime tutoring. They spoke constantly with his mom. It all worked—sort of.

Lucas ended the year on-track, though barely. He failed just one semester of a core class (World Studies). He ended the year with mostly C's and D's. "He really scraped by by the skin of his teeth," Pavona said. Still, she considered his case a clear success. He remained on-track to graduate with just one semester course to make up during summer school. As important, he finally kicked into gear toward the end of the year, turning in assignments and showing up regularly to tutoring.

Lucas described his evolution as a student as having three phases: In the first, he was trying to do well because his parents wanted him to (and his dad had promised him an iPhone if he pulled his grades up). In the second, he was trying to do just enough work to get his parents and teachers off his back. In the third, he gave it everything he had, for himself. "It was really me wanting to do a lot way better. I knew I had the potential, so I said, 'Okay, let me really give this a try.' I started going all the time to Scholar Hour. Started checking my grades online all the time. Started doing my assignments. That was sometime in April or May."

Lucas couldn't really pinpoint what precipitated his transformation. "It just sort of popped into me one night," he said. "I realized, you know, I really need to change." Pavona didn't mind that Lucas didn't make the connection between all of the support he had received from his teachers and his end-of-the-year surge. If Freshman OnTrack was working effectively, it should be "nearly invisible" to students, Pavona believed. The fact that Lucas ended the year feeling capable of manufacturing his own academic success was proof that Freshman OnTrack was working at Hancock. "At one point he was failing four classes. He ended up with just one failure," she said. "It's just so wonderful to see systems work."

CHAPTER 9

"Marcus Clark's math score went up about twenty points," Jenny, the City Year corps member, noted. "I love that kid."

On a Thursday afternoon in the last week of April 2016, Jenny, Swinney, and Holmes were seated around the conference table in Swinney's office while they crafted a Freshman OnTrack plan that would carry them through the rest of the year. The city was gearing up to host the NFL Draft that weekend, to be held in Grant Park, the stately "front yard" of the city's business district. Meanwhile, the school system was gearing up for another teachers strike.

The teachers' contract resulting from the 2012 strike had expired in June 2015, and the two sides remained at loggerheads, particularly over how to address the $9 billion deficit in the teachers' pension fund. The CTU had rejected the district's most recent offer, which would have increased salaries but also required teachers to pick up a greater share of their pension costs. The pension situation had reached a crisis point. CPS's payments to the fund were eating up a greater and greater percentage of its operating budget. In 2015, CPS had contributed $634 million to the fund. Just a decade earlier, the district had contributed zero.

Schools had been feeling the squeeze all year. CPS had cut school budgets by nearly 5 percent in the middle of the school year and had also instituted three district-wide furlough days. On the previous day, CTU vice president Jesse Sharkey had said that the "majority" of members would want to strike "immediately" if CPS discontinued its practice of picking up the majority of teacher pension payments. "We would respond accordingly and it would be on," Sharkey declared.

Still, despite the looming threat of a teachers strike and the gray, chilly weather outside, the mood was light inside Swinney's cozy purple and yellow office. Also, there were snacks.

"I think part of it is Emani," Holmes said. "Some of his behavior is shifting because she just doesn't tolerate that stuff."

Swinney grinned. "*Ohhh*, they are dating? I like when girlfriends have influence over their little boyfriends," he said, availing himself of a cookie.

Emani, a self-possessed freshman who had transferred from a local charter school to Tilden during second semester, had begun dating Marcus in March. Emani's former high school handed out demerits for every minor infraction: sporting an untucked shirt, chewing gum, drinking soda, eating outside the lunchroom, texting or other use of a cell phone, engaging in public displays of affection, arriving tardy to class.... The list seemed endless and petty to Emani. Demerits led to detention, which led to calls home. Emani's mom had grown tired of all the demerits and calls regarding her generally well-behaved daughter, especially after administrators gave her grief for keeping Emani home for consecutive days when her grandmother died. When Emani's family moved mid-year to a house in the Tilden attendance zone, it made sense to start afresh.

Marcus liked Emani from the first time she walked into Ms. Holmes's English class. She wasn't silly or loud. She had a kind smile and quiet confidence. She seemed like a person of substance, a quality he hadn't necessarily been looking for in a girlfriend but had come to see as essential. "She doesn't like drama, she's A-1," Marcus said earnestly.

She noticed him straight off as well. She recalled her first impressions of Marcus as the two of them downed double-scoop cones at a South Side ice cream shop a few months after their initial meeting. "I

thought he was *bad*. I was like, 'He must don't get whuppings.'"
Emani had gone to school in Iowa before her family moved back to
Chicago. "I've been gone for a long time. I've been in a different envi-
ronment. I thought, This is how these kids act in public school?
Throwing books?"

"Who did?" Marcus demanded.

"You!"

"When?"

"I don't recall."

"Oh, yeah . . . well," Marcus conceded, "I came in late that day. It
was Darius started it. Then Lee, then—"

Emani softened. "I did notice he was smart though. Especially in
math."

Marcus nodded his agreement.

"He's real sweet, but real ignorant. But only to other people. Not
to me. He curse people out. He be messing with them."

Marcus adopted an injured expression. "I don't think you
like me."

"You do be messing with people. *Say* you don't mess with
people."

"That's why I don't say nothing. I don't deny it."

"And if I didn't like you, I wouldn't be wasting my time. *Duh*."

Marcus polished off the last bit of his ice-cream cone and
smiled a sleepy, contented smile. He reached for her hand. "Every
time I get around you, what do I do?"

"Fall asleep."

"Right. 'Cause I'm so comfortable."

Marcus asked Emani out "about one hundred times" before they
finally got together on March 29, 2016. Marcus has a gift for recalling
dates, and he could rattle off this one as easily as his own birthday.
Emani still thought he was "ignorant, *real* ignorant," but she also saw
his essential goodness. "His words—he's real, real sweet," she said.
"He really is, more than what you think." Like Marcus's teachers, she
tried to convince him to see himself as she saw him.

One afternoon, riding in the backseat of a car together, his head on her shoulder, he pointed out the church he had attended in his childhood. He admitted that he had been thrown out of the church for fighting. "See, I'm real bad," he said.

"I don't think you're bad," Emani said softly.

"I love you," Marcus said. "But I am bad."

"I don't believe in all bad or all good."

"What if I stole something," Marcus challenged, "wouldn't I be bad?"

"No, everyone makes mistakes."

"You're an intelligent, beautiful woman," Marcus said. A moment later, he added, "And I have always been bad."

Emani might not have been fully able to convince Marcus that he was good, but she had persuaded him to start acting better. She had told him in no uncertain terms that she wasn't looking to date someone who was likely to end up dead or in jail. "There's a whole bunch of girls crying because they lost their boyfriend," she told him with feeling. "You wanna die? I might as well kill you."

Marcus listened. He distanced himself as much as possible from his old friends in his gang. "Basically, once you're in [a gang], you're always in it," Marcus explained. "I'm still in it. I just move myself around. I don't be around. Basically, if everybody be on the block, I don't be on the block." He felt isolated from his old life and hurt that his friends had stopped texting or calling, but Emani made up for it.

Emani's family was tight-knit and supportive. Tilden's teachers observed that her home situation was far more stable than Marcus's was. But the family had also experienced its share of heartache and loss. In addition to losing her grandmother that fall, Emani had nearly lost her young cousin, who had been shot. Marcus and Emani often talked on the phone until two or three o'clock in the morning about silly things and about serious things they had never told another person. "She's a great listener," Marcus said. "I tell her everything."

One spring day shortly after he began dating Emani, Marcus, Ms. Holmes, and a sophomore boy sat in Ms. Holmes's class kvetching about the sophomore's love life. The boy had been heartsick ever since his girlfriend had broken up with him, and Ms. Holmes had been trying to counsel him through it.

"Forget her," Marcus said dismissively. Then he glanced up at the lovesick teen and registered the pain on his face.

"Oh, you love her?" Marcus said solemnly. "I love my girl too. And I don't care who knows it. Lemme tell you how to get her back. . . ."

The small group that was gathered in Swinney's office on that gray April day passed around the chocolate chip cookies as they contemplated one of their biggest success stories of the year.

"I love Marcus. He's grown so much," Jenny said. "He used to walk into the City Year room and immediately cause chaos. Now he's so respectful."

"Oh, he was the best student in Ms. Parson's class the other day," Swinney added enthusiastically. "He modeled how he solved problems. He was like, 'Do you all understand?' It was so good."

Indeed, Marcus's classmates had started relying on him to help them in math. Marcus's second-semester math teacher was young and inexperienced, and students complained that she didn't "teach right." Marcus, who would take the class step-by-step through a multipart problem, checking for comprehension along the way, was sometimes a more effective instructor than the new teacher was. Marcus often complained that Tilden was not challenging enough. Teaching his classmates was the one thing that truly energized him. "I really like to learn something that I don't know how to do, so I can understand it and then teach it to someone else."

"He likes demonstrating how smart he is," Holmes observed. "He thinks we think he's stupid. Not at all. 'We think you're smart. We're just frustrated when you don't show it.'"

"I'm worried about Jakiyah," Jenny said, switching to a less hopeful topic. Jakiyah was the basketball player who wanted to be a teacher. She had ended the previous semester on-track, but things had deteriorated for her during second semester. "She hasn't been here since April fifth. I didn't know if you heard about that."

"She's on my list," Swinney confirmed. He had an orange marker out and was writing the names of students, including Jakiyah's, on his whiteboard.

"I think she's still in a shelter," Holmes said. "She's been running away. She and her mom are going through some stuff." Jakiyah and Holmes had grown close throughout the year. It pained her to see her suffering.

"I'll email her teachers," Jenny offered.

Swinney stepped back from the board and perused the names he had written. "We had our typical third-quarter meeting with NCS around Freshman OnTrack," Swinney told Holmes and Jenny. "They created what they called an 'orange' group [of] POT-NOTs, 'Previously OnTrack–Not OnTrack.' We had twenty kids who were on-track who are now off-track. So what we talked about was, Who are these kids? What might be the reason they are off-track? And how do we address the issue?"

"Mmm," Holmes sighed. She knew that every one of those "POT-NOTs" had a reason they had fallen off track. Sometimes those reasons, lined up one after another, overwhelmed her. She helped herself to another cookie.

Swinney, Holmes, and Jenny attempted to divvy up the POT-NOTs by the source of their failure. Was it attendance? Behavior? Or solely academic challenges? After they had subdivided the list, Swinney queried the group. "What behaviors might *we* exhibit to help kids be more on-track?" The emphasis on "we" was more a reminder to himself than to the people in the room. He sensed that he was slipping into that mode where he wanted to blame someone else—the kids, the parents, the district, whomever—for that list of names written in orange.

When there was no immediate response to his question, he continued. "I had thought about sitting with Ms. Dominguez, asking her to call parents and say, 'Hey, Mom, your child was doing very well first semester. We have x weeks left. Here are the things we need from the student and family.'"

"Sometimes parents are a good thing," Jenny agreed, "but I know we call those parents every day and no one picks up. We call Jakiyah's mom every single day."

"Also, I'm thinking we need to start calling kids directly," Holmes suggested. "For example, Alyssa has not been here in two weeks. We called her mom. No answer. But then Jordan told me Alyssa was on Snapchat eating an Italian beef! So I got her number from Jordan and just called her directly. I think we may need to start harassing them ourselves."

"A lot of the people in orange, most it's only one class, and it's a really high F," Jenny said, optimistically.

A long silence followed as the group considered all the names on the board and the circumstances that had led the teens to be there.

Holmes dropped her pencil to the floor. She rummaged around for it. She sighed a deep sigh. The mood in the room had curdled. The rest of the cookies remained in the middle of the table, untouched.

Swinney moved toward the computer on his desk and let out his own sigh. "Let me see if I have any time on my calendar," he said. "I'm having an overwhelmed moment. To be honest, I'm tired, and I don't really want to talk to anybody," he said with resignation. "This moment will pass, but right now, I don't want to do this."

He pulled up his calendar, which was populated with meetings and obligations that had nothing to do with students. "My frustration . . . whenever I feel like I don't have enough time, I get mad at CPS. There are way too many things to try to fix. Because [in Louisiana,] I managed five hundred freshmen," Swinney said, referring to his school there, "but there were certain systems and ways that my district had to make sure I could do my job."

Swinney did feel overwhelmed by all that he was asked to do and achieve as a principal in Chicago, even as his resources to accomplish the tasks dwindled. Like most educators in the city, he was being asked to do more with less. In addition to the expiration of Tilden's three-year School Improvement Grant (the same one Hancock received), his budget had been slashed by nearly $200,000 this year due to declining enrollment and other budget line cuts. But more than that, he felt emotionally drained, both by events in his own life and ones in his students' lives. Swinney had adopted a phrase to describe how he was managing to limp through this most difficult year: "Leading while bleeding." He borrowed it from T.D. Jakes, founding pastor of an evangelical megachurch whose sermons Swinney admired. It was a reminder that leaders were often called to minister to others even as they grappled with their own pain. Swinney had long suspected that thirty-seven, his current age, would somehow be a milestone year for him. He couldn't specify why, just that he felt it in his bones. Call it a premonition or a hunch; whatever it was, it had proved prophetic. Thirty-seven was a milestone year all right, as well as the hardest one he had ever experienced.

That January, his father had died. As Swinney mourned his loss, he was mourning both the relationship they had had and the relationship they might have had if circumstances had been different. Swinney had grown up in a tight-knit family in a tight-knit New Orleans neighborhood, the type where someone would block off the street and before you knew it, there was a shrimp boil underway. His mostly working-class neighbors were mechanics, security guards, and bus drivers, with some teachers and other professionals mixed in. They took care of and kept tabs on one another.

"There was communal responsibility. When I was in trouble, everyone knew," Swinney recalled. "I remember cutting class and seeing my cousin on the bus. She took one look at me and my friends and yelled, 'I'ma tell your Mama!'" Two sisters in the neighborhood founded the Young Black and Successful Club for all the children on the block. The sisters brought them on field trips to the zoo, organized volleyball tournaments, and introduced them to local black professionals. "We were taught we were brilliant and smart as young black kids," Swinney recalled.

The tenor of the neighborhood, his family, and his childhood changed when crack cocaine became readily available in New Orleans in the late 1980s and early 1990s, and his father became addicted to the drug. "My dad always said all was well until crack hit the streets," Swinney recalled. "Crack was the reason my mom and dad broke down. You want to oppress someone? Take away their resources and take away their role models."

Swinney and his father were estranged for years. They had finally reconciled when Swinney was in his late twenties. "I realized my dad had his own story," Swinney said, "his own struggles." Swinney thought it was important to share the details of his relationship with his dad with his students, many of whom had their own complicated relationships with family members.

In March, the school held an event for the community where many students participated in a spoken-word performance. Swinney received the loudest applause of the evening when he took the stage.

"I actually just wrote this poem in the back," Swinney told the crowd of students and parents. "I actually found one called 'Ninth Grade' that I wrote back in 2009, but I decided this one is better because it's about my father."

Dad told me when crack hit the street
Pancakes and karate, sittin' on the sofa, taken from under my feet
Little time riding on his back.
He had a new best friend. His name was crack.
We stopped talking for many, many years.
No more walkin', no more spending time,
No more of my father addressing my fears.
But nine months before he died in January
I didn't realize that he saw me through his own eyes.

*You saw the best in me, when you saw my flaws, you saw the best
   in me.*
*You decided to love me, and you recognized that the greatness you
   could not pursue was already in your son.*

Swinney went on to talk about their reconciliation. How his father
had expressed his love for Maurice on his deathbed, and how Maurice had come to forgive him. "Because I *love* my daddy," Swinney
declared.

How could I phase myself out? How could I have let you go?
*How could I not understand you were struggling with your own life
   that had nothing to do with my own?*
*What's important for me to remember, and what's important for me
   to accomplish means nothing if I don't have you inside of me.*
Maybe it's a sign so I can now see your eyes to see through me.

The students hollered their appreciation as Swinney stepped off
the stage.

"I identify with Tilden kids *so* easily," Swinney said. Most Tilden
students had experienced some form of trauma. So had he. Swinney
had recently taken the Adverse Childhood Experiences question-
naire, a ten-question quiz designed to measure how much trauma
you experienced as a child. Swinney scored a 5, meaning that he had
experienced five of the ten categories of abuse, neglect, or household
instability. Research shows that high ACE scores like Swinney's are
strongly tied to poor life outcomes. As ACEs accumulate, so does the
risk of experiencing depression, heart disease, cancer, obesity, unem-
ployment, domestic violence, drug and alcohol abuse, teenage pregnancy, trouble in school, and dozens of other issues. Among those
with an ACE score of 4 or higher, 51 percent had learning or behavior
issues in school. Those statistics helped explain some of the behaviors that Swinney's Tilden students were exhibiting, and some of the
trouble Swinney had gotten into as a teen. "All the things that my
Tilden kids do now, I've done," Swinney said. "I started doing some
of those things in middle school."

Swinney said that quantifying his childhood trauma turned out to be therapeutic. "It exposed me to the fact that what I had experienced was not normal. It might be normal for the students in this space. But it's not normal. It actually helped me to know that it's not normal. Because it helped me to stop judging myself. It helped me realize, okay, maybe that's why it took me five years to finish what should have taken me four."

Swinney tried to provide that same sense of perspective for his students. He wanted to help them understand why they might sometimes feel the way they felt or act the way they acted. He believed he was particularly well-suited to help them in a way that recognized their struggle but did not diminish their strength or potential or uniqueness. "Everybody doesn't have that same tough upbringing," Swinney said. "And if you haven't had that upbringing, you might have sympathy, but not necessarily empathy. Sympathy is 'My heart bleeds for you.' Empathy is 'I am sorry this happened to you, and I can find a way to connect to your experience, and we're going to get through this together.' Empathy requires a little more vulnerability. And when a person learns they are not alone—for real—when they can say, 'Wow, this happened to you too?,' that can lead to a whole new way of being."

Swinney's approach was powerful, but it also took a toll. It required a tremendous emotional investment, and this year, as he tried to process his father's death, he didn't have as much emotional reserve to spare. Swinney's approach also concentrated the burden for helping students onto himself, Holmes, and those who had the largest stores of empathy. If he had had more resources—for an extra counselor, for a full-time Freshman OnTrack coordinator—he might have been able to distribute that burden a little more evenly. Or if he had had fewer students with extraordinary needs, maybe he wouldn't have required those extra resources. Freshman OnTrack was supposed to be about pinpointing students' social, developmental, and academic needs in order to prevent failure. But sometimes—like today—it only served to highlight his failure, the school's failure, even the system's failure, to meet those overwhelming needs.

As Swinney stared at his calendar, hoping some free time would materialize, Jenny from City Year asked about the status of home visits. "How often are those happening?"

"You have to talk to the attendance team about that," Swinney said.

"If that's not happening frequently, maybe that could be a way to start—"

"Yes, *and*," Swinney interrupted, "I'm having my own moment because I know how to push kids. I've never had that problem. But I am grappling with my own capacity. I have always, always pushed kids and gotten them in the presence of a teacher who can help them. But when we look at some of these failures, it's related to actually being at school. So there could be some things we are doing to push kids to not want to be around us. So I think my first step is, I have to check in with all of these kids this week." Swinney may have been having an overwhelmed moment, but he wasn't about to give up on those POT-NOTs, which meant that he wasn't going to stop asking what else he and his staff could be doing.

"Do you have the capacity to do that?" Jenny asked.

"If I don't, then I'm putting it into other people's hands that don't have the same leverage. I know I can push kids, whether it's with a heavy hand or a soft touch," Swinney said. "Has anyone talked to Sierra, by the way? Didn't her friend just get killed?"

"Yeah, we were talking about that yesterday," Holmes confirmed.

"She was really working and trying in math," Swinney said. "I saw a couple of times where she just zoned out, when I assumed she was thinking about that."

Holmes closed her eyes and shook her head slowly. "These babies."

"I was talking to Ms. Kennedy the other day," Swinney said. "And she said, 'When does the second shift come in?' And so that's what I'm wondering today. 'When does the second shift come in?'"

A few days later, Swinney walked purposefully through the halls, a list of POT-NOTs in his hand. As he made his way to Ms. Holmes's English class, he saw a security guard drag a student out of his classroom. The student appeared irate and was struggling to extricate himself from the guard's grip. Swinney walked over to see what was going on. He put his head close to the teen's head and whispered something inaudible. The teen shoved Swinney angrily. Swinney pushed him back gently. Swinney whispered something again. Finally, the boy smiled, the tension dissolving from his face. He offered his hand to Swinney, who took it. "Firmer," Swinney admonished. The boy tightened his grip and looked Swinney in the eye.

"Can I get a bus pass?" the boy asked, as he tucked in his shirt.

"Could be, could be," Swinney replied. "If you're looking put together like that when you come to my office."

The boy returned to class without a security escort. Swinney returned to the task at hand.

"See that?" Swinney said. "We don't get credit for that, for improved behavior. He came from a therapeutic day school. Last year he would have exploded."

Swinney walked along the third-floor hallway until he arrived at Ms. Holmes's class. "Can I speak to Sierra?" he asked. "It will only take two minutes."

Sierra sauntered out the door, closing it softly behind her.

Swinney turned his attention to Sierra, who was wearing a high ponytail; a wide, glittery headband; and pink lipstick.

"Hi, how are you?" Swinney asked.

"Heyyyy," Sierra said, sociably.

"Two questions. First, how are you doing since your friend passed?"

Sierra's smile faded.

A sixteen-year-old friend of Sierra's had been shot and killed a few weeks before. He was one of several of her friends who had been killed this year. Reflecting at the end of the school year on all the deaths, she displayed her characteristic mix of strength and sensitivity: "It's really hard, but you just have to stay on your feet. You can't just break down," she said. "I just learn to live with it. But it's real hard.

"The first day you feel horrible, you can't stop crying. After so long, I have to get back on my feet, have to stop crying. I try to tell myself, 'You want the best for me. You were my friend.' I know my friend would want me to continue to go to school, to do something with my life."

Sierra would say all that later. With Swinney, she was succinct. "It's been kinda hard, but I'm okay," she said.

"If you ever need to talk to somebody about it, I can get someone for you to talk to," Swinney said.

"Mr. Walker, he don't never be here no more. Whenever I come into his office, he don't be here," Sierra complained.

This was a common grievance among Tilden freshmen. They all loved Mr. Walker, the Peace Room coordinator—they just wanted more of his attention. Walker split his time between Tilden and another high school. He knew Tilden needed him full-time. In fact, they probably needed two of him. Tilden's one full-time counselor spent most of his time with seniors helping them apply to college, or processing paperwork for students with learning disabilities. An additional counselor was top on the list of services and supports Swinney would add if he had additional funds.

"He did email me to say to check in with you," Swinney said. "Your attendance is high, but it's slumped a little this quarter. You used to be 100 percent and then [your attendance went down] to 95 and now it's 83. What do you think happened?"

"Um, coming late?"

"Have you fixed the tardy issue?"

"Noooo," Sierra's said, her eyebrows rising in unison with the pitch of her voice.

"And why not?" Swinney probed.

"*Becaauuuse,*" Sierra whined, "I be *tired.*"

"I'm gonna have Ms. Dominguez come pick you up at, what? Six thirty?" Swinney replied with a poker face. Sierra couldn't make out whether he was serious or not.

"Ain't nobody gonna pick me up!" she cried.

"We could have her wake you up. Now let me tell you why I'm concerned about the tardy. You already know why."

"Mm-hmm."

"You tell me why."

"'Cause my first-period class."

"Mm-hmm," Swinney agreed mildly. "What's up with that?"

"I don't know—get up too late?"

"You do know that this is a class if you fail, you have to take it again."

"I know," Sierra said soberly. Her first period class was Algebra, which was often called the "gatekeeper course" for high school because it was necessary for more advanced math, and students often failed it.

"This is one of those extremely important classes," Swinney reiterated. "So what time are we going to start getting to school?"

"Eight o'clock," Sierra intoned.

"All right. I'm going to track your attendance. And your check-in time. Do you want me to call your mom and make sure you're getting up?"

"No! I can get up!"

"So, what are you doing?"

"You know it takes a lot in the morning 'cause I be eating, and getting dressed, and when I first get up, I don't just start getting ready," Sierra explained.

"I lay around for a few minutes, myself," Swinney admitted.

"I'm on my phone. Probably watching an episode I fell to sleep to last night."

Swinney nodded seriously. "So, well, think about this," he said. "School ends on June twenty-second, right? Six weeks. Which is worth it? Is it better to get to school on time for six weeks or have to repeat the class?"

"Get to school on time," Sierra said.

"Okay, so I'm going to check in on you next week. And you're going to also tell me the conversation you had with Ms. Parsons about getting here on time."

"I *told* her she can make me a math packet and I'm gonna do it at *hooome*," Sierra pouted, managing to draw out the monosyllabic word for a full three seconds.

"And what happened after that?" Swinney inquired.

"She said okay but she never did it, and I ain't gonna keep reminding her because I ain't a big fan of math," Sierra admitted.

Swinney raised an eyebrow at her. "Whose grade is it?"

"My grade."

"Let me tell you something," Swinney said. "Sometimes when I *need* something, I have to go back and ask again. So, we're going to have a check-in again, and I want to see a higher grade in math. Even if it's not totally passing, it needs to be higher."

Sierra nodded. They shook on it.

Sierra was indeed struggling with math, as she had the last semester. She didn't think the teacher explained it right, and there was no point in coming to class if she wasn't going to learn anything anyway. Still, she hadn't totally given up on learning Algebra. She continued to work diligently with Evan, the preternaturally cheerful City Year corps member who tutored her in math. But she had lost all enthusiasm for school after an incident that happened in late February.

That afternoon, Sierra boarded the number 47 bus, just as she did every day. Four other Tilden students—three girls and a boy—boarded just behind her.

"Ain't no security around now," one said ominously, trying to catch Sierra's eye. Sierra stared resolutely at her phone. If they weren't going to talk to her directly, she wasn't going to give them the satisfaction of a response. For the next few minutes, the four of them made a series of similar threats, all ostensibly vague but clearly directed at Sierra. Finally, the bus pulled over at the regular stop of one of the other girls. All four remained seated. Sierra's pulse quickened. She wasn't exactly scared—she knew how to defend herself—but now she knew for sure a fight was coming.

The group followed her when she got off the bus, then followed her to the Red Line station where she typically transferred for the second leg of her trip home.

"Hey, Sierra," one of the girls called. "I heard you been talking about me." Sierra whirled around, and the girl swung at her.

Sierra blocked the blow, and the two fell to the floor, punching and clawing at one other. The other three jumped into the scrum. One took out a bottle of mace and sprayed it in Sierra's eyes. Another took out an eyebrow archer and tried to stab her with it. A bystander from school took out his cell phone and began to record the fight.

One of Sierra's friends took out her cell phone and called the school. Tilden's security staff called the police. By the time the police arrived, the fight had broken up. Sierra was left with bruises, burning eyes, a broken phone, and ripped clothing. But the worst part was returning to school the next day. The student who had videotaped the fight had sent the video to friends, who had sent it to more friends. By the afternoon, it seemed like everyone at school had seen the video.

"That kind of did upset me," Sierra said. "Like, 'Why you doin' that? You're making it worse.' I already was upset because I got jumped, and I didn't even know why. But then you're sending the video out to everyone? And everyone's asking me about what happened, and I don't even know why we were fighting, and everyone be asking me like, 'Why you fightin'?'" Sierra's voice cracked. "I mean, I don't know why!"

Her teachers marveled that she had shown up to school the day after the fight. Sierra said she never considered staying home. "When I came back to school, everybody's like, 'You're in school? I thought you had black eyes and stuff.' And everyone was so surprised. But, no. I'm the type of person, you might think you hurt me, but you didn't hurt me or do anything to make me feel that I'm not me."

Adding insult to injury, the fight also ended her friendship with Marcus, a loss she felt acutely. Sierra believed that Marcus's sister, Briana, had been the ringleader of the fight. Sierra didn't want the fight to end her relationship with Marcus, but it did. "We was friends," Sierra said. "We was best friends. We would take pictures together, do everything together every day, but when she came, and started drama because this thing that [her friend] didn't like me . . . after so long. . . . Me and Marcus, we just . . . drift away like, he don't say nothing to me, and I don't say nothing to him. I know it's not his fault, but at the same time, it's weird. I can't have this friendship with you, you know, friends do things together, and I didn't want to have to see her because I just . . ." Sierra trailed off.

Though Sierra didn't like to admit it, seeing her attackers in the hallways every day was difficult. One of the girls had been suspended and left the school, but the others returned after their suspensions. Mr. Walker attempted to bring the group together in the Peace Room. Sierra tried to engage in the process, but she was still struggling with the whole thing.

"Briana, Marcus's sister, she said she was just playing. She said she was sorry and she don't usually do nothing like that. The other girl, Teresa, convinced her to do it, something like that," Sierra said.

Walker asked her if she thought she could move forward. Sierra responded that that was what she was trying to do. "But as far as being friends with her? I don't think I could ever be friends with someone who tried to hurt me, especially for no reason. So, her crying, saying she's a good person? I didn't really—yeah, whatever. I can't tell you you're a bad person. It's just some people don't make good decisions. Some people do things without thinking. She's saying people in the school are calling her ugly and things like that. I didn't even say nothing about her!" Sierra insisted.

"She said she was just mad because everyone told her I was talking about her. And my thing is, if somebody say something, I'm not just going to instantly believe what other people say, because I know people want a reaction and want something to happen. So I'm not going to just attack you based on what somebody else said. I'm going to find out for myself. I'm not going to just come at you like that if I don't know it's the truth."

At the end of the intervention, Sierra addressed Briana. "I don't forget, but I forgive you. I'm over it. Don't think that I'm plotting to get you back. Don't ever feel like it's not safe because I have people who are going to jump you. Me? I'm on to something bigger and better, therefore, you can move on with your life," She concluded, with dignity, "I'm trying to continue to do me."

Mr. Walker told her she had done an excellent job. He was proud of her for not retaliating physically and for assuring Briana that the fight was over.

But taking the high road had taken its toll on Sierra. "In this school, people don't allow you to just cry without them thinking, 'Oh, she's weak.' Without looking at you and laughing. I just be feeling like I need a breaking point sometimes. There's just so much I be holding in," she said later, reflecting on all the drama of the year.

Tilden's teachers noted a clear shift in her mood and behavior after the fight. "Ever since then, she's down," Ms. Dominguez observed. "She's different. I told her, 'I understand what happened to you.' I tried to get her to talk about it. She's hanging out with different people now, the 'cool' kids . . . the older boys. She's a freshman, hanging with seniors."

Dominguez said she had seen a hardening in Sierra, like she was gradually becoming the very person her tormentors had accused her of being. "I don't know why women are the way they are,"

Dominguez said. "They jumped her for no actual reason except she's pretty and confident. Yeah, she was the pretty girl when she started here, but I don't think she knew it at the time. Now she knows it. She carries herself so different, like, 'I know I'm the shit.' But her grades are suffering, everything is suffering. She's always late. Her attention is somewhere else now instead of [in] class. I sit upstairs in the lunchroom, and I can just watch the other kids gravitate to her. They try to pull her into their world. I think they already have," she concluded regretfully.

It was looking increasingly like freshman year was going to be the "break it" year for Sierra—the social identity she was crafting for herself was more negative than positive. She had come to school with a fixed mindset around math, convinced she was bad at it and disinclined to try, and she was still displaying that orientation seven months later. She had forged strong relationships with a number of teachers and staff, but fraying relationships with her peers had left her feeling disconnected from school. It was hard to know what, if anything, the school could have done better to support her during this time. Dominguez, Holmes, Walker, Swinney, Yafah Levy (one of the school's deans)—all of them had reached out to her repeatedly. Now it was up to Sierra.

"Am I in trouble?" David asked without preamble as he entered Swinney's office, weighed down, as usual, by his oversized backpack.

"I don't know. Are you?" Swinney replied, rising from his desk to greet David with a handshake.

"I don't know, I got called down here."

David was on Swinney's list of students he wanted to talk to one-on-one. Unlike the POT-NOTs on the list, however, David was excelling this semester. Swinney and his staff had discussed at length what to do about David's first-semester grades, three F's and a D. They had discussed his case with CPS administrators and had finally determined that if he was able to get A's and B's this semester, they would change his grades from last semester in math and English. But Swinney wanted him to take ownership of the process.

"Have a seat," Swinney offered.

"Right here? Yes, sir," David said, as he removed his backpack and lowered himself into the chair across from Swinney's desk.

"What was our last conversation about?" Swinney prompted.

"About getting my grades up?"

"Unh-unh," Swinney contradicted.

"Not about getting my grades up, but about talking to Mr. Persaud about getting the credit?"

Swinney nodded. "Tell me how that went."

"It went well. He just told me I needed to have an average higher than a B," David said.

"Mm-hmm."

"And Ms. Holmes said I had to be higher than a B"

"So they said to you, if you pass my class with a B, they will go back and retro your grade?"

"Mm-hmm."

"Do you know why they are doing that?"

"The improvement that I made?" David ventured.

"That, *and* what you did in first semester is always coming up in second semester. So, let's say you study fractions in first semester, right? Do you do *y* equals *mx* plus *b*, all that stuff? Like, and plotting lines. So all of the things we thought you couldn't do—"

"I'm actually doing it this semester," David finished.

"Right," Swinney agreed, "so we know you have mastered those skills. Pretty sweet deal, huh?"

Swinney asked if David had spoken yet to his first semester Biology teacher, Ms. Anderson. He hadn't.

Swinney was masterful at striking a balance between supporting students and coddling them, one of the hardest balances to get right with Freshman OnTrack. Coddling was doing for them. Supporting was teaching them how to do for themselves.

"Talk to Ms. Anderson," Swinney advised. "Say, 'Hey, I know I failed your class.' Whenever I talk to somebody, what I do is, I own whatever I did. Right, wrong, or indifferent. So, I would go to Ms. Anderson, and I would say, 'Hey, Ms. Anderson, I know I failed this class, and I really want to find a way to make up the work before the school year ends.'"

"Is there a possible chance I could do that?" David asked hopefully.

"Mm-hmm, mm-hmm. And who is your favorite City Year person?"

"Ms. Lyana, since she's my mentor," David said.

"Right, so what if you and Ms. Lyana came to Ms. Anderson together and said, 'Hey, if you could put this stuff together for me, I will make sure I get it done and I could prove that I am actually learning these things.' I think Ms. Anderson would be open to helping you."

David practiced his pitch. "So, I'm like, 'Ms. Anderson, I know I failed your class first semester. Is there any way you could get me any work so I could make up the credit?'"

"Mm-hmm," Swinney confirmed. "When you failed last semester, how low or how high was the credit?"

"Fifty percent?" David guessed.

"So, it's probably not that much missing stuff. So, I'm going to put a whisper in her ear when I see her tomorrow after school. But when I talk to her, she should have already told me that you two have had a conversation. Got it?"

"Got it."

"And right now you are passing everything, right?"

"Yes, sir."

"That was easy," Swinney said.

"Yeah, it was. Have a good day, Mr. Swinney," said David as he gathered his things to leave.

Actually, doing well in school turned out to be a lot easier than David had expected. His attendance began to improve when he moved in with his father and his father's girlfriend, who dropped him off at school and picked him up every day. Pretty soon, attending class became a habit, just as ditching class had become a habit first semester. Other than one court date in February, he had not missed a single day of school second semester.

He was also engaging much more deeply with his schoolwork, completing all his assignments and actively participating in class. He volunteered to read aloud in English and called out answers in math. He was an enthusiastic public defender arguing a mock capital punishment case in social studies class. He had belatedly realized that participating was simply more interesting than sitting with his head down on his desk all period. In fact, he actually wished he had *more* work. "Only Ms. Holmes's class really challenges me—the books we read, the annotations we have to make, the essays we have to type. It's a lot of thinking and writing." He also thought he could handle more classes at one time. Tilden's block schedule, which gave him four courses each semester rather than the standard seven, also seemed too easy now. "The four classes doesn't really seem like nothing, like, I don't know . . . I kind of like to be challenged now!" he marveled, as if he had surprised even himself.

Just as it proved to be more enjoyable to pay attention than to zone out, it also turned out to be far more enjoyable to excel than to fail. When asked about a month into second semester what his favorite day of school was, he replied, "Probably today. Because when I walked in, I got two donuts and hot chocolate, so that was alright. Then I looked at my math test I took, and I got [a] 100, so it made me feel proud." The only other day he could recall enjoying so much was Field Day in elementary school, when they competed in athletic contests all day.

He also was reveling in his new reputation as the "turnaround kid." "Even some teachers I've never met have come up to me and said, 'I've been hearing good things about you,'" David said with pride. One day in March, prior to his discussions with Swinney about first-semester grade changes, he had intercepted the principal in the hallway and inquired, "Hey, Mr. Swinney, have you heard about me?" Swinney assured him that he had. David nodded approvingly.

David exemplified why Freshman OnTrack was such a powerful intervention. When Roderick's research was first published, there were plenty of people who questioned her interpretation of ninth grade as a critical intervention point. Sure, students were struggling with the transition to ninth grade, but those who were failing might have been different in some fundamental (but unmeasurable) way from those who sailed through. David was proof that well-timed interventions could permanently alter the ways students see themselves in relation to school, which could in turn alter their academic trajectories.

As he experienced academic success for the first time in years, David allowed himself to start thinking more about his future. He wanted to transfer to a school with a stronger academic reputation and then go on to college. The teachers at Tilden were good, he said, but the kids were too distracting. Now that he was serious about school, it bothered him that other students weren't. He thought it was a gigantic waste of time how every class started ten or fifteen minutes late, "because teachers aren't going to just teach to the five or six kids who are actually there on time."

Though he talked about transferring to a high school closer to his father's house, he also began to increasingly feel a part of the larger Tilden community. His friend Dominic had left school, which Tilden teachers thought was good for David. With Dominic gone, David started making friends with other freshmen. In the cafeteria he began sitting with a group of "nice" kids who got good grades.

He built a strong rapport with several of the City Year corps members, particularly Jess Enriquez, whose childhood home was at Laflin and 47th, just a mile from Tilden. Tilden would have been her neighborhood school, but she had attended Jones College Prep, a selective enrollment high school, instead. She went on to earn a prestigious Posse scholarship to attend Connecticut College.

The students appreciated her because she came from the neighborhood, though they sometimes noted that she was different from them. "You didn't go to a bad school like Tilden," they would tell her. Mostly they liked her because she was a really good listener. She and David, in particular, grew close. When she missed a day of school to attend a conference, he emailed inquiring about her whereabouts and demanding a valid excuse for her absence. "He was keeping me accountable," Jess recalled, smiling at the memory. "It was good to see he's modeling what I do, because I would have done that to him too."

Jess said that one thing that stood out to her about David from the beginning was that he knew how to advocate for himself. "He was always willing to raise his hand and say 'I need help,'" Jess said. Even before he came to Tilden, David had close relationships with some of the adults at the local Boys & Girls Club. "Having those sorts of resources helped him," Jess said, "because even before he really knew me, he was able to see me as a resource."

With second semester conferences approaching, David had begun to use his advocacy skills to ensure that the teachers said nice things about him to his dad. "What are you going to tell my dad? What are you going to tell my dad?" he pestered Ms. Holmes. Holmes assured him that she would have nothing but nice things to tell his dad, but David was still worried. He had never actually disclosed to his dad the full extent of his failure the previous semester.

On the appointed day, David arrived with his father and older brother to the conferences, which were held in the Tilden cafeteria. His brother was there to translate if necessary. His dad was dressed in jeans and a button-down striped shirt. He appeared grave, as if bracing for bad news.

Holmes greeted them enthusiastically when they came to her table.

"DAVID, David, I LOVE David!" Holmes said brightly. David's dad looked slightly bewildered by her exuberance.

"I love David, in case you didn't know," she added for good measure.

"My name is Joe, David's older brother."

"You should be very proud of your brother," Holmes said. "He's done a complete three-sixty, I mean one-eighty. He is kicking butt."

Joe smiled.

"He has two A's and two B's," Holmes said. "He's worked really, really hard. He's been coming to school on time, doing all his work. If he doesn't finish it, he comes back during lunch to finish. He's just awesome. He's been doing really, really well, and I'm really proud of him. Last semester he did not pass reading, but he's doing so well, we're going to retroactively change his grade if he pulls off an A because he's doing so well."

David's dad nodded.

"So, do you have any questions for me?" Ms. Holmes asked.

"No, everything you say sounds good," David's dad said formally. "Thank you."

"I'm serious," Holmes enthused. "He's one of my favorite kids, and he makes my day." She turned to David. "See what you're capable of?"

David's turnaround was one of the things carrying Holmes through the school year. Unfortunately, it seemed like more students were going in the wrong direction. In mid-May, the week after Swinney went from classroom to classroom to talk to his POT-NOTs, he convened another meeting of freshman teachers and City Year staff in his office. Not much had changed. Most of the POT-NOTs from last meeting, including Sierra, were still failing at least one course.

"These students are all still off-track," Swinney said. He was wearing a blue Tilden polo shirt, jeans, and bright orange Nike sneakers, which matched the color of the names written on the board and added a bit of levity to an otherwise somber meeting.

"The kids in this group, they seem to be the ones—they're not on-again, off-again, but *OFF* for a few weeks. Does that sound right to y'all?"

"Yep," Holmes sighed. She was tired. No, it was more than that. She was weary. Since about January, she had wondered whether she had the energy to return the next year. Lately, she had been talking more seriously with her partner about quitting. She didn't have another job lined up, but she didn't believe she could make it through another school year like this one. All of the counseling and mentoring and advocating had taken a toll. "Sometimes I feel like I have to go, for my own mental health," Holmes confided in early May. "Honestly, sometimes I feel like I've been abused. The constant trauma that is playing out in the classroom, it wears you down."

But when Holmes talked about leaving, she spoke less about her students and more about the other teachers in the building. "The teacher support, it's not as good as it should be," Holmes said. "We're not as understanding or flexible with each other, and I don't like the way some teachers treat some kids."

Most of all, it bothered her that not everyone was philosophically aligned around the Freshman OnTrack work. She thought some Tilden teachers were still too quick to fail students, particularly first semester freshman year. "They don't take the research seriously," Holmes lamented. "They don't get it that if you fail a kid, they get off track, and they get discouraged, and they are more likely to drop out, and that's a LOT of power you have over a kid. When you give that F, you are basically saying, 'Okay, you are going to fail life.' And I am just of the opinion that first semester, when you are teaching transitions and a reading class, unless that kid isn't here, you shouldn't fail that kid. I don't care what they do in class, how they act, until they've gotten into the real school. Because I think about kids like David. That kid exemplifies why we should not fail kids in first semester, because it takes a while for things to click. And when it clicked for him, it CLICKED. He went from all F's to A's and B's."

The Marcuses and Davids of the world were why Holmes couldn't quite bring herself to quit. They were the reason she continued to lead the Freshman OnTrack work. As Holmes looked at the list of POT-NOTs, she tried to divine who was the next David on the list, just waiting for things to click.

"There are two outcomes I would like to see," Swinney said, breaking the meeting's silence. "A phone call made by one of us to talk to parents and get some info. And second, put that information in the log."

The group began divvying up the names on the list.

Deja, a tomboyish freshman who wore her hair in two long braids that reached midway down her back, was first on the list.

"She's always here," Jenny offered optimistically.

"OMG! She's *always* here," Holmes agreed, snapping out of her funk with a rueful laugh.

"She's a sweetheart," Jenny insisted.

"No, she's a nice kid," Holmes conceded. "But she whines, and I cannot *stand* whining."

"I don't even teach the girl, and she comes and says, 'Heeelllp me,'" Persaud said, affecting a high-pitched moan.

"YES! That's how she does it!" Holmes laughed.

Holmes agreed to call her mom. It would be an easy call. Deja was whiny, to be sure, but she was motivated, and her mom was on top of her academically.

Sierra was next on the list.

"I'll take her too," Holmes offered.

"No, I'll take her," Swinney said grimly. "I had a talk with her grandma yesterday when she came to pick up Sierra's phone." Everyone in the meeting was worried about Sierra.

Holmes then agreed to check in with Jakiyah, who still hadn't returned to school. Holmes knew Jakiyah had been sleeping away from home recently. She had a pit in her stomach just thinking about it. She suspected Jakiyah was sleeping around, likely for money.

Persaud volunteered to contact the parents of the three students who were failing his class. After someone from the group had claimed each of the orange names, Swinney pointed to another group of names written in red. These were the students who had ended the previous semester off-track.

"The shining star of this group seems to be David," Swinney said.

Swinney looked at the other names on the list, wondering aloud if any of them might be similarly salvageable.

Jackson Klein, the school's data strategist and scheduler, nodded, noting that if they could get three or four of the red students back on track, it would make a significant difference in their overall on-track rates. "It would virtually lock us in to 80 percent," he said, encouragingly. "I'm looking at the kids who didn't fail a lot first semester. Mateo Rodriguez only failed algebra first semester but he's failing everything now."

Swinney shook his head sadly. "Something is edgy about him. He went from being silly or frivolous to angry."

"He's definitely talking a lot more about gangs, about being about that life," Holmes agreed. "He's talking a lot about getting shot at and shooting people. Yeah, there's been a definite shift. You're not imagining that."

"Aniyah?" Swinney said hopefully.

Holmes shook her head. Aniyah had failed all of her classes first semester and was on her way to failing all of them second semester. She had aged out of elementary school, meaning that she was promoted to high school because she was too old to remain for another year, not because she had passed. She was already sixteen and seemed both more mature and more jaded than her classmates. When she received her third-quarter report card, full of failing marks, she had announced loudly to the class, "See, this is why

I'm gonna be a stripper." On the other hand, she constantly dogged Mr. Swinney to let her make the school announcements over the intercom. Swinney took that as a hopeful sign that she still had some connection to school.

Like so many of her peers, Aniyah named Ms. Holmes as her favorite teacher. "She be on my heels," she explained gratefully. "She want me to pass her class even though I be coming late. She always be trying to motivate me to come to her class." Even if Holmes couldn't convince Aniyah to stay in school, she hoped she could influence her to "stay away from the pole," as she put it.

Swinney took another long glance at the names in red. "Here's what I'm asking about from this group," he said carefully. "Are there some kids, and this is going to sound kind of cruel, are there some kids we need to focus on and some kids we should not give as much intentional attention to? That's a hard, hard—"

"No." Holmes interrupted bluntly. She wasn't objecting to Swinney's plan, but to his reluctance to implement it. She was ready to start prioritizing. Unfortunately, Freshman OnTrack was sometimes about making bets about which kids were salvageable and which were not. Teachers' time and resources were not unlimited. In the past, before teachers received and discussed real-time data on students' course grades and absences, dropout prevention resources were often allocated indiscriminately or to the toughest cases. Freshman OnTrack helped educators realize that the best way to address the dropout crisis was to put more effort into those students who were most likely to respond.

"It's hard for me to say," Swinney said. "I know you are boots on the ground, so you've had more contact with them." Swinney looked at the remaining names on the list.

"Sebastian?"

"Maybe," Persaud said. "If he comes to tutoring."

"Caleb?"

"No," said Holmes with finality.

Daniel Bailey?

"No," Persaud and Holmes said in unison.

"Okay, then," Swinney said. "I think we have our list."

The group agreed to reach out to each student individually, call their parents, and escort them to mandatory tutoring sessions during lunch. Jenny from City Year agreed to contact each of the students' teachers and gather their makeup work into one place.

As they readied to leave, Jenny thought of another incentive. "Some kids are obsessed with *Ghost Hunters*. They think there are ghosts in the basement. Maybe we could take all the kids who get back on-track on a ghost hunt down there?"

It was a good reminder that they were still fourteen- and fifteen-year-olds, after all.

"Sure," Swinney said with a smile. It was worth a shot.

A few days after the meeting, Holmes called Jakiyah, who had missed the previous week of school. First semester, Jakiyah had gotten A's and B's and played on a sports team. She had been one of the high-risk students who had met in the Peace Room to talk about her first-semester success. She had even been moved up to Honors Math and English second semester. Persaud said she was one of his most capable math students. But now she rarely came to school.

"Hello, Jakiyah," Holmes chirped. "Are you asleep?"

"Yeah," Jakiyah replied groggily. It was 11:00 a.m.

"Why didn't you come to school today?"

"Because it's not school today."

"But you need to make up your work."

"I am."

"When? I'm really concerned about your grades. You're not passing Math or Biology. What are we gonna do, little homey?"

"I'm gonna do it."

"You promise?"

"Yes!"

"You mad I woke you up?"

"Yes."

"I still love you though."

"I love you too."

"You going home? When you going home? Today?"

"Yeah."

"Promise?"

Long pause.

"I'm going to call you today. You better be home."

Holmes hung up, feeling sad. The cheer she had mustered on the phone had evaporated. "I'm tired. Just really tired. Where are the parents? Who is the mama?" she asked rhetorically, putting her head in her hands. Jakiyah was one of the students who reminded Holmes most of herself in high school—a smart-mouthed loner who wanted to fit in but could never quite connect with her peers. "I'm just having a moment," Holmes said.

Later that week, Sierra ambled into Swinney's office and flashed a hopeful smile. Swinney was calling the parents of all the POT-NOTs this day, telling them he would be asking their children to stay after school for tutoring until they got their grades up. Students filed one by one into his office, and he called their parents while they sat nearby. Sierra's cheerful façade evaporated when Swinney told her the purpose of the meeting. "I don't live with my mama," she reminded him. He told her he would try her grandma. She shrugged an okay.

Despite her promises the previous week, Sierra had not managed to improve her on-time arrival rate. Swinney had a new trump card, though. He knew Sierra was eager to have the school adopt "Dress-down Fridays," when students could attend out of uniform. Swinney thought he could use that as leverage.

"What did you ask me about today in the lunch line?" Swinney asked.

"Um, something about Dress-down Day," Sierra mumbled.

"I'm considering it," Swinney said. "At least on some Fridays. But you also made me think, What are Sierra's grades? What do you think I found?"

"That I'm failing first period still?"

"You are correct. Girl, where have you been?"

"But I also got two B's and a C, right?"

"You actually have an A, a B, and a C. That's good. Do you need me to wake you up? I thought we talked about this."

"Unh-unh! No, no, no. I got here on time today! And I'm gonna get here on time for the rest of the week! And I'm starting to stay at City Year and I'm gonna stay with Ms. Parsons during lunch. Well, she ain't here today but—"

"So you're going today after school with City Year? Okay, if you go to City Year every day this week, this school gets a Dress-down Day."

"Why?" Sierra protested. "Why you gotta put it on me?"

"I'll even put you on the announcement," Swinney promised.

"No, no, no, no! Don't put me on the announcement! Why you gotta do that to me?" Sierra cried, mortified.

"Because you advocated. You're the one who wanted to make sure it got done for the school!"

"Unh-unh, unh-unh, unh-unh," Sierra objected. "I don't want that either. I will just feel good because I know I'm the reason. Nobody got to know it was me."

"Okay," Swinney agreed, "nobody has to know it was you."

"So, I can start tomorrow, right?" Sierra ventured.

"Today! Today!"

Sierra giggled.

"You told me you were staying today! Those were your words. You just told me that."

"Okay, okay," Sierra conceded.

"The whole school is depending on you, I'm telling you. If they don't get it, I'm gonna tell them it was you," Swinney threatened.

"*Okaaay.*"

"You can handle it. You need me to come knock at your door at three fifteen and be like, ''C'mon?'"

"Um, I don't need that. I'm responsible."

"All right, we got a deal. See you after school. I'll be there after school about three forty-five."

"Okay, okay," Sierra said, laughing.

Sierra did show up that day after school to work with City Year, but she continued to ditch her first period class. She never did earn that Dress-down Day. Some days she even made it to school in time for her math class but lingered at her locker or outside Ms. Holmes's door until first period ended.

"I can be on time. I really can. I choose not to," Sierra admitted a week before the last day of school. She had resigned herself to failing math. She had the opportunity to do makeup work, but was resisting. "I'm not going to be at home with a big ole packet," she scoffed.

She blamed her failure on her math teacher, a first-year teacher who was clearly struggling. "I do it on purpose because when I get in her class, I don't like the way she teach." Sierra claimed her teacher occasionally checked YouTube to figure out how to solve problems in the math book. "I'm like, 'Oh my God! What are you doing? You don't know how to do it. I definitely don't know how to do it. We both don't know how to do it!'"

"It's cool, Ms. Holmes," Marcus drawled. It was the day before the last day of classes. Finals were over, and students and teachers were saying their goodbyes. Ms. Holmes's classroom overflowed with her groupies. "It's cool. I'm used to being let down."

"Unh-unh," Holmes objected. "I'm not having that. Don't be guilting me like that."

"Like someone say they going to be there for you, then they quit. It makes you feel some type of way," Marcus replied, doubling down on the guilt trip. "I ain't coming to school tomorrow, Ms. Holmes."

"I'm gonna throw you out the window," Holmes countered.

"Did you hear that? That's a threat," Marcus said with mock outrage.

He gave Holmes a bear hug.

"You still leaving, Ms. Holmes?" asked a girl from the back of the room.

"Yep, I'm out," Holmes replied, with much less sentiment than she felt.

"You can't quit. I'ma drop out," the girl countered.

When she finally made the decision to quit in late May, Holmes had decided to tell each of her classes individually. She had wanted to wait until after City Year left, a couple of weeks before the end of the school year, since their departure was always traumatic for students who had grown to depend on them as tutors and mentors. But another teacher had let Holmes's plans slip to her class, and word had spread through the school rapidly. "You can't leave!" students insisted. "I won't let you." At least a dozen threatened to drop out without her.

As the school year came to a close, Holmes still hadn't fully processed her decision. "I don't know," Holmes said. "I just feel like it's just so much. I just feel like . . . I mean, I don't even have another job. I haven't looked for one. Part of the reason I haven't looked for one is I haven't really made my peace with it. I just struggle every day. It's just so much. It's really hard."

As expected, Marcus ended his freshman year on-track. David had A's and B's and ended up on-track after his first-semester grades were updated. Sierra failed math and ended up off-track.

Reflecting on the year, Marcus rattled off his grades. "First quarter I had two D's and two C's. Second quarter I had one D, two C's, and a B. Third quarter was three C's and a D. Fourth I ended up with an A, a B, and two C's. At least I'm making some sort of progress," he said modestly.

An incident toward the end of the school year indicated just how much progress he had really made. It started in band class. Some boys were harassing a girl, teasing and touching her inappropriately. The girl picked up a music stand to defend herself. Marcus stepped in to try to de-escalate the incident. He tried to take the

music stand out of her hand, knowing that she might end up getting herself into trouble if she were to hit someone with it. At that
point, though, the girl was so upset, she implicated Marcus along
with the other boys. The other boys refused to admit to their part in
the incident.

In the past, the injustice of it all would have infuriated Marcus.
But instead of getting mad, Marcus wrote the girl a heartfelt apology note. He said he knew he should have just stayed out of it, but
he also didn't want her to get into trouble. He said he was very sorry
for making the situation worse. Walker said it was one of the most
impressive displays of maturity he had ever witnessed.

"He was frustrated because he didn't do it and also frustrated
because some of the other boys were not owning up to their part. It
took a lot for him to put his frustrations on the shelf around all those
things, to write an apology letter. If Marcus were super-cynical, he
wouldn't have written it. It also took a lot of perspective-taking. He
put himself in her shoes when the other boys couldn't. It wasn't just
impressive for Marcus Clark from the South Side of Chicago. It
was impressive for anyone."

Marcus, who had been listening to Walker's recitation, smiled.

"She probably threw the note away," Marcus said.

"Nah, she may have framed that joint," Walker said, grinning.

Marcus ended the year with a summer job through One Summer
Chicago, the city's youth employment program, and planned to
spend the rest of his time with Emani and her family, whom he loved
to be around. His teachers still worried about him. He had come so
far, and yet he was still prone to fits of anger, and still drawn to the
friends he had spent much of second semester trying to avoid. He
worried about himself, too. He wrestled with just how much control
he truly had over his own destiny. "The road you take, that's where
you are now," Marcus said philosophically. "You get killed in a gang?
Shouldn't have been gangbanging. You get lung cancer? You shouldn't
have been smoking." He paused. "But then, I knew a guy who got

Swinney wondered if they had devoted too much time and re-sources to the toughest cases. "When I think of kids who were heavily off track, as a system or a structure, we probably spent way too much time on them," Swinney acknowledged in July. Moving forward, he wanted his freshman teams to operate more like Han-cock's freshman teams do, focusing on students on the bubble who only had one or two failures. Realistically, those were the students who could truly benefit from classroom-based interventions. Kids with multiple failures generally needed a good social worker be-fore they could benefit from good teaching. If he had spent less time on those kids, maybe he would have had more time to devote to Sierra, who, for much of the year, was on the brink.

"The Mateos, the Aniyahs just have a lot going on," Swinney said. "I don't know what the right balance is for having teachers take on a task like that. Jakiyah? She's selling her body. That's a lot. And these are *not* bad kids," Swinney clarified. "They just have a lot going on."

He went on to observe that "there are probably better ways to manage the system in terms of supporting kids and following up. I think that was part of Sharon Holmes, in this fourth year, breaking down. She was just like, 'Why don't some of the adults get it?' But when I would sit with adults, they seemed to get it. So, some of that was just compassion fatigue."

He continued, "One of my takeaways from this particular year was, number one, I was dealing with my own trauma of my dad passing and leading up to his passing. So I was dealing with my own trauma, and then my secondary trauma from what my kids were experiencing," he said. "I realized I didn't have the bandwidth to focus on freshmen like I normally do. And what I mean by that, I'm usually much more . . . in their face, much more personable and in-teractive."

At the same time, he recognized that more than just a herculean effort on his part was needed. Perhaps his greatest takeaway from the year was that if he was going to do more, then he needed to have *more*. More help. More time. More emotional bandwidth. And all that started with more resources. If Freshman OnTrack was a baseline measure for how well kids were being supported, then Swinney had his answer. At least 30 percent needed more than they were able to give this year. And already he was worried about next year, when he would not have Holmes or City Year, the two pillars of Freshman OnTrack at Tilden. With his dwindling student population, Swinney simply could not afford City Year's annual fee.

Swinney had a number of ideas about how to put in place even stronger systems and structures next year for supporting freshmen. He had simple solutions, such as a cart filled with the makeup work for every student that could be pushed from classroom to classroom so it wouldn't always be such a heavy lift every time they tried to get students the makeup work they needed from each class. He also wanted to hold more regular success team meetings. The lag time between monthly meetings made it difficult to maintain continuity from one meeting to the next. He also was increasingly convinced that Tilden needed to go to standards-based grading, which he hoped would eliminate some of the subjectivity around grades and make it clearer to teachers and students alike what it took to pass a class.

This year had made Swinney recognize that as a principal he needed to be both the building leader and its chief advocate. He was determined to take an "activist stance," fighting for equity and justice in the larger system on behalf of his students. He needed an additional social worker who had the time to do more than just the compliance work mandated around students with disabilities. He also needed an additional staff member who could run in-school suspensions. Swinney knew issuing out-of-school suspensions didn't accomplish a thing besides getting a problem kid out of class for a few days. But as it stood, Tilden didn't have the capacity to issue in-school suspensions, where students could do both schoolwork and restorative work with teachers or students they had wronged. Finally, Swinney wanted to advocate for a different funding formula, one which recognized that certain students simply needed much more help than others. Give schools a bump for every student with learning disabilities, for English language learners, for every student who had ever been listed as homeless. Suddenly, the kids no one wanted to admit would be the kids everyone was fighting for.

Swinney leaned back in his chair and became reflective.

"People are always like, 'Why don't you leave, why don't you leave?' The district has offered me opportunities. . . . But I feel like, as a district, we love to put new people in places and inspire people to do stuff so there is the appearance that everything is about to be better and newer and fresher. But there is nothing new about the resources, there is never a change in that. So we are so quick to be like, 'Yeah, this is great,' and then you get someone else who comes in with this fresh energy, but it doesn't create sustainable change. I at least have one or two years left. I'm learning so much about equity and treatment of people."

Swinney had thought a lot recently about the district's choice system, which ended up concentrating so many of the highest-need students into neighborhood high schools with dwindling student populations. He figured there was a way that the district could make that work, but only if they acknowledged that those kids needed more than they were getting. "We know who our kids are. There could be an advantage to having high-needs kids in smaller schools in some places, but if they are going to be in one place, we also need to make sure they have what they need. It's about equity. It really is."

CHAPTER 10

As Freshman OnTrack survived one upheaval after another and district leaders moved from one priority and crisis to the next one, Roderick and the Consortium researchers marveled at the steadily rising FOT rates. "Why is this happening? What does this mean? Is it real?" Roderick asked in meeting after meeting with her staff. "I've never seen a system shift of this magnitude before." In 2012–13, the year of the teachers strike and Brizard's resignation, the Freshman OnTrack rate had reached 82 percent, a 25 percentage-point increase from the 2006–07 school year. That increase represented 6,900 additional students *annually* who ended freshman year in good standing.

Roderick was hopeful that the life trajectory for these 6,900 students had truly changed for the better, but she was also wary. For years in Chicago, Roderick and her Consortium colleagues had played the role of policy spoilers. It was the Consortium's research that in 1995 had called CPS's high schools "institutional failures." It was Roderick's research that had revealed the flaws in Vallas's signature "Ending Social Promotion" initiative; and it was her research that had prompted a notorious 2006 front-page *Chicago Tribune* headline that decried, "Of 100 Chicago Public School Freshmen, Six Will Get a College Degree" (a headline that Roderick despised, despite the attention it drew to her work and the Consortium; she felt it was demoralizing to schools and didn't provide any information that would build their capacity to improve). And so, as Freshman OnTrack rates improved year over year, she celebrated but also worried: What if the system was being gamed? What if teachers were simply handing out D's rather than F's? What if more freshmen were passing ninth grade, only to fall off-track in subsequent years and drop out? In short, what if Freshman OnTrack hadn't really worked at all, despite those impressive numbers?

By the end of the 2013 school year, enough time had elapsed to allow Roderick to test these concerns empirically. A group of twenty schools had begun making substantial progress on Freshman OnTrack in the school years ending in 2008 or 2009. Those early cohorts of freshmen had now reached the age when they should have graduated, allowing Roderick to examine whether graduation rates had in fact improved when Freshman OnTrack rates improved.

Roderick first analyzed the data for the three "primary mover" schools: Hancock, Kirby's Kenwood, and Steinmetz College Prep, on the city's Northwest Side. Each had experienced improvements of at least 10 percentage points in the 2008 school year compared with the averages of their previous three years. Roderick found the initial gains were sustained when those freshmen became sophomores in 2009 and juniors in 2010. In 2011, after the cohort completed their senior year, graduation rates improved at all three schools, with increases ranging from 8 to 20 percentage points. Among the seventeen "secondary movers," Freshman OnTrack rates increased by an average of 11 percentage points in 2009, compared with the baseline cohorts; in 2012, graduation rates at these schools jumped by an average of 13 percentage points. Crucially, at those those schools there hadn't been any major demographic shifts or changes in the ninth graders' prior academic achievement that might have accounted for the gains.

The results of the analysis prompted Roderick to start telling everyone who would listen that "Chicago had solved its dropout problem." They indicated that Freshman OnTrack was indeed a crucial lever for moving graduation rates, just as the researchers had predicted a decade earlier. They also addressed some of the concerns that popped up periodically that had suggested that the system was being gamed. The fact that the improvement had carried through to the students' sophomore and junior years seemed to belie those concerns. Since schools weren't being held accountable for the performance of their sophomores or juniors, it was unlikely that the freshman year gains would have held up in subsequent years if the schools had been artificially inflating their Freshman OnTrack rates.

To double-check, Roderick also ran an analysis of how freshman year grades had shifted. She figured she would find a big increase in the number of D's that students had earned if teachers had been simply passing students along. She didn't. Instead, she found a significant decline in the percentage of students with F or D averages, from 33 percent to 22 percent. At the same time, the percentage of students with B's or better—a key marker for college readiness—improved from 28 to 37 percent. "There is little evidence, on average, that the increase in on-track rates in these schools was driven by simply focusing on turning F's into D's or on trying to move students at the margins," the researchers wrote.

The finding that really got to her—the one that reliably made her voice break, no matter how many times she repeated it—was the statistics on African American and Latino boys, who had made the greatest gains of any subgroup of students. The Freshman OnTrack rates of African American males had improved by 28 percentage points, from 43 percent in 2005 to 71 percent in 2013. Latino males had made the second-highest gains, improving 25 percentage points, to 77 percent. When she thought about the additional 6,900 students annually who were finishing freshman year with significantly better odds of breaking the cycle of poverty, she thought about all the people and all the work that had contributed to those gains. She thought about her Fall River research and her early days at the University of Chicago, the pioneering research at the Consortium, the founding principals of the Network for College Success, all the district administrators who had helped operationalize the work, and many dozens of other people. But most of all she thought about Malik, a black teen from the South Side, and Alex, a Latino teen from the West Side. And she wished she could tell them that they had helped to change an entire system, and that because of them, another generation of black and Latino boys from those neighborhoods would not have to experience the anonymity and neglect that they had experienced as freshmen.

Roderick was eager for the findings be known nationally, but she was even more concerned about getting the word out locally. She was anxious, as she always was when there was turnover at the top of the district, that the new CEO might not grasp the significance of Freshman OnTrack and would do something—probably unintentionally—to undermine efforts to support freshmen. Roderick knew that even new policies that on their face had nothing to do with freshmen or graduation could have unintended consequences, and so she was determined that the new CEO, Barbara Byrd-Bennett, hear about her findings and think carefully about how any new initiatives might directly, or indirectly, impact the work.

Already, high schools were grappling with the unintended consequences of Mayor Emanuel's signature initiative—the introduction of a longer school day across CPS high schools and elementary schools. Emanuel had campaigned in 2011 on a promise to lengthen Chicago's school day, which was among the shortest in the nation. He had also vowed to make the longer day a more well-rounded one, reintroducing art, music, recess, and other "extras" that had been cut as schools scrambled to maximize instructional time, particularly in tested subject areas like math and reading. In 2012, Emanuel rolled out the longer day, which added an hour and fifteen minutes to the elementary day, and half an hour to the high school day.

Like so many large-scale, top-down initiatives before it, the longer school day contained the germ of a good idea, but it was insensitive to the realities on the ground. The mandate to reintroduce recess, for example, caused huge logistical challenges for schools without play-grounds or a safe outdoor space for children to run in. Nor was the one-size-fits-all mandate particularly sensitive to the diversity of schools in the system. Parents in wealthy neighborhoods complained that their kids were already overprogrammed. Parents in crime-ridden neighborhoods, meanwhile, complained that the longer school day prevented their children from safely participating in after-school activities, which now took place at a later hour and required them to return to their neighborhoods after dark.

The biggest stumbling block to successful implementation was funding. With the district facing a $1 billion budget shortfall, schools simply could not afford to hire additional staff or pay teachers extra for the extended day. This had become one of the sticking points in the 2012 strike. To resolve the issue, CTU and the Emanuel admin-istration had agreed to a plan to reengineer the workday. Teachers who had been required to arrive at school at least half an hour be-fore students arrived were now contractually obligated to arrive and leave at the same time as students. This significantly cut down on the common planning time and teacher collaboration that had previously occurred before students were in the building. Thus, the longer school day effectively cut down on a key component of Fresh-man OnTrack and school improvement generally. "It was one of those times when people could just get some *stuff* done together, and that disappeared," Sarah Duncan from NCS said. "It was just one of those crazy things. The list goes on and on."

To stave off further upheaval, Roderick was keen to present her preliminary findings on the twenty early movers to Byrd-Bennett. In December 2012, shortly after Byrd-Bennett took office, she got her chance. The meeting had been brokered by two of the early Freshman OnTrack devotees who had since risen to leadership roles in the district, Kirby of Kenwood and Craven, the former area offi-cer whose area had competed with Area 21. Roderick presented the research and then brought along Pitcher from NCS to speak to the crucial role that networks and cross-school collaboration played in the gains.

Byrd-Bennett was receptive to the research, but she did not draw the conclusions from it that Roderick had hoped. Though she did end up making Freshman OnTrack a large part of the new accountability system her administration rolled out in August 2013—a move that was crucial to keeping the district focused on the metric—she also latched on to the idea of extending Freshman OnTrack to all grades, a move Roderick opposed. Reasoning that what had worked so well in high school would translate to the earlier grades, Byrd-Bennett decided to hold elementary schools accountable for an on-track metric that the district had developed based on attendance. Roderick was dismissive of this new elementary metric, which did not have a strong research basis behind it. There was a substantial research base showing ninth grade offered a unique intervention point for students, but there was scant evidence to support the idea that an elementary on-track indicator would work as a lever for graduation in the same way that Freshman OnTrack had. Freshman OnTrack began with a documented problem (widespread freshman course failure) and slowly evolved into a solution through collective problem solving. Elementary on-track began as a solution imposed on a never clearly articulated problem.

Taking a page from her predecessors' playbooks, Byrd-Bennett also moved to put her signature on the network structure, another move Roderick opposed. Byrd-Bennett was eager to end the practice of having separate elementary and high school networks, arguing that combining the two would allow for better coordination between the lower and upper grades. The rationale made little sense in Chicago, where traditional feeder patterns between elementary and high schools no longer existed. Under the plan, networks would go from groups of schools working on common problems to groups of schools that had little or nothing in common. In October 2013, CPS announced the new network structure, which reduced the number of networks from nineteen to thirteen and shifted them to a preK–12 configuration.

Under Byrd-Bennett, the networks lost their common focus. "She came in right after the teacher strike, and things were just really disjointed under her," Craven, a network chief, recalled. "She removed a lot of the people who were there under Ron and Jean-Claude. She changed the network structure again. And so it just felt like people were out there doing their own thing."

In many ways, the challenges under Byrd-Bennett were a retread of earlier challenges under Vallas, Duncan, Huberman, and Brizard. Shifting priorities. One-size-fits-all mandates. Policies stacked one on top of another, with little consideration given to how they fit together. In each case, Freshman OnTrack had overcome these challenges. But after Roderick began touting her findings publicly in early 2014, Freshman OnTrack had to face another challenge.

The mayor loved it.

In other circumstances, this might have proved to be a boon. But in this case, it proved to be more of a liability, as the mayor was already struggling with a credibility problem stemming from the way his administration had handled a highly controversial mass school closure of forty-nine elementary schools. The mayor's support, therefore, left Freshman OnTrack wide open to ad hominem attacks.

The mass closure had been the single largest school closure in the nation's history. Emanuel and Byrd-Bennett had insisted that the move was necessary to "right-size" a district with a gaping budget hole and declining enrollment. They targeted schools that were under-enrolled and low-performing, and vowed to send students to higher-performing schools. The closures were concentrated in neighborhoods on the South and West Sides, primarily affecting African American students who were already among the district's most vulnerable and who had already been "reformed upon" the most.

Parents and community members were devastated by the loss of important neighborhood institutions and fearful of sending their children to unfamiliar schools. Many students would have to attend a school farther away from their homes. Some would have to cross gang lines to get to school. All of them would lose established relationships with teachers and classmates.

The public also became increasingly skeptical of the numbers the Emanuel administration proffered to explain the closings. Raise Your Hand for Illinois Public Education, a nonprofit grassroots advocacy group, pointed out that the formula relied on large class sizes (assuming every homeroom should have thirty students) and also failed to account for the fact that schools across the district utilized space differently. Self-contained special education classrooms, for example, were required to have lower teacher-to-student ratios and might therefore contribute to the appearance of underutilization.

"For months, CPS and the City have told Chicagoans that our district has too many underutilized schools requiring it to be 'right sized.' In recent weeks however, numerous sources have refuted the key arguments and data that have been used to bolster the school closing strategy. As parents and taxpayers, we deserve facts and an open, honest discussion," Wendy Katten, a CPS parent and founder of Raise Your Hand, wrote in an open letter to Byrd-Bennett that was published in an article by Valerie Strauss in the *Washington Post.*

Facts were hard to come by—at least in their entirety. Though the Emanuel administration had marshaled a barrage of data to support the closing plan, those data tended to be incomplete and one-sided. For instance, administrators generally omitted the fact that a primary factor contributing to the underutilization of schools was the board's decision to open new schools—many of them charter schools—in depopulating areas. The total number of CPS schools increased from 597 schools in 2000 to 681 schools in 2013. The district was set to open 13 new schools in the fall.

District officials also appeared to be dealing in strategically culled facts in their pledge to send all displaced students to schools that performed at higher levels than the ones they had previously attended.

The schools that the district had targeted for closure were among the lowest-performing schools in the district, and a key justification for the closings was that it would benefit student achievement. The pledge to send students to higher-performing schools was a response to previous research from the Consortium, which found that in earlier rounds of closings, displaced students were generally shuffled from one low-performing school to another. As a result, student achievement remained flat after the closings. But the researchers had also found that the small portion (6 percent) of students who had transferred to substantially higher-performing schools (those in the top quartile in the district) did make significant academic progress. Citing this research, the Emanuel administration vowed to send students to higher-performing schools, arguing that the closures were not just about the district's footprint but also about school quality.

The challenge to fulfilling that promise was that there was a dearth of high-performing schools that were both geographically close to the closing schools *and* had enough open seats to accommodate an influx of new students. Of the fifty-five designated receiving schools, just six were in the top quartile in achievement, the threshold the Consortium had identified as leading to improving test scores.

Still, the administration was able to claim it had fulfilled its pledge to send students to higher-performing schools by pointing to the total points each school had earned on its arcane rating system. Each receiving school had had the same or more total points on the district's school performance policy during the 2011–12 school (two years prior to closing) compared with its respective closed school. The point differential "varied substantially," from zero points, in one instance, to 64 points. On average, the differential was 21 percentage points. However, it was exceedingly difficult to tell what, if anything, that point differential meant in terms of quality. The performance policy in place at the time awarded points based on school test scores, student growth on test scores, test score trends, and attendance. But even the district didn't think those criteria were the best measures of school effectiveness. In the 2014–15 school year, CPS scrapped the performance policy and replaced it with a new one.

CTU president Karen Lewis, who led the charge against the closings, took every opportunity to hammer away at the numbers the administration had put forth. "We do not have a utilization crisis. What we have is a credibility crisis," she said at a press conference at Mahalia Jackson Elementary School, one of the schools slated for closure. "CPS continues to peddle half-truths, lies and misinformation in order to justify its campaign to wipe out our schools and carry out this corporate-driven school reform nonsense."

Lewis, who had gained widespread local and national attention during the 2012 teachers strike, was emerging as Emanuel's chief political opponent and a viable candidate to run against him in the 2015 mayoral election. As Lewis was gaining prominence, Emanuel's education record was rapidly becoming a political liability. In a *Chicago Tribune* public opinion poll taken shortly after the school closure vote in May 2013, 60 percent of respondents said they disapproved of Emanuel's handling of the school system.

So it was no surprise that Emanuel seized upon Roderick's Freshman OnTrack findings as a glimmer of good education news. The new Freshman OnTrack research offered Emanuel a conveniently timed opportunity to remind voters that there were in fact good things happening in classrooms across Chicago.

With a phalanx of news cameras trained on him, Emanuel opened an April 2014 press conference to announce Roderick's Freshman OnTrack findings by recalling former federal secretary of education William Bennett's declaration that Chicago was the single worst school system in the country. "Today, I'd like to give him a one-way ticket back to the city of Chicago to take a look at what's happened in our city. Because we aren't the worst, we're the biggest turnaround. We're on our way. And not just as a city—all these kids now, because of being on-track for high school, they're on track to a life of possibility."

From that point on, Freshman OnTrack was increasingly associated with Emanuel. An *Economist* article in June 2014 which praised him for the tough calls he was making to address the city's colossal unfunded pension liability and for his education track record specifically cited Freshman OnTrack. "He closed 50 schools last year: largely bad, half-empty ones in depopulated neighbourhoods. . . . Many parents were deeply upset about the closures. In some poor, black neighbourhoods, teaching was one of the few middle-class jobs." The article went on to assert, "Yet there are signs that, overall, the city's schools are on the right track." To support the claim, the article showed a graph of rising Freshman OnTrack rates between 2002 and 2013. The graph was labeled "Brighter."

In August 2014, Lewis filed the official paperwork to run for mayor. As the 2015 mayoral race grew closer, Emanuel repeatedly invoked Freshman OnTrack to buttress his education track record, which had otherwise become a liability. "He frequently cites the city's improved high school graduation rate under his watch, mentioning a statistic that projects 80 percent of high school freshmen being on track to graduate," a *Chicago Tribune* article noted.

That is not to say the mayor's support for Freshman OnTrack or his focus on graduation rates was purely politically motivated. "The mayor cared about the school system having a great reputation because that's what will keep the middle class in the city and draw in business. So did the mayor care about big headlines? Yes. And to be frank, those can be a distraction if you don't focus on the real ingredients of the meal," Brizard argued. "But the mayor also cared about those other ingredients. He cared about the smaller levers like Freshman OnTrack." To an extent, his support was useful for keeping practitioners focused on the metric and for attracting investments from private and public sources that might be allocated to help freshmen transition to high school, conduct additional research on Freshman OnTrack, or support the Network for College Success.

But no matter how genuine his support, any education number used to buttress an election campaign becomes more susceptible to manipulation. Critics of high-stakes accountability and testing in education often cite Campbell's Law, put forth by social scientist Donald T. Campbell in a paper first published in 1976, which states that "the more any quantitative social indicator is used for social decision-making, the more subject it will be to corruption pressures and the more apt it will be to distort and corrupt the social processes it is intended to monitor."

Though the indicator had been used in the district for years, political pressure to keep the numbers moving in the right direction increased under Byrd-Bennett, even as support for the work decreased with the shift to K–12 networks. "The last year and a half in the district? It was just a cluster," Dozier said in a 2015 interview. "Nothing really happened besides compliance. Nobody was talking about the work. They were just talking about, 'You need to get these numbers.' But it wasn't done in a strategic way. We weren't reading anything. We weren't getting any coaching. At one point in the year, our kids were at 60 percent on-track at the end of the quarter. I get a phone call from the network, 'I need you to pick up your on-track rate.' Um, *yes*. But is there any coaching behind that? Are we going to get together and talk with people? At the same time, we had NCS really talking about the work. We were lucky we had that, but lots of people didn't. A lot of it depended on the chief. Ours was an elementary chief. She had no idea how to move it. She just said, 'Move it. Get it up.'"

There were whispers that some schools were responding to the pressure to move the metric in ways that did not truly benefit students. One of the strengths of Freshman OnTrack was that it was malleable, meaning that it was easier to influence than some other metrics, such as standardized test scores. This malleability was what made it so attractive to educators who recognized that improving Freshman OnTrack rates could create momentum for school improvement generally. But the metric's strength could also be its weakness. Its malleability also made it vulnerable to manipulation by principals or other administrators who wanted to game their ratings.

From the beginning of the Freshman OnTrack movement in Chicago, there were periodic complaints that teachers were under pressure to change grades upward or to pass students who had not really earned it. It could be difficult to determine when this type of pressure crossed the line and became unethical. Hancock teachers frequently complained about Glynn's crusade to reduce failure rates. Likewise, the CTU filed a grievance against Kirby because as network chief she required teachers in her network to show evidence of having created an intervention plan for students before issuing a failing grade. Kirby—like Glynn—was unapologetic about creating obstacles to issuing F's. She argued that life offered plenty of safety nets for middle-class and wealthy kids. "When you go to elite schools, they won't let you fail," she said. "Why don't kids in public schools, poor kids, deserve a chance?"

But some schools' practices went well beyond simply giving students a few extra chances. During Byrd-Bennett's tenure, at least four high schools engaged in attendance data fraud, artificially inflating their attendance rates, according to a report by the Office of Inspector General (OIG) for the Board of Education. Like Freshman OnTrack, attendance figured into a school's performance rating. It also affected the amount of funding schools received. Two of the principals told the inspector general that pressure from their network chief contributed to their decision to engage in these practices.

The practices uncovered at the four schools cast doubt on all the district's data. "Given the number of times we've reported on problems with attendance data and transfer data, the office does have broad concerns about the accuracy of the information reported system-wide," inspector general Nicholas Schuler said. Though the attendance figures were not directly tied to Freshman OnTrack rates, it was easy to draw a line between the two. Three of the four schools cited in the OIG report had also made significant gains in their Freshman OnTrack rates around the time they were manipulating their attendance numbers.

Indeed, the Inspector General investigation was prompted in part by an article about Chicago's improving Freshman OnTrack rates that appeared in *The Atlantic* magazine. Reporter Kate Grossman described an attendance recovery program at one of the schools that the inspector general later deemed fraudulent. "It's all data-driven and whatever they can do—lie, fudge, and steal—they'll do to get the numbers up," Marilyn Parker, a Manley teacher, told Grossman. Manley, Sean Stalling's old school, which had been one of the first schools to closely track freshman performance, was one of the four schools cited in the report. Under Stalling, the school had never managed to keep more than 55 percent of its freshmen on-track, due in part to high rates of absenteeism. But between the 2012 and 2013 school years, Manley's Freshman OnTrack rate soared from 50 percent to 92 percent. The inspector general recommended firing the Manley principal, who at the time of the report was running a district elementary school.

Much-touted district-wide graduation rates were also coming under scrutiny. Reporters began to question the district's practice of counting students who earned a diploma from one of the district's "alternative schools" as graduates. Students generally transferred to these schools when they were far behind in credits. The schools were advertised as more intimate environments where students could make up classes quickly, but neither the state nor the Consortium counted the holders of alternative diplomas as graduates, because the credential was not equivalent to a traditional high school diploma. For years CPS had not counted these students as graduates, either, but beginning in 2007 the district had changed its formula. "The end result of this numbers game is that the graduation rate tends to hide the fact that a good number of students who start as freshmen at a school, don't wind up walking across the stage to get their diploma at the same school—but nevertheless get counted as one of that school's graduates," one article explained.

"Emanuel touts graduation rate" was the headline of another article questioning the legitimacy of the city's graduation rates, this one jointly reported by the Better Business Bureau and Chicago's local public radio affiliate. The article reported that between 2011 and 2014, at least 2,200 students from twenty-two high schools were incorrectly coded as transfer students rather than as dropouts. Transfers are factored out of the district's graduation rate formula, so the misclassification artificially inflated the graduation rate. "This is not the first time Emanuel's administration has come under fire for doctoring figures," the article noted.

In April 2015, Emanuel was elected to his second term as mayor, surviving a formidable challenge from Jesus "Chuy" Garcia, a Cook County commissioner who ran to the left of him and hammered away on education issues. Garcia had been recruited to the race by Karen Lewis, who had discontinued her campaign after being diagnosed with brain cancer the previous fall. Though he lacked Lewis's name recognition, Garcia managed to force a runoff in the five-way February mayoral election, "a rare humbling experience for [Emanuel,] a longtime Washington insider not known for humility."

Throughout the campaign Garcia had attacked Emanuel's education record, particularly his decision to close schools and redirect money to "elite private schools founded by his big campaign contributors." (Garcia's education rhetoric was often imprecise and bombastic. He was actually referring to public charter schools, not "elite private schools.") Though Garcia's campaign ultimately came up short, his attacks on Emanuel's education record seemed to resonate, at least among those most invested in public education in the city. Garcia was backed by the majority of voters with children in CPS, according to a survey of voters leaving the polls on Election Day.

Then, shortly after Emanuel was elected to his second term, the city was battered by an education scandal that further eroded whatever trust in the system remained. Amidst a federal probe, Barbara Byrd-Bennett pleaded guilty to a single felony count of wire fraud for directing a $20.5 million no-bid contract to her former employer, SUPES Academy, in exchange for a promise of $2.3 million in future payments. SUPES Academy had provided professional development sessions for principals and other administrators, who had publicly complained the training was a colossal waste of time. "I have tuition to pay and casinos to visit (:," Byrd-Bennett allegedly wrote in one email discussing the kickback scheme, a phrase that immediately entered Chicago political lore, alongside Abner Mikva's "We don't want nobody nobody sent."

That very same month, responding to reports of incorrectly labeled transfers, the district opted to restate its graduation figures going back to 2011. Rates were adjusted downward between 2 and 3 percentage points for the 2011, 2012, 2013, and 2014 school years. The restatement also led to an adjustment of the district's Freshman OnTrack rates for those years. The recalculation did not change the overall picture of rising graduation rates, but by then few people were inclined to give the district the benefit of the doubt.

Indeed, the kickback scheme and the graduation rate adjustment had been lumped together in the public imagination, part and parcel of the type of corruption Chicagoans had come to accept as the natural order of things, like cooler-by-the-lake temperatures and potholes on city streets. Calling for an independent audit of all district finances and operations in the wake of Byrd-Bennett's indictment, *Chicago Tribune* columnist John Kass wrote, "Rahm wants some $500 million from tax-strapped Illinois taxpayers to fill a fiscal hole. But the Democratic Boss of Illinois, House Speaker Michael Madigan, is said to not trust CPS numbers.... Boss Madigan is no fool. And he has good reason not to trust CPS numbers. CPS inflated its five-year graduation rate—happy numbers released

during Emanuel's re-election campaign—only to revise them downward earlier this month. The number was dropped to 66.3 percent
for the 2013–14 school year. A failing grade."

Yet Chicago schools were not, in fact, failing, even if it did make for a
snappy line in a newspaper column. The clear thrust of most of the
articles about the city's graduation rates was that the numbers had
been politicized and therefore could not be trusted. But politics cut
both ways, and the truth of the story was more nuanced than reporters or the Emanuel administration let on. To be sure, reporters had
uncovered shady accounting at some high schools. And the district's
2007 decision to count graduates of alternative schools as graduates
(a decision made under Daley, not Emanuel) was a less conservative—
and arguably also less accurate—way of calculating graduation rates
than the method the state and Consortium used. Neither, however,
invalidated the fact that Freshman OnTrack rates and graduation
rates had risen dramatically. What should have been a story about
educators and administrators coming together to improve the lives
of students instead became a "gotcha" story intended to discredit the
mayor, who, truth be told, really didn't have much to do with rising
graduation rates in the first place, except that he liked to talk about
them.

   In 2016, the Consortium released a comprehensive review of
graduation rate trends in Chicago over the previous two decades that
placed the emphasis back where it belonged—on schools. The research had been designed to test every assumption about graduation
rates in the city. It found that rising Freshman OnTrack rates had
indeed led to rising graduation rates, just as Roderick's more descrip-
tive 2014 study had found. It also demonstrated that the improvements in high schools were real and not simply a numbers game.

   "Even the most conservatively estimated rates, where all transfer students and students at alternative schools are counted as non-
graduates, show large improvements in the percentage of students
earning a diploma, especially in the last six years. Data coding issues

could account for some of the improvements in graduation rates between 2005 and 2008, but not in subsequent years. This does not
mean that data records are completely accurate in recent years—just
that they could not account for the improvements in graduation
rates in the most recent years," the researchers found.

Elaine Allensworth, the report's lead author and one of the original on-track researchers, had been at the forefront of the local and
national movements to improve how states and districts tracked graduation rates. There was no one more passionate about the importance
of accurate graduation data. She appreciated the impulse that had led
reporters to delve into the district's graduation-rate data. But she was
also angry that the focus on gaming the system had cast doubt on the
real progress being made in the district, particularly since her research found that graduation rates were up at the same time that other
indicators, such as test scores, attendance, and college-going, were
also improving. It was a truly remarkable confluence—more students
were graduating, and at the same time, graduates were more qualified
than in the past. "I feel like this should be a time when we're celebrat-
ing because our schools have improved so much," she said.

Discounting or denying progress can be every bit as problematic
as overstating it. If the Freshman OnTrack numbers were a sham and
the graduation rate improvements they were helping to fuel were a
scheme, then the district needed an entirely new high school strategy, and this did not seem to be the case. Failure to acknowledge real
improvement when it happens contributes to the relentless policy
churn that plagues education, as well as contributing to the perva-
sive pessimism that greets new initiatives. In this case, it also
fueled the perception that Chicago schools were unfixable and un-
worthy of public or private investment, particularly among those
already predisposed to think real progress in city schools was not
possible.

"The simple fact is that when you look objectively at the state of
Chicago Public Schools, many of them are inadequate. Many of them
are woeful, and some are just tragic. Many of them are basically

almost crumbling prisons. They're not a place a young person should be educated," Illinois Republican governor Bruce Rauner told a downstate audience in June 2016. Rauner and Emanuel were locked in a battle over funding for Chicago's schools. Rauner was arguing that downstate tax dollars shouldn't be diverted to shore up Chicago's education budget, given the city's poor education track record.

Emanuel retorted that Rauner "may have a stereotype that plays to his political philosophy, but those are not the results." He then referred Rauner and the media to Allensworth's report on improving graduation rates. "Now, I know you're gonna try to play a political game and some rhetoric. [But] I ask all of you to do the responsible thing and put the data out about what the results are. It's a University of Chicago report that talks about graduation rates, college attendance that are hitting remarkable highs."

Yes, they were.

Researching and reporting are both by their nature skeptical activities. The reporter's motto is "If your mother says she loves you, check it out." Research begins as well with the "null hypothesis," that a proposition is not true until proven true. Politics, of course, breeds skepticism, even cynicism. And education, when done right, imbues students with healthy skepticism and the critical thinking skills to distinguish between what they believe to be true and what is verifiably true.

And yet the movement that occurred in Chicago to support freshmen hinged not on skepticism, but on belief. Data-based belief, but belief nonetheless. Belief that the dropout crisis was something that could be solved. Belief in the research that showed ninth grade was the make-or-break year for high school graduation. Belief that careful monitoring and support in ninth grade could set students on entirely new trajectories. Belief that, with the right coaching and support, Chicago teachers could be sophisticated problem solvers. Belief that employing trust, collaboration, and personalization—

qualities that are tough to measure or quantify—could result in measurable, quantifiable change. Belief that schools could learn from one another. Belief that such a simple idea as supporting students in their transition to high school could spark such widespread system change.

Roderick, for her part, was still astonished by that one. "I've been arguing against silver bullets my whole career—but this is one," Roderick marveled. "Failure is horrible; it's overwhelming for every kind of kid. But a kid who passes is off to a good start in high school. And it turns out, if you keep children in front of teachers they actually learn."

As Roderick pointed out, Freshman OnTrack was about belief in kids: the belief that it was possible to keep most kids on-track for graduation and lives of opportunity. Ultimately, all of this belief trickled down to the students, who were the ones who most required belief. The belief that they belonged in school. The belief that school could get them where they wanted in life. The belief that they could succeed. Those beliefs, if established freshman year, could propel students through to graduation.

In a speech to her graduating class, Hancock student Fatima Salgado articulated the role that belief had played in getting her fellow students onto that stage to accept their diplomas. Salgado, a 2012 graduate of Hancock, had begun her high school career at a neighboring high school. Then she failed math. She was devastated. Her parents were devastated. "In my culture, you can't fail a class. You have to become a doctor. You have to become the first sibling to graduate from college. It put a lot of pressure on me to make sure I had straight A's. My parents were like, 'Why can't you do this?' It made me feel so guilty."

The school hadn't provided her with much support, despite her pleas for extra help. They advised her to drop down a level in math. "That made me feel, kind of, like it was not a solution, it was just another label put on me that said, '[Y]ou can't do it.' It was not said in those words, but that's how I understood it." The whole experience turned her off of math—and school generally. "I had PTSD in math, in a figure of speaking. I felt like I was set up for failure basically."

At the end of the year, her mom transferred her to Hancock, where the vibe was entirely different. When she struggled, there was a whole cadre of teachers who reminded her that she *could* do it— even if she could not do it *yet*. "They taught me there might be more than one way to teach or learn something. I had thought that unless you were a super brainiac, you couldn't succeed in math. I learned that's actually not the case." She graduated from Hancock with a 4.0 grade average.

At the graduation ceremony in June 2012, Salgado addressed her classmates, about two hundred in all. They were freshmen during Pam Glynn's tumultuous first year at Hancock. Roughly 72 percent of them had ended freshman year on-track to graduate, and 64 percent of them ended up graduating, up from 56 percent in the previous class.

At the graduation ceremony, Salgado, who had taught herself English by listening to cartoons on television, who had struggled throughout elementary school to understand what her teachers and classmates were saying in English, who had failed high school math, issued a rousing pep talk to her fellow graduates:

> Is it really that difficult to find in ourselves the motivation and perseverance to keep fighting for a brighter future? All it takes is to believe that it is possible—that it is possible for us to achieve our goal, our dream. Our past is crucial for our future. We must use our past experiences to transform ourselves into an intellectual, responsible man or intellectual, responsible woman. . . . .
>
> I believe that a person who endures unexpected challenges and hardship, yet emerges with an undefeated smile and a modest character, is a great leader. We must believe that we can be like those leaders and surpass what life gives us. Believing in ourselves is the greatest challenge. But believing in ourselves can also be our greatest accomplishment.

EPILOGUE

On a Sunday morning in the spring of his sophomore year, Marcus's Facebook profile page erupted. "WTF happen to my boy?" "Dam what happen?!!" His friends were frantic, having heard through social media and word of mouth that Marcus had been shot earlier that morning. They posted prayers for his recovery and pleas for more information. They told him to stay strong and expressed disbelief that just a few hours earlier, he had been goofing around on Facebook Live.

Later in the day, Marcus's mother posted a reassuring note. Marcus was going to be okay. He was recovering in the hospital. She was sorry, but she was not allowing anyone but family to see him.

He had been shot once in his arm and once in his foot as he walked down the alley near his house that morning. He said he heard gunfire, then felt a searing pain. He didn't know who had shot him.

The evening after the shooting, Marcus took to social media, posting a live video from his hospital bed. He was groggy and in pain, but he responded to each friend who had offered sympathy on Facebook. "Hey, Jackie. Hey, Cha Cha. Hey, Bailey—Yeah, I'm okay. I got shot." Every so often, he would offer reassurances that he was too "hardbody" to die. You know I'm gonna live regardless," he said with a weak smile.

"I can still flip," he reassured me shortly after he was released from the hospital. Marcus was one of at least 246 shooting victims under the age of seventeen in Chicago in 2017. Thirty-eight of those shooting victims were killed, including Marcus's classmate Kejuan Thomas, who was murdered while playing basketball with his brother on a summer day shortly before the start of his junior year. Marcus never returned to Tilden. Fearing for his life, his mother sent him to live with relatives. He now attends high school in another state. Marcus was proud to report that he earned all A's and B's last semester. He plans to enlist in the Marine Corps when he graduates from high school.

All three of the Tilden freshmen profiled in this book ended up leaving Tilden. Sierra transferred to Bowen High School, another high school that is potentially slated for closure due to low enrollment, before her sophomore year, in large part to escape the "drama" she had encountered. She says Bowen is not much of an improvement on that front, but as of December 2017, she remained committed to getting her high school diploma.

Midway through his sophomore year, David transferred to Curie Metropolitan High School, which enrolls nearly three thousand students, roughly twelve times as many as at Tilden. Though he missed the teachers and students at Tilden, he was glad to be at Curie, which he found more academically challenging than his old school. David hopes to graduate in 2019 and enroll in college.

In October 2017, leaders from the nation's large public school districts convened at the Hilton Cleveland Downtown Hotel to hear Bill Gates, the billionaire philanthropist, outline the Bill & Melinda Gates Foundation's new education strategy. The leaders were in Cleveland for the annual conference of the Council of the Great City Schools, which represents sixty-nine large city school districts. Since 2000, the Gates Foundation had invested $1 billion in the districts gathered in the room, and many more billions in education nationwide. Bill Gates had become one of the most influential and controversial figures in education by pouring money into—and providing much of the momentum for—the type of "silver bullet" reforms that had dominated the past two decades of education reform: the Common Core State Standards, the small schools movement, and teacher evaluation, to name a few.

Standing beneath an arched bouquet of blue, white, and yellow balloons, Gates announced his intention to invest $1.7 billion over the next five years in K–12 education. But the tone of his speech was more measured and reflective than celebratory. He acknowledged that some of the foundation's past investments in education had come up short. Small schools had improved graduation rates in New York City, but the political and economic costs of replacing large high schools with smaller ones were too high, and "the chance of this having a super-large impact was limited." The foundation's push to measure and identify components of effective teaching and develop new methods of evaluating teachers had led to useful insights and tools, but just focusing on the work of teachers in the classroom was not enough "to get the full result we want." He continued to believe in the Common Core's purpose to establish a shared vision of the skills and knowledge students need to succeed in college and life, but he acknowledged that more needed to be done to fully realize its potential.

Based on the successes and failures encountered during seventeen years of investing in education, the foundation would be shifting toward a different type of improvement model, one that resembled the scaling up of the Freshman OnTrack movement in Chicago. Over the next five years, the foundation planned to direct 60 percent of its $1.7 billion toward networks of schools working together to identify solutions to local problems and using data to drive continuous improvement. "The actual tactics about great teaching, about how to reform the schedule, how to get students who are off track on track—those will be driven by the schools themselves. Other than an approach of continuous improvement and really being driven by the data, we will let people come to us with the set of ap-

proaches they think will work for them in their local context," Gates
said. It was an explicit pivot away from the one-size-fits-all approach
that had dominated not just the Gates Foundation's agenda but also
the national school reform agenda for nearly two decades.

Then Gates cited Chicago's Freshman OnTrack movement as an
exemplar of this new type of work his foundation would be supporting. He described the Consortium's Freshman OnTrack research
and the mediating role that the Network for College Success had
played in helping to translate the research to practice: "Taking
those insights that came from the data, the school leaders in Chicago
partnered with the University of Chicago to create their Network
for College Success, and that network of schools is really using
data to identify strategies that educators can use. From 2007 to
2015, the percentage of students on-track to graduate from those
high schools rose from 61 to 85 percent, and four-year college enrollment rates went from 36 percent to 44 percent, so that, you
know, is a substantial increase compared to the current national
situation that's largely flat.

"So these kinds of approaches, where groups of schools or networks of schools have the flexibility to propose the approaches
they want, we think that this will lead to more impactful and durable systemic changes that, with luck, will be attractive enough to be
widely adopted by other schools. We're seeing more examples of
this all the time."

It was, to say the least, a moment for Chicago and Freshman
OnTrack.

"Hold up, did @BillGates just shout out @ChiPubSchools @
UChiConsortium as great ex. of using data & research 2 improve
stud outcomes?#cgcs17" CEO Janice Jackson, who was representing CPS at the conference, tweeted gleefully almost as soon as the
words had left Gates's mouth.

After the Consortium published the Freshman OnTrack research in 2005, a number of states, districts, and networks of

schools across the country adopted the indicator in one form or another. Illinois, Oregon, Delaware, and Connecticut, for example, have placed Freshman OnTrack in their states' accountability systems. But Gates's speech illustrated that the indicator itself is only a small part of the larger lesson to be gleaned from the Chicago-led movement to improve freshman course performance. The approach can be applied to a range of other challenges that districts face, from chronic absenteeism to enrollment and persistence in college.

Broadly, the approach has three central tenets:

1. Focusing on a research-based, high-leverage problem, rather than on a specific program or tool.
2. Building teachers' and principals' capacity to use data to engage in continuous improvement.
3. Sharing knowledge and know-how through networked communities.

This approach fits within a larger movement in education to spend less time fighting over the merits of one policy over another and more time on helping schools "get better at getting better." Leading the charge is Tony Bryk, the UChicago Consortium founder who now heads the Carnegie Foundation for the Advancement of Teaching. Bryk is a proponent of improvement science, sometimes called "continuous improvement," which has driven advancements in sectors from manufacturing to health care. Improvement science eschews "silver bullet" solutions imposed from on high and instead focuses on uncovering the systemic causes of the problems that schools and districts face.

To accomplish this, networks of educators (teachers and administrators) partner with researchers to work on a specific problem of practice, like ninth-grade course failure in Chicago. These networks develop and implement modest changes in their schools and classrooms that are designed to affect whatever common problem they are trying to tackle, and they collect data to assess whether or not those changes are working as intended. As educators learn from what works and, as importantly, what doesn't work across a variety of settings, the interventions are continuously refined. "With subsequent cycles of redesign and testing, a better understanding evolves about the actual problem(s) to solve, and more productive changes are more likely to emerge. Consequently, it is sensible to think about these inquiries as cycles of learning to improve."

It was the type of work Ponder had catalyzed in CPS when she advised the Freshman OnTrack coordinators to act as if they were researchers on a project dedicated to figuring out the root causes of freshman course failure, and that Glynn had initiated when she told Hancock teachers that reducing freshman course failure was a starting point for uncovering many other systemic problems facing the school. Bryk characterizes this approach as "learning-by-doing. . . . It guides us toward starting small, learning quickly, and thereby minimizing the likelihood of harm in case we have it wrong."

It is the opposite of the type of reforms that Gates and many other reformers had previously supported: big solutions to big problems that paid insufficient attention to how those solutions might actually be integrated into schools and classrooms. Carnegie's 2017 Summit on Improvement in Education drew more than four hundred organizations, including schools, nonprofits, colleges and universities, private corporations, and most of the major players in education reform. After two decades of change and upheaval in education, there was clearly an appetite for an orientation that emphasized learning-by-doing, steady improvement over time, and the ability of educators to solve their own problems when given the right tools and support.

The national graduation rate has improved every year for the past decade, increasing from 73 percent in 2006 to 84 percent in 2016. During that same time period, Chicago's graduation rate improved even faster, from 57 percent to 74 percent, in part because Chicago was leading the charge around the use of early warning indicators like Freshman OnTrack.

Robert Balfanz, the graduation rate expert from Johns Hopkins, argues that the uneven improvement nationally—some states and districts have made much more progress than others, and some have actually gone backwards—proves that improvement stems largely from "the people doing the work" rather than from any large-scale social, economic, or demographic change. "I think the patchwork reflects differential of efforts, of focus, or sticking with it and picking the right things to do."

Specifically, most states and districts have begun to use early warning indicators such as Freshman OnTrack, attendance rates, behavior information, and course grades to monitor students' progress toward graduation. During the 2014–15 school year, about half of the nation's school districts reported using early warning systems.

"It's really a fascinating story," says Balfanz. "If you go back to ten years ago, to 2007, you would only really find modern work to improve graduation rates happening in a few high schools in Chicago and a few middle schools in Philly, and now it's fairly ubiquitous."

Balfanz, who has helped states and districts develop early warning systems, says their implementation has been uneven, but most successful systems have three core principles: teams of teachers with common students who monitor attendance and grades, time in the day set aside for these teachers to meet, and a focus on using the data to solve problems at both the individual and the school levels. ("You can't individually intervene your way out with 200 kids. You have to look at the larger problems of failure," Balfanz explains.) His next generation of work will share another commonality with the Freshman OnTrack movement in Chicago—he hopes to build people's capacity to implement early warning systems through networked communities.

Meanwhile, in Chicago all signs indicate that the city's graduation rate will continue to improve. In 2017, the Freshman OnTrack rate reached 89 percent, putting an 80 percent graduation rate in three years within reach. It's unclear how much further Freshman On-Track rates can climb in the district, but the focus on supporting freshmen is unlikely to waver in the near term. "I think Freshman OnTrack is here to stay," said Janice Jackson. "I might just be too immersed in it, but I can't even fathom this district not talking about FOT as part of its accountability structure. I don't know what would happen that would make anyone think that that makes sense. It would be like not tracking attendance or something. I think it's that much part of the system and how we think about success."

Beginning in December 2017, it became Jackson's call to make. That month, Forrest Claypool, the mayor's longtime political ally who had followed Barbara Byrd-Bennett as the district's CEO, resigned after the district's inspector general accused him of engaging in a "full-blown cover-up" of an aide's ethics violation. Jackson was named his replacement, becoming the ninth CEO that the Chicago high-schoolers who have been discussed in these chapters have experienced during their CPS tenure.

A CPS graduate who had been a teacher, principal, and network chief, Jackson was the first CEO to come up through the system since the mayoral takeover of schools. She had seen how Freshman OnTrack worked at every level of the system. She appreciated how it had started broader conversations about the importance of grades and getting freshmen off on the right foot, but more broadly, she appreciated how it had been implemented.

"I think when reforms work . . . there is obviously the training and support to go along with that. There is an attempt to make sure the people on [the] ground who actually have to implement it understand it and believe it, and part of that belief comes from it being research-based. I think the more proof points you can point to, the greater the likelihood of people embracing it is. I think it has to be high-leverage. If people have to do a lot of work, but it's not high-leverage, they're not going to do it. I think FOT was one of those things. Yes, it added more work, more meetings, but when people saw the impact, it was hard to not do it, and I think in education we do a lot of things that take up a lot of time and don't necessarily move the needle, but in Freshman OnTrack you could see a lot of progress quickly."

Though CPS overall is making progress, the district continues to be made up of "the haves and the have nots." Increasingly, Hancock has become one of the "haves." Beginning in the 2015–16 school year, Hancock was designated by CPS as a selective enrollment school, meaning it would no longer accept everyone within its attendance boundary. Instead, as the city's eleventh selective enrollment high school, it would be reserved for those with qualifying grades and test scores. "I thought we could get successful and stay off the radar," said Karen Boran, who had taken over as principal in 2012 from Glynn. "Nope . . . we got too successful too fast, and our alderman fell in love with us." The absence of a selective high school on the city's heavily Latino Southwest Side had for years angered local activists, and the move by Central Office seemed designed to shore up political support just months before the mayoral election.

The move infuriated proponents of neighborhood high schools. "You can understand trying to shake up a school that is not performing, but shaking up something that is working really well, it looks like you're trying to undo it or reduce its effect," NCS's Sarah Duncan said at the time. "The conspiracy theorists might say they're undermining high-achieving neighborhood schools on purpose. It kind of looks like that."

Though privately Boran was piqued, publicly she played the good soldier, rationalizing that she was still serving the "kids who live in 60629." She and the Hancock staff spent the summer working to adapt their systems and structures to serve students with much stronger academic track records than those previous classes of Hancock students had. Boran looked to Freshman OnTrack to anchor the work, recognizing that many of the same systems that she had put into place to prevent failure could also be used to promote college-going.

Led by the Network for College Success, Boran and other principals who had knocked their Freshman OnTrack rates out of the park for several consecutive years embarked on a plan to turn Freshman OnTrack into a college readiness strategy—what they called "B's or Better." Once again drawing on Consortium research, which showed high school grades—far more than test scores—were the best predictor of whether students would graduate from college, "B's or Better" featured the same types of monitoring and support for students earning C's that failing students had previously received. "On-Track is so close to the bone for us. It's not even a strategy anymore. It's part of our DNA," Boran said a few weeks prior to the school's reopening as a selective enrollment school. "It's who we are. It's *still* who we are."

At the end of the school year in 2017, Boran moved on to a new job in Madison. Hancock had posted two consecutive years of nearly perfect Freshman OnTrack rates, and the staff was now focused on ensuring that the level of instruction was rigorous enough to prepare students for highly competitive colleges. It was the next step on the journey that Glynn had started for the school a decade earlier. "Karen would always say that every policy she made for a long time was about on-track and once we figured out on-track it was about B's or better and now I would say it's about quality instruction, every single thing about quality instruction," Pavona said.

Tilden, meanwhile, continued to fight for its survival. In 2017, the school enrolled just 250 students in a building with the capacity to hold 1,900. At the start of the 2017 school year, the 2,300 high-school-aged students who lived within the school's attendance boundaries had fanned out to 147 different schools. The loss of students, along with expiring federal grants, had issued a blow to Tilden's budget, which had been cut by about $2.6 million since 2014. The loss of funding has made it impossible for Tilden to offer the array of classes, support services, and extracurricular offerings that most high school students—inside and outside Chicago—take for granted. Not coincidentally, Freshman OnTrack rates have declined from the 82 percent achieved in 2014 to 64 percent in 2017. As the district nears the end of a school-closing moratorium imposed after the last round of school closings, Tilden is a clear candidate to be permanently shuttered.

Still, even as Tilden's future remains uncertain, Swinney and the staff continue to provide each student with the individualized support that has become the school's hallmark. And he will continue to advocate for Tilden's kids, no matter where they end up. "Even if the school's closed, the types of children who need support are going to end up somewhere—so a new building, a combined building, a distribution will only hide a bigger issue if we're not intentional about how we design something to ensure the kids, my kids and other principals' children, are landing in spots that will nurture, cultivate, inspire, and protect them," he says.

As for the UChicago Consortium researchers, they continue to try to chip away at the biggest challenges facing Chicago's educators and students. With high school graduation rates and college enrollment rates at record highs, and growing evidence that the average Chicago student actually learns more than his peers in other large urban districts, the researchers have turned their attention to building the system's capacity to produce college-ready graduates. If a student needs a 3.0 grade point average to have a reasonable chance of succeeding in college, what would it mean for teachers across the district to work to support students to reach that goal, much as they supported students to prevent their failure? They don't have the answers yet, but they are asking the right questions.

ACKNOWLEDGMENTS

The Make-or-Break Year was a direct outgrowth of my time as the communications director at the University of Chicago Consortium on School Research. The Consortium profoundly influenced not just my understanding of Freshman OnTrack but of what matters in education generally. I cannot overstate the intellectual contributions that Consortium researchers (both those named and unnamed in these pages) made to this book. If I am able to contribute to the national conversation on education and school reform in a productive way, it is in large part because I was lucky enough to spend five years learning from such brilliant, dedicated, mission-driven researchers.

Thank you in particular to Elaine Allensworth, Melissa Roderick, John Easton, Shazia Miller, Camille Farrington, Jenny Nagaoka, Penny Bender Sebring, David Stevens, David Johnson, Eliza Moeller, Julia Gwynne, Marisa de la Torre, and Thomas Kelley-Kemple, whose work on non-cognitive factors, high schools, data use in schools, and freshman year were critical to my understanding of the dropout problem and Chicago's educational landscape. Thank you also to Bronwyn McDaniel and Lauren Sartain for helping me track down key historical documents and academic articles.

Thank you to the Network for College Success for providing me with a framework for thinking about how research and policy trickle down to schools and classrooms. Thank you, too, for connecting me with so many teachers and administrators who were willing to talk to me because they trusted you so deeply.

My deepest appreciation to Maurice Swinney and Karen Boran for providing me with unfettered access to Tilden and Hancock. Opening up your school to scrutiny is a tremendous risk that many educators are unwilling to take. I hope I have done your schools, your work, and your beautiful students justice.

Thank you to the many educators who spent countless hours talking to me about their experiences with Freshman OnTrack. Thank you especially to Maurice Swinney, again, who was unflaggingly thoughtful, gracious, and generous with his time, even as he was being pulled in ten different directions at once; to Pam Glynn, whose hospitality and passion for the work are unparalleled; and to Heather Pavona, who taught me so much about how this work lives in schools during our long talks.

Thank you to the Spencer Foundation, which provided me with the initial funding to research and report on the Freshman OnTrack movement in Chicago. Without the foundation's generous support, this book would not have been possible. Thank you especially to John Easton, for shepherding the project at Spencer, and to Diana Hess, whose initial support and enthusiasm for the book gave me the confidence to pursue it. Thank you also to the Education Writers Association, which helped manage the grant financials.

Thank you to Eliza Moeller, Jane Fleming Fransson, Jeff Gaunt, Lila Leff, and Linda Lutton, who all provided invaluable feedback on drafts of this work. Writing a book can be a very lonely process indeed, and each of you provided vital feedback, friendship, and support when I needed it most.

Thank you to my amazingly dedicated agent, Emma Borges-Scott, at McCormick Literary. You "got" this project before almost anyone outside of my small Chicago education world got it. I am eternally grateful for your editorial feedback, patient coaching, and cheerleading. I am so lucky to have you!

Thank you to my editor, Tara Grove, at The New Press. This book is a better book because of your thoughtful edits.

Thank you, Mom and Dad, for believing in me always and for putting a roof over our heads for the past nine months.

Thank you to my husband, Tom, who fiercely believed in this project and in my ability to get it done—confidence I didn't always share. You say it often to me, and it applies equally to you: "You sacrifice so much of your life, in order for this to work." This book truly was a team effort.

Thank you, most of all, to Marcus, Sierra, and David. Getting to know the three of you was the greatest gift this book has given me. Thank you for your humor, your honesty, your time, and your friendship.

NOTES

Introduction

3 **how Eric thought of himself** The names of all minors in this book have been altered to protect their privacy.

3 **solid academic records before high school** Elaine M. Allensworth and John Q. Easton, *The On-Track Indicator as a Predictor of High School Graduation* (Chicago: Consortium on Chicago School Research, 2005), ccsr.uchicago.edu/publications/p78.pdf.

3 **$670,000 more** C.E. Rouse, "Quantifying the Costs of Inadequate Education: Consequences of the Labor Market," in *The Price We Pay: Economic and Social Consequences of Inadequate Education*, ed. C.R. Belfield and H.M. Levin (Washington, DC: Brookings Institution Press, 2007), 99–124.

3 **more likely to vote** Sandy Baum, Jennifer Ma, and Kathleen Payea, *Education Pays 2010: The Benefits of Higher Education for Individuals and Society* (New York: College Board, 2010), trends.collegeboard.org/files/Education_Pays_2010.pdf.

3 **less likely to live in poverty or be institutionalized** Andrew Sum, Ishwar Khatiwada, Joseph McLaughlin, and Paulo Tobar, *An Assessment of the Labor Market, Income, Health, Social, and Fiscal Consequences of. Dropping Out of High School: Findings for Illinois Adults in the 21st Century* (Boston: Center for Labor and Market Studies, 2007), 30, 45.

3 **healthier** U.S. Department of Health and Human Services, Centers for Disease Control and Prevention, National Center for Health Statistics. *Vital and Health Statistics: Summary Health Statistics for U.S. Adults: National Health Interview Survey*, by J.R. Pleis, B.W. Ward, and J.W. Lucas, Series 10, Number 249 (Hyattsville, MD: 2009), www.cdc.gov/nchs/data/series/sr_10/sr10_249.pdf.

3 **live longer** S. Jay Olshansky, Toni Antonucci, Lisa Berkman, Robert H. Binstock, Axel Boersch-Supan, John T. Cacioppo, Bruce A. Carnes, Laura L. Carstensen, Linda P. Fried, Dana P. Goldman, James Jackson, Martin Kohli, John Rother, Yuhui

Zheng, and John Rowe, "Differences in Life Expectancy Due to Race and Educational Differences Are Widening, and Many May Not Catch Up," *Health Affairs* 31, no. 8 (2012): 1803–1813.

3 **For many consecutive years** S. Luppuescu, E.M. Allensworth, Paul Moore, Marisa de la Torre, James Murphy, and Sanja Jagesic, *Trends in Chicago's Schools across Three Eras of Reform: Summary of Key Findings* (Chicago: Consortium on Chicago School Research, 2011), files.eric.ed.gov/fulltext/ED524669.pdf.

4 **"the dismal state of public schooling"** "Dismal School Dropout Study," *Chicago Tribune*, February 11, 1985.

4 **"intellectual genocide"** Rudolph Unger, "Hispanic Dropout Rate Put at 57%," *Chicago Tribune*, February 13, 1985.

4 **"African-Americans leave"** Lori Olszewski, "1 in 5 Blacks Drop Out: African-Americans Leave City's Public Schools at Staggering Rate," *Chicago Tribune*, November 3, 2003.

5 **almost always dropped out** Shazia Rafiullah Miller, Stuart Luppescu, Robert M. Gladden, and John Q. Easton, *How Do Barton Graduates Perform in CPS High Schools?* (Chicago: Consortium on Chicago School Research, 1999), consortium.uchicago.edu/publications/how-do-barton-graduates-perform-cps-high-schools.

5 **more predictive than all of those factors** Allensworth and Easton, *On-Track Indicator as a Predictor*.

6 **Since 2007** Melissa Roderick, Thomas Kelley-Kemple, David W. Johnson, and Nicole O. Beechum, *Preventable Failure: Improvements in Long-Term Outcomes When High Schools Focused on the Ninth Grade Year: Research Summary* (Chicago: UChicago Consortium on School Research, 2014), consortium.uchicago.edu/publications/preventable-failure-improvements-long-term-outcomes-when-high-schools-focused-ninth.

6 **Freshman OnTrack efforts produced** Roderick et al., *Preventable Failure*.

000 Rahm Emanuel, "Chicago's Focus on Ninth Grade On-Track Triggers Climb in High School Graduation Rates," press release (University of Chicago Consortium on Chicago Research), April 24, 2014.

17 **"killer binaries"** Joseph P. McDonald, *American School Reform: What Works, What Fails, and Why* (Chicago: The University of Chicago Press, 2014), 21.

Chapter 1

21 **It wasn't until 1940** U.S. Department of Education, Office of Educational Research and Improvement, National Center for Education Statistics, *120 Years of American Education: A Statistical Portrait*, ed. Thomas D. Snyder (Washington, DC: 1993), 55.

22 **economic or moral necessity** S. Dorn, *Creating the Dropout: An Institutional and Social History of School Failure* (Westport, CT: Praeger Publishers, 1996), 37.

22 **the public's expectations for high schools** Dorn, *Creating the Dropout*.

22 **reached 70 percent** U.S. Department of Education, *120 Years of American Education*, 55.

22 **a grave national problem** Dorn, *Creating the Dropout*, 78.

22 **President Kennedy warned** John F. Kennedy, *Taped Remarks for Television on School Dropouts and Draft on School Dropouts for the Department of Agriculture*, audio tape (Washington, DC: White House Audio Recordings, 1963), JFKWHA-209-003.

22 **article lamented** "Dropout Tragedies," *Life*, May 2, 1960, 106–113.

23 **In the popular imagination** Dorn, *Creating the Dropout*, 65–80.

24 **Royko ended his rant** Mike Royko, "Drop Nonsense About Dropouts," *Chicago Tribune*, August 10, 1984.

24 **Studies label these factors** R. Rumberger, "Why Students Drop Out of School" in *Dropouts in America*, ed. Gary Orfield (Cambridge: Harvard Education Press, 2004), 131–155.

25 **Fall River Public Schools** Melissa Roderick, *The Path to Dropping Out: Evidence for Intervention* (Westport, CT: Auburn House, 1993), 47–48.

26 **"early drops"** Roderick, *Path to Dropping Out*, 62.

26 **average fourth-grade GPA** Roderick, *Path to Dropping Out*, 62–63.

27 **At the time** Luppuescu et al., *Trends in Chicago's Schools*.

28 **taught his case** All the quotations from the interviews in the Student Life in High School Project come from the case studies written by Melissa Roderick and her team of researchers at the School of Social Service Administration at the University of Chicago. Reprinted with permission from Melissa Roderick.

28 **278 children and young people** A.M. Garza, "Deadly Trend Is Cited in a Murderous Year," *Chicago Tribune*, January 4, 1995.

29 **"South Side High"** "South Side High School" is the pseudonym Roderick assigned to the school.

30 **when they entered ninth grade** Melissa Roderick and Eric Camburn, "Risk and Recovery from Course Failure in the Early Years of High School," *American Educational Research Journal* 36, no. 2 (1999), 303–343.

31 **no one seemed to notice** Melissa Roderick and Eric Camburn, "Academic Difficulty during the High School Transition," in Penny Bender Sebring, Anthony S. Bryk, Melissa Roderick, Eric Camburn, Stuart Luppescu, Yeow Meng Thum, BetsAnn Smith, and Joseph Kahne, *Charting Reform in Chicago: The Students Speak* (Chicago: Consortium on Chicago School Research, 1996), 52.

31 **"If you fail, you just fail"** Roderick and Camburn, "Risk and Recovery," 304.

33 **Omar** Melissa Roderick, Michael Arney, Michael Axelman, Kneia DaCosta, Cheryl Steiger, Susan Stone, Leticia Villarreal-Sosa, and Elaine Waxman, *Habits Hard to Break: A New Look at Truancy in Chicago's Public High Schools* (Chicago: School of Social Service Administration, University of Chicago, 1997), 3.

33 **Oscar** Roderick et al., *Habits Hard to Break*, 9.

33 **missed two or more weeks of instruction** Roderick et al., *Habits Hard to Break*, 8.

33 **at least two weeks of class** Roderick et al., *Habits Hard to Break*, 8.

37 **"West Side"** A pseudonym assigned by Roderick.

43 **42 percent of freshmen** Roderick and Camburn, "Academic Difficulty During the High School Transition," in Sebring et al., *Charting Reform*, 49.

43 **At one particularly troubled high school** Roderick and Camburn, "Academic Difficulty During the High School Transition," in Sebring et al., *Charting Reform*, 54.

43 **performing *at grade level*** Roderick and Camburn, ""Academic Difficulty During the High School Transition," in Sebring et al., *Charting Reform*, 65.

43 **"The overall picture"** Roderick and Camburn, "Academic Difficulty During the High School Transition," in Sebring et al., *Charting Reform*, 65.

44 **"North Side High"** A pseudonym.

Chapter 2

48 **"furnish facilities for the very best instruction"** Elizabeth A. Patterson, "Edward Tilden Career Community Academy High School," Chicago Historic Schools, last modified August 26, 2013, chicagohistoricschools.wordpress.com/2013/08/26/tilden-career-community-academy-high-school.

49 **Ever since, students and visitors** John Hagan, Paul Hirschfield, and Carla Shedd, "Shooting at Tilden High: Causes and Consequences" in Mark H. Moore, Carol V. Petrie, Anthony A. Braga, and Brenda L. McLaughlin, eds., *Deadly Lessons: Understanding Lethal School Violence* (Washington, DC: The National Academies Press, 2003), 188, https://doi.org/10.17226/10370.

50 **book on how students' social lives** Robert Crosnoe, *Fitting In, Standing Out: Navigating the Social Challenges of High School to Get an Education* (New York: Cambridge University Press, 2011), 138.

50 **the "linchpin"** Crosnoe, *Fitting In*, 138.

50 **believe that they do not belong** Crosnoe, *Fitting In*, 138.

51 **"school-kid identity"** Nilda Flores-Gonzalez, *School Kids/Street Kids: Identity Development in Latino Students* (New York: Teachers College Press, 2002), 12.

51 **warned St. Amant freshmen** C.J. Futch, "Freshmen Get Help Dealing for 'Year 9,'" *The Advocate*, August 10, 2011, www.theadvocate.com/baton_rouge/news/communities/ascension/article_dce419fe-bdb9-5cd9-a955-2f262f30754a.html.

52 **he assured them** Futch, "Freshmen Get Help."

54 **"portfolio approach"** Paul Hill and Christine Campbell, "Growing Number of Districts Seek Bold Change with Portfolio Strategy," CRPE at the University of Washington, June 2011, www.crpe.org/sites/default/files/GrowingNumberofDistrictsSeekBoldChangeWithPortfolioStrategy_June2011_1.pdf

55 **high schools for 100,670 students** Linda Lutton and Becky Vevea, "Chicago Has a High School with 13 Freshmen," *WBEZ*, October 27, 2015, www.wbez.org /shows/wbez-news/chicago-has-a-high-school-with-13-freshmen/dd7ebcb5-c22f -4b21-be36-583d0ad8bb6f.

55 **Less than one-quarter** Kate Grossman, "Reviving a Hollowed-Out High School," *The Atlantic*, April 8, 2016, www.theatlantic.com/education/archive/2016/04 /reviving-a-hollowed-out-high-school/477354.

55 **one clear result** Brian Metzger and Linda Lutton, "The Big Sort," *WBEZ*, July 16, 2014, www.wbez.org/shows/wbez-news/the-big-sort/d198b0c7-b490-4041-94fc -b9d10666f127.

55 **citywide pecking order** Metzger and Lutton, "The Big Sort."

55 **live within the school's geographic boundary** Lutton and Vevea, "Chicago Has a High School."

56 **consequence of school choice** Geoff Hing and Jennifer Richards, "Data: Chicago Public High Schools' Enrollment Crisis in Charts," *Chicago Tribune*, November 3, 2015.

56 **Tilden students** Illinois State Board of Education, "Tilden Career Community Academy: Illinois State Report Card," last accessed May 3, 2018, www.illinoisreportcard.com/school.aspx?source=studentcharacteristics&Schoolid=150162990 250044.

63 **"dis-identification"** Claude M. Steele, "Race and the Schooling of Black Americans," *Atlantic Monthly*, April 1992.

Chapter 3

78 **"interventions that have truly scaled"** Sarah D. Sparks, "How to Find Evidence-Based Fixes for Schools That Fall Behind," *Education Week*, September 27, 2016, www.edweek.org/ew/articles/2016/09/28/how-to-find-evidence-based-fixes-for -schools.html.

78 **only twenty-nine interventions** Sparks, "How to Find."

79 **"kicked from one end of the 1990s to the other"** Charles M. Payne, *So Much Reform, So Little Change: The Persistence of Failure in Urban Schools* (Cambridge, Harvard University Press, 2008), 8.

79 ***Nation at Risk* report** U.S. Department of Education, National Commission on Excellence in Education, "A Nation at Risk: The Imperative for Educational Reform" (Washington, DC: 1983), files.eric.ed.gov/fulltext/ED226006.pdf.

79 **"solutionitis"** Anthony S. Bryk, Louis G. Gomez, Alicia Grunow, and Paul G. LeMahieu, *Learning to Improve: How America's Schools Can Get Better at Getting Better* (Cambridge: Harvard Education Publishing, 2015), 24.

79 **the next "big idea"** Bryk, Gomez, Grunow, and LeMahieu, *Learning to Improve*, 5–6.

81 **1995 overhaul** This move toward mayoral control largely reversed the landmark 1988 school-reform law. The law had radically decentralized the country's third largest school system and placed each school in the control of a locally elected council made up of parents, teachers, and community members. The idea was that local schools, led by principals who served at the pleasure of elected school councils, would be far more nimble and attuned to the needs of the community than schools run by Central Office, which was viewed as bloated and inefficient. Seven years later, mayoral control recentralized power, radically swinging the reform pendulum back away from the more grassroots approach of the late 1980s.

81 **buffer schools from the back-scratching** Larry Cuban and Michael Usdan, eds., *Powerful Reforms with Shallow Roots: Improving America's Urban Schools* (New York: Teachers College Press, 2003), 1.

82 **He called on them** Caroline Hendrie, "Chicago Board to Consider Plan to Overhaul High Schools," *Education Week*, March 5, 1997.

82 **The task force included** Michael Martinez and Janita Poe, "Chicago Grade Schools Pull Off Test Turnaround High Schools Perform Poorly," *Chicago Tribune*, June 4, 1996.

82 **Vallas added** Elizabeth Duffrin, "Reform Groups In, Teachers Out at First," *Catalyst*, March 1997, 10.

82 **only slightly mollified** Duffrin, "Reform Groups In," 1.

82 **concrete recommendations and sketchy aspirations** Elizabeth Duffrin, "Board Downshifts on High School Plan," *Catalyst*, March 1997, 1.

83 **"It was a joke"** Duffrin, "Reform Groups In," 10.

83 **Vallas and his team trumpeted** Michael Martinez, "Chicago Might Open 6 More High Schools," *Chicago Tribune*, March 27, 1997.

83 **plan had two key tenets** Alfred G. Hess and Solomon Cytrynbaum, "The Effort to Redesign Chicago High Schools: Effects on Schools and Achievement," in Valerie E. Lee, ed., *Reforming Chicago's High Schools* (Chicago: Consortium on Chicago School Research, 2002), 19–20.

83 **"try something"** Veronica Anderson, "High Schools Told: Get Goin' on Freshmen," *Catalyst*, February 1997.

83 **long-standing program** Janita Poe and Michael Martinez, "It's Back to Basics for City High School Reform," *Chicago Tribune*, December 6, 1996.

83 **electives and remedial courses** Poe and Martinez, "It's Back to Basics."

83 **now be required** Hess and Cytrynbaum, "Effort to Redesign," 33.

84 **Vallas declared** Janita Poe and Michael Martinez, "School Reform to Enter Key Year, Time for Students to Show Benefits from the Changes," *Chicago Tribune*, August 28, 1997.

84 **complained—publicly and privately** Hess and Cytrynbaum, "Effort to Redesign," 38.

85 **implementation of a single advisory period** Maureen Kelleher, "Probation Program Sluggish, Advisory Proposal Rejected," *Catalyst*, September 1997.

85 **Sharon Rae Bender called a meeting** Kelleher, "Probation Program Sluggish."

86 **"a sense of compliance"** Hess and Cytrynbaum, "Effort to Redesign," 26.

86 **little time to plan** Anderson, "High Schools Told."

86 **simply paid lip service** Hess and Cytrynbaum, "Effort to Redesign," 97.

87 **the promotion gate** Hess and Cytrynbaum, "Effort to Redesign," 29.

87 **test's ambiguity** Ben Joravsky, "Getting Testy," *Chicago Reader*, February 18, 1999.

87 **intended to reuse the test** Joravsky, "Getting Testy."

87 **legal battle dragged on** Ben Joravsky, "Before Mayor Rahm There Was a Big Boss Man at CPS Called Paul Vallas," *Chicago Reader*, July 10, 2013, www.chicagoreader.com/Bleader/archives/2013/07/10/before-mayor-rahm-there-was-a-big-boss-man-at-cps-called-paul-vallas.

87 **the conclusion of the lawsuit** Ben Joravsky, "Test CASE/The Schmidt Report," *Chicago Reader*, October 24, 2002, www.chicagoreader.com/chicago/test-casethe-schmidt-report/Content?oid=910126.

87 **a model for the nation** "Chicago Schools Elated by Praise," *Chicago Tribune*, January 20, 1999.

87 **significant gains on state tests** Chicago Tribune Editorial, "A Light at the End of the Tunnel," *Chicago Tribune*, May 21, 1999.

88 **a damning report** Michael Martinez and Ray Quintanilla, "Despite Reforms, City's High Schools Failing, Study Says," *Chicago Tribune*, March 10, 2001.

88 **at high schools on probation** Martinez and Quintanilla, "Despite Reforms."

88 **initially attempted** Martinez and Quintanilla, "Despite Reforms."

88 **"wouldn't want to use Chicago as a model"** Greg Hinz, "New Student Dropout Report Shakes Up Biz," *Crain's Chicago Business*, March 17, 2001.

88 **"champion of the previous school reform agenda"** Hinz, "New Student Dropout Report."

88 **"get away from that box entirely"** Hinz, "New Student Dropout Report."

89 **"Six years is enough"** Jodi Wilgoren, "Chief Executive of Chicago Schools Resigns," *New York Times*, June 7, 2001.

89 **"The biggest thing"** Wilgoren, "Chief Executive."

94 **correctly identified** Elaine M. Allensworth and John Q. Easton, *The On-Track Indicator as a Predictor of High School Graduation* (Chicago: Consortium on Chicago School Research, 2005), ccsr.uchicago.edu/publications/p78.pdf.

95 **"dropout factory"** Lisa Watts, "Number of 'Dropout Factories' Declines," *Johns Hopkins Magazine*, February 28, 2011, archive.magazine.jhu.edu/2011/02/number-of-"dropout-factories"-declines.

96 **two different and powerful ways** Elaine Allensworth and John Easton, *What Matters for Staying On-Track and Graduating in Chicago Public High Schools* (Chicago: Consortium on Chicago School Research, 2007), 2.

96 **"we've missed the boat"** Karoun Demirjian, "Freshmen Schooled on Need to Attend; Report Links Early No-Shows, Dropout Rates in Chicago's Public System," *Chicago Tribune*, August 15, 2007.

97 **distributed highlights** Karoun Demirjian, "Freshmen Schooled on Need to Attend; Report Links Early No-Shows, Dropout Rates in Chicago's Public System," *Chicago Tribune*, August 15, 2007.

98 **Steve Gering, a CPS educational consultant** All quotations attributed to Steve Gerring come from author interview on April 27, 2017.

98 **"If you were a principal or an area officer"** Author interview with Paige Ponder, July 2, 2015.

98 **served as** James Janega and Carlos Sadovi, "Duncan to Join Obama Cabinet," *Chicago Tribune*, December 16, 2008.

98 **need to build the professional capacity** Joseph P. McDonald, *American School Reform: What Works, What Fails, and Why* (Chicago: University of Chicago Press, 2014), 36.

98 **tapped into private funds** McDonald, *American School Reform*, 37.

99 **reputation as a pragmatist** Sam Dillon, "Schools Chief from Chicago Is Cabinet Pick," *New York Times*, December 15, 2008.

99 **"I started tracking through my experiences"** Author interview with Sean Stalling, April 26, 2017.

102 **"there were weird fissures in most systems"** Author interview with Robert Balfanz, December 4, 2017. These data reports were part of a national movement in education around "early warning indicators": data points like Freshman OnTrack that could predict students' likelihood of later academic success or failure. The goal was to use early warning indicators to systematically address the dropout problem and historic achievement gaps between white and minority students. Chicago, with its focus on Freshman OnTrack, was at the forefront of that movement.

The EWI movement picked up steam around 2008, after the Consortium released its *What Matters for Staying On-Track and Graduating* report, and Ruth Neild, Robert Balfanz, and Liza Herzog from Johns Hopkins released a similar report from Philadelphia (2007). Balfanz and Neild had followed a cohort of 14,000 Philadelphia students from sixth grade through high school graduation. They found that a sixth grader with any *one* of four signals had a 75 percent chance of dropping out of high school: a final grade of F in math, a final grade of F in English, attendance below 80 percent for the year, or significant behavior issues in at least one class. Balfanz began promoting the use of the ABCs (Attendance, Behavior, and Course Performance) to predict dropout.

103 **fixation on these unproven fixes** John Hattie, "What Works Best in Education: The Politics of Collaborative Expertise," Pearson, June 2015, www.pearson.com /content/dam/corporate/global/pearson-dot-com/files/hattie/150526_ExpertiseWEB _V1.pdf.

104 **work together effectively** Hattie, "What Works Best."

104 **politics of collective action** Hattie, "What Works Best."

Chapter 4

109 **"a picture postcard"** Charles Kouri, "Domestic Tranquility: West Elsdon Preserves Americana of the '40s," *Chicago Tribune*, September 20, 1991.

109 **one-third of them never made it** Chicago Public Schools five-year cohort graduation rate data, 2008.

109 **fewer than half enrolled** University of Chicago Urban Education Insitute To & Through project, toandthrough.uchicago.edu/tool/cps/2017/school/1200/details/# /college-enrollment/breakdown?igr_qual=qual-any.

109 **failed to show up to class** Chicago Public Schools attendance data 2008.

110 **Iles had told a reporter** Janita Poe, "A Magnet School Fails to Attract: Neighbors Repel Hancock High Plan," *Chicago Tribune*, June 30, 1998.

111 **"solid students"** Poe, "Magnet School Fails."

111 **became a "surprising success story"** Poe, "Magnet School Fails."

112 **"It was so crushing"** All quotes in book from Hernandez come from author interview, December 11, 2015.

121 **he phrased it more charitably** Author interview, December 23, 2015.

121 **"my background as opposed to hers"** Author interview, December 23, 2015.

122 **the instructional "core"** Richard F. Elmore, *Getting to Scale with Good Educational Practice: School Reform from the Inside Out* (Cambridge: Harvard Education Press, 2004), 8.

122 **"They tend to be places"** Charles M. Payne, *So Much Reform, So Little Change: The Persistence of Failure in Urban Schools* (Cambridge, Harvard University Press, 2008), 23.

123 **"think about demoralized schools"** Payne, *So Much Reform*, 61.

125 **"No one's going to check on you"** All quotations attributed to Castillo come from author interview on October 20, 2015.

126 **"rate buster"** Payne, *So Much Reform*, 22, 76.

129 **debate around the issue** M.A. Mac Iver, "When Minimum Grading Policies Backfire: Who Decides Whether to Let Students Fail?" in M. Gottfried and G. Conchas, eds., *When School Policies Backfire* (Cambridge: Harvard Education Press, 2016), 69–84.

130 **had filed a lawsuit** Mac Iver, "When Minimum Grading Policies," 69–84.

130 **hard-line grading practices** Mac Iver, "When Minimum Grading Policies," 69–84.

132 **linked students' responses** Thomas J. Kane, "Ask the Students," *Brookings Institution*, April 10, 2013, www.brookings.edu/research/ask-the-students.

Chapter 5

139 **practices and systems might be contributing** Roderick and Camburn, "Risk and Recovery," 337.

139 **transitions generally** John W. Alspaugh, "Achievement Loss Associated with the Transition to Middle School and High School," *Journal of Educational Research* 92, no. 1 (1998): 20–25; J.S. Eccles and C. Midgley, "What Are We Doing to Early Adolescents? The Impact of Educational Contexts on Early Adolescents," *American Journal of Education* 99, no. 4 (1991): 521–542; Roderick and Camburn, "Risk and Recovery."

139 **"risk of getting stuck"** R.C. Neild, "Falling Off Track During the Transition to High School: What We Know and What Can Be Done," *The Future of Children* 19, no. 1 (2009): 56.

140 **as eighth graders** Aprile D. Benner and Sandra Graham, "The Transition to High School as a Developmental Process Among Multiethnic Urban Youth," *Child Development* 80, no. 2 (2009): 356–376; Todd Rosenkranz, Marisa de la Torre, David W. Stevens, and Elaine M. Allensworth, *Free to Fail or On-Track to College: Why Grades Drop When Students Enter High School and What Adults Can Do About It* (Chicago: University of Chicago Consortium on School Research, 2014).

140 **ninth-grade "bottleneck"** Neild, "Falling Off Track."

140 **teachers decrease** Rosenkranz et al., *Free to Fail*, 5.

140 **but barely noticed** Rosenkranz et al., *Free to Fail*, 6.

140 **"Teachers in eighth grade pushed us"** Rosenkranz et al., *Free to Fail*, 6.

141 **"that's your choice"** Rosenkranz et al., *Free to Fail*, 7.

141 **a "work in progress"** "Teenage Brain: A Work in Progress (Fact Sheet)," National Institute of Mental Health, last modified September 10, 2010, www2.isu.edu/irh/projects/better_todays/B2T2VirtualPacket/BrainFunction/NIMH-Teenage%20Brain%20-%20A%20Work%20in%20Progress.pdf.

141 **major changes to the limbic system** Laurence Steinberg, *Age of Opportunity: Lessons from the New Science of Adolescence* (New York: First Mariner Books, 2015), 72.

141 **conundrum for teens** Frances Jensen and Amy Ellis Nutt, *The Teenage Brain: A Neuroscientist's Survival Guide to Raising Adolescents and Young Adult* (New York: Harper Collins, 2015), 37.

142 **proliferation of dopamine receptors** Steinberg, *Age of Opportunity*, 72.

142 **brain chemical intimately tied to motivation** Jensen and Nutt, *Teenage Brain*, 54.

142 **"feel better during adolescence"** Steinberg, *Age of Opportunity*, 73.

142 **cravings can be overwhelming** Steinberg, *Age of Opportunity*, 74.

142 **"starting the engines"** Steinberg, *Age of Opportunity*, 70.

142 **Even during late adolescence** Steinberg, *Age of Opportunity*, 71.

143 **"split-second decision making"** Carolyn Gregoire, "Why Are Teens So Moody and Impulsive? This Neuroscientist Has the Answer," *Huffington Post*, December 6, 2017, www.huffingtonpost.com/2015/06/14/teenage-brain-neuroscience_n_7537188 .html.

143 **"he could do them without even thinking"** Author interview, May 3, 2016.

143 **heat of the moment** Gregoire, "Why Are Teens?"

143 **the mental calculus** Steinberg, *Age of Opportunity*, 92–95.

149 **fatally shot in the back** Steve Schmadeke, "Friend Describes Slaying of Endia Martin at Trial of Shooting Suspect's Uncle," *Chicago Tribune*, January 26, 2016.

155 **Steinberg calls adolescence** Steinberg, *Age of Opportunity*, 95.

Chapter 6

163 **guy with a heart** Ryan Blitstein, "Numbers Man," *Chicago Magazine*, July 21, 2009, www.chicagomag.com/Chicago-Magazine/August-2009/Numbers-Man.

163 **well-run system of data analysis and measurement** Blitstein, "Numbers Man."

163 **Results were color-coded** Greg Marietta, *Performance Management in Chicago Public Schools* (Cambridge: Harvard Education Press, 2012), 5.

164 **Marilyn Stewart argued** Carlos Sadovi and Dan Mihalopoulos, "Daley Standing by School Chief Choice: Huberman Appointment Called Political," *Chicago Tribune*, January 28, 2009.

164 **Huberman acknowledged** Rebecca Harris, "Huberman to Chicago Principals: Do Performance Management, School Improvement Will Follow," *Catalyst*, February 5, 2010, chicagoreporter.com/huberman-chicago-principals-do-performance-management -school-improvement-will.

164 **unveiled his education plan** Ron Huberman, *Ron Huberman, CEO, Chicago Public Schools*, audiovisual tape (Chicago: City Club of Chicago, 2009), www.youtube .com/watch?v=Ae5mTSxJW4g.

164 **"Let's pretend"** Huberman, *Ron Huberman, CEO*.

165 **how much he cares** Linda Lutton, "Huberman Named CPS Chief," *WBEZ*, January 28, 2009, www.wbez.org/shows/wbez-news/huberman-named-cps-chief /4e48eb4d-8c57-4558-b6b0-d2b735930d27.

166 **Huberman explained** Marietta, *Performance Management*, 5.

166 **"you have a plan"** Marietta, *Performance Management*, 6.

168 **"we had to do something"** Carol Felsenthal, "CTU President Karen Lewis: Race, Class at Center of Education Debate," *Chicago Magazine*, November 2011, www

.chicagomag.com/Chicago-Magazine/Felsenthal-Files/November-2011/CTU-President
-Karen-Lewis-Race-Class-at-Center-of-Education-Debate.

169 **blast Huberman and previous administrations** Steven K. Ashby and Robert Bruno, *A Fight for the Soul of Public Education*: ILR Press, 2016, 69.

169 **teachers admitted** Rosalind Rossi and Art Golab, "Grades: I'm Giving Them; Students Aren't Earning Them," *Chicago Sun-Times*, August 30, 2009.

169 **"how many kids are learning"** Rossi and Golab, "Grades: I'm Giving Them."

169 **"The Mayor should know"** CORE Press Release—March 2010, www.coreteachers.org/2452-2.

170 **"principals have been left high and dry"** Noreen Ahmed-Ullah, Tara Malone, and Rex Huppke, "Chicago Schools Chief to Leave Post This Month," *Chicago Tribune*, November 3, 2010.

170 **"a real superintendent"** Ahmed-Ullah, Malone, and Huppke, "Chicago Schools Chief."

170 **"loss in a unifying vision"** Whet Moser, "The Chicago Teachers Union Strike Has Been Building for Awhile," *Chicago Magazine*, September 6, 2012, www.chicagomag.com/Chicago-Magazine/The-312/September-2012/The-Chicago-Teachers-Union-Strike-Has-Been-Building-For-Awhile.

170 **average tenure of an urban superintendent** Madeline Will, "Average Urban School Superintendent Tenure Decreases, Survey Shows," *District Dossier* blog, *Education Week*, November 6, 2014, blogs.edweek.org/edweek/District_Dossier/2014/11/urban_school_superintendent_te.html.

170 **"I think the challenge in CPS"** Author interview, October 19, 2017.

171 **"When I talked to principals"** Unless otherwise specified, all quotations from Brizard come from author interview, October 5, 2017.

172 **"We were all searching for system change"** Author interview, March 30, 2016.

175 **identification of "bright spots"** Bryk et al., "Learning to Improve," 145.

175 **"create a sense of moral urgency"** Bryk et al., "Learning to Improve," 148.

176 **"these kids deserve a spot in the middle class"** Author interview, September 10, 2015.

177 **"It created a demand for help."** Author interview, May 9, 2017.

177 **NCS and Area 21 began** Mary Ann Pitcher, Sarah J. Duncan, Jenny Nagaoka, Eliza Moeller, Latesha Dickerson, and Nicole O. Bechum, *The Network for College Success: A Capacity-Building Model for School Improvement* (Chicago: University of Chicago Consortium on School Research, 2016), 14.

178 **checklists for all their routine procedures** Atul Gawande, "The Checklist: If Something So Simple Can Transform Intensive Care, What Else Can It Do?" *New Yorker*, December 10, 2007.

179 **"obsessed at the network with systems and structures"** Carl Vogel, "Learning a New Way," *SSA Magazine* 19, no. 1 (2012), ssa.uchicago.edu/ssa_magazine/learning-new-way.

180 **Jackson had attended** Lauren Fitzpatrick, "How Janice Jackson Rose from Chicago Public Schools Student to Its CEO," *Chicago Sun-Times*, December 11, 2017.

180 **later named her the founding principal** Fitzpatrick, "How Janice Jackson Rose."

180 **hoped someday to lead** Fitzpatrick, "How Janice Jackson Rose."

182 **networks have gained attention** Anthony S. Bryk, Louis G. Gomez, Alicia Grunow, and Paul G. LeMahieu, *Learning to Improve: How America's Schools Can Get Better at Getting Better* (Cambridge: Harvard Education Publishing, 2015), 5–6.

182 **"'lateral capacity building'"** Michael Fullan, "Change Theory: A Force for School Improvement" *Center for Strategic Education Seminar Series Paper No. 157*, November 2006, 7, michaelfullan.ca/wp-content/uploads/2016/06/13396072630.pdf.

182 **"weak on capacity building"** Fullan, "Change Theory," 7.

183 **"schools compete with each other"** Michael Fullan, "The Big Ideas Behind Whole System Reform," *Education Canada* 50, no. 3 (2010), 26.

183 **"So much of what we were looking at"** Author interview, October 25, 2017.

184 **highest Freshman OnTrack rate** Network for College Success, Lead Partner Application for School Improvement Grants, www.isbe.net/Documents/univ_chgo_lead.pdf.

184 **rechristened them "networks"** Sarah Karp, "As Part of District Shakeup, Brizard to Hire Schools Portfolio Office," *Catalyst*, July 27, 2011.

184 **CPS's policy for years had been pushing** Karp, "Part of District Shakeup."

184 **"share what they've learned"** Vogel, "Learning a New Way."

186 **two sticking points** Dana Liebelson, "What Happened with the Chicago Teacher Strike, Explained," *Mother Jones*, September 11, 2012, www.motherjones.com/politics/2012/09/teachers-strike-chicago-explained.

186 **Karen Lewis said** Monica Davey, "Teachers' Leader in Chicago Strike Shows Her Edge," *New York Times*, September 11, 2012.

186 **"agenda of blaming teachers"** Ben Goldberger, "Karen Lewis, Street Fighter," *Chicago Magazine*, October 2, 2012, www.chicagomag.com/Chicago-Magazine/November-2012/Karen-Lewis-Street-Fighter.

186 **He had pushed** Valerie Strauss, "The Problem with Rahm's School Reforms in Chicago," *Washington Post*, September 11, 2012.

187 **"reinvigorated a national teachers movement"** Ashby and Bruno, "Fight for the Soul," 1–2.

187 **longer school day and more leeway** Greg McCune, "Chicago Teachers Union Ratifies Deal That Ended Strike," *Chicago Tribune*, October 4, 2012.

188 **Reflecting later** "Interview with Jean-Claude Brizard," *Flypaper Blog*, August 23, 2013, edexcellence.net/by-the-company-it-keeps-jean-claude-brizard.

188 **Kotlowitz argued** Alex Kotlowitz, "Are We Asking Too Much from Our Teachers?" *New York Times*, September 14, 2012.

189 **"but teachers can't do it alone"** Kotlowitz, "Are We Asking?"

190 **"Quality schools and quality teaching"** Kotlowitz, "Are We Asking?"

Chapter 7

196 **a clear link** Carol Goodenow, "Strengthening the Links Between Educational Psychology and the Study of Social Contexts," *Educational Psychologist* 27, no. 2 (1992): 177–196.

197 **"whether or not a teacher was supportive"** Rosenkranz et al., *Free to Fail*, 9.

201 **non-cognitive factors** Paul Tough documented some of the efforts to improve non-cognitive skills in his bestselling book *How Children Succeed*, which brought the academic literature on non-cognitive factors into the mainstream.

201 **Researchers define** Camille A. Farrington, Melissa Roderick, Elaine Allensworth, Jenny Nagaoka, Tasha Seneca Keyes, David W. Johnson, and Nicole O. Beechum, *Teaching Adolescents to Become Learners: The Role of Noncognitive Factors in Shaping School Performance: A Critical Literature Review* (Chicago: University of Chicago Consortium on School Research, 2012), 2–8.

202 **how well students will fare later** W.G. Bowen, M.M. Chingos, and M.S. McPherson, *Crossing the Finish Line: Completing College at America's Public Universities* (Princeton: Princeton University Press, 2009); Melissa Roderick, Jenny Nagaoka, Elaine Allensworth, Vanessa Coca, M. Correa, and G. Stoker, *From High School to the Future: A First Look at Chicago Public Schools Graduates' College Enrollment, College Preparation, and Graduation from Four-Year Colleges* (Chicago: University of Chicago Consortium on Chicago School Research, 2006).

202 **grades clearly capture** S.M. Brookhart, T.R. Guskey, A.J. Bowers, J.H. McMillan, J.K. Smith, L.F. Smith, M.T. Stevens, and M.E. Welsh, "A Century of Grading Research: Meaning and Value in the Most Common Educational Measure," *Review of Educational Research* 86, no. 4 (2016): 32.

202 **failure to exercise self-discipline** Angela L. Duckworth and M.E.P. Seligman, "Self-discipline Outdoes IQ in Predicting Academic Performance of Adolescents," *Psychological Science* 16, no. 12 (2005): 939.

203 **"growth mindset"** C.S. Dweck, G.M. Walton, and G.L. Cohen, "Academic Tenacity: Mindsets and Skills That Promote Long-term Learning" White Paper (Gates Foundation, 2011).

203 **classroom and school contexts** Farrington et al., *Teaching Adolescents*, 32.

203 **"Positive academic mindsets"** Farrington et al., *Teaching Adolescents*, 9.

204 **four specific mindsets** Farrington, et al., *Teaching Adolescents*, 10.

205 **evidence linking students' self-efficacy** Dweck, Walton, and Cohen, "Academic Tenacity," 5.

205 **When students think they will fail** Farrington et al., *Teaching Adolescents*, 29.

210 **"there's not going to be a conversation every time"** Author interview, June 10, 2016.

214 **"He knew"** Author interview, May 3, 2016.

Chapter 8

223 **"SMART" goal** SMART is an acronym designed to guide the creation of targeted goals. It stands for Specific, Measurable, Achievable, Measurable, and Timebound.

225 **seeking out challenge** Camille Farrington, "Sweating the Soft Stuff: Qualities Needed for Learning and How to Nurture Them," Q&A (Chicago School Policy Forum Series, Chicago, October 30, 2012).

227 **"Yeah, I was guilty of that"** Author interview, December 11, 2015.

227 **this motley crew came together** Author interview, July 22, 2016.

229 **"We understand that you are frustrated"** Author interview, July 22, 2016.

Chapter 9

241 **the district had contributed** "Chicago Public Schools Fiscal Year 2017 Budget: Pensions," *Chicago Public Schools*, last modified May 26, 2017, cps.edu/fy17budget /Pages/pensions.aspx.

242 **"it would be on"** Juan Perez Jr., "Chicago Public Schools Making Contingency Plans for Possible Strike," *Chicago Tribune*, April 27, 2016.

248 **budget had been slashed** Kate Grossman, "Reviving a Hollowed-Out High School," *The Atlantic*, April 8, 2016.

250 **As ACEs accumulate, so does the risk** "About the CDC-Kaiser ACE Study," *Centers for Disease Control and Prevention*, last modified June 14, 2016, www.cdc.gov /violenceprevention/acestudy/about.html.

250 **learning or behavior issues in school** David Brooks, "The Psych Approach," *New York Times*, September 27, 2012.

265 **"Having those sorts of resources helped him"** Author interview, May 12, 2016.

276 **"she may have framed that joint"** Author interview, May 24, 2016.

Chapter 10

282 **"Of 100 Chicago Public School Freshmen"** Jodi S. Cohen and Darnell Little, "Of 100 Chicago Public School Freshmen, Six Will Get a College Degree," *Chicago Tribune*, April 21, 2006, www.metrosquash.org/docs/CPS_Article.pdf.

283 **graduation rates improved** Roderick et al., *Preventable Failure*.

283 **that might have accounted** Roderick et al., *Preventable Failure.*

284 **researchers wrote** Roderick et al., *Preventable Failure.*

284 **to 77 percent** Roderick et al., *Preventable Failure.*

286 **the longer school day** Sara Neufeld, "A Longer School Day in Chicago, but with What Missing?," *Hechinger Report*, January 21, 2014, hechingerreport.org/a-longer-school-day-in-chicago-but-with-what-missing.

286 **now contractually obligated** Sara Neufeld, "More Time in School, with a Drain on Chicago's Teachers," *Hechinger Report*, January 22, 2014, hechingerreport.org/more-time-in-school-with-a-drain-on-chicagos-teachers.

288 **"She came in right after the teacher strike"** Author interview, October 25, 2017.

288 **single largest school closure** Marisa de la Torre, Molly F. Gordon, Paul Clark, and Jennifer Cowhy, *School Closings in Chicago: Understanding Families' Choices and Constraints for New School Enrollment* (Chicago: University of Chicago Consortium on School Research, 2015), 5

289 **open letter to Byrd-Bennett** Valerie Strauss, "Questions About School Closings," *Washington Post*, January 3, 2013.

289 **primary factor contributing to the underutilization** Becky Vevea and Linda Lutton, "Fact Check: Chicago School Closings," *WBEZ*, January 3, 2013, www.wbez.org/shows/wbez-news/fact-check-chicago-school-closings/81734980-e9fb-4c05-8605-af207b43d8c9.

290 **did make significant academic progress** Marisa de la Torre and Julia Gwynne, *When Schools Close: Effects on Displaced Students in Chicago Public Schools* (Chicago: University of Chicago Consortium on Chicago School Research, 2009).

290 **just six were in the top quartile** Vevea and Lutton, "Fact Check."

290 **difference "varied substantially"** De la Torre et al., *School Closings.*

291 **replaced it with a new one** De la Torre et al., *School Closings.*

291 **"corporate-driven school reform nonsense"** Karen Lewis, "CTU President Karen Lewis Statement on CPS School Closings" press release (Chicago Teachers Union, March 21, 2013), www.ctunet.com/media/press-releases/ctu-president-karen-lewis-statement-on-cps-school-closings.

291 **disapproved of Emanuel's handling** Rick Pearson, "Tribune Poll: Voters Give Emanuel Low Marks on his School Policies," *Chicago Tribune*, August 15, 2014.

291 **"they're on track to a life of possibility"** Rahm Emanuel, "Chicago's Focus on Ninth Grade On-Track Triggers Climb in High School Graduation Rates," press release (University of Chicago Consortium on Chicago Research, April 24, 2014).

292 *Economist* **article** "Rahmbo's Toughest Mission," *The Economist*, June 14, 2014.

292 *Chicago Tribune* **article** Juan Perez Jr., Bob Secter, and Bill Ruthhart, "Differences over Chicago Schools Stir Mayor's Race for Emanuel, Garcia," *Chicago Tribune*, March 28, 2015.

292 **"But the mayor also cared about"** Author interview, October 5, 2017.

293 **Donald T. Campbell** D.T. Campbell, "Assessing the Impact of Planned Social Change," *Evaluation and Program Planning* 2, no. 1(1979): 67–90.

293 **"Nothing really happened besides compliance"** Author interview, August 6, 2015.

294 **"deserve a chance"** Kate Grossman, "What Schools Will Do to Keep Students on Track," *The Atlantic*, July 6, 2015, www.theatlantic.com/education/archive /2015/07/chicago-graduation-rates/397736.

294 **according to a report** Nicholas Schuler, Office of Inspector General Chicago Board of Education Annual Report FY 2016, 12, www.chicagotribune.com/news/ct -chicago-public-schools-inspector-general-report-20161214-htmlstory.html.

294 **told the inspector general** Schuler, *Annual Report*, Appendix A, 5–6.

294 **"broad concerns about the accuracy"** Kate Grossman, "4 CPS High Schools Dramatically Inflated Student Attendance: IG," *Chicago Sun-Times*, October 6, 2016.

295 **"whatever they can do"** Grossman, "4 CPS High Schools."

296 **one article explained** Sarah Karp, "Tinkering with the High School Graduation Rate," *Catalyst*, February 26, 2015, chicagoreporter.com/tinkering-with-the -high-school-graduation-rate.

296 **incorrectly coded** Sarah Karp and Becky Vevea, "Emanuel Touts Bogus Graduation Rate," *WBEZ*, June 10, 2015, www.wbez.org/shows/wbez-news/emanuel-touts -bogus-graduation-rate/7891382c-6069-4bdb-ad7c-a34fd67895e2.

296 **force a runoff** Bob Secter, "Political Dynamics Change as Emanuel, Garcia Move into Runoff Campaign," *Chicago Tribune*, February 25, 2015.

296 **often imprecise** Bill Ruthhart, "Fact-Checking Garcia Education Attack Ad Against Emanuel," *Chicago Tribune*, February 25, 2015.

296 **Garcia was backed** Julie Bosman, "Rahm Emanuel Wins Runoff Election to Secure 2nd Term as Chicago Mayor," *New York Times*, April 7, 2015.

297 **Barbara Byrd-Bennett pleaded guilty** Jason Meisner, "Ex-CPS Chief Barbara Byrd-Bennett Pleads Guilty, Tearfully Apologizes to Students," *Chicago Tribune*, October 14, 2015.

297 **"tuition to pay and casinos to visit"** Sun-Times Staff, "Feds: Byrd-Bennett Said 'Tuition to Pay and Casinos to Visit' Led to Kickbacks," *Chicago Sun-Times*, June 24, 2016.

297 **Rates were adjusted downward** Becky Vevea, "Admitting Dropouts Were Miscounted, Chicago Lowers Graduation Rates," NPR, October 2, 2015, www.npr.org /sections/ed/2015/10/02/445152363/admitting-dropouts-were-miscounted-chicago -lowers-graduation-rates.

297 **adjustment of the district's Freshman OnTrack rates** Juan Perez Jr., "Chicago Public Schools Downgrades Four Years of Inflated Graduation Rates," *Chicago Tribune*, October 2, 2015.

297 **John Kass wrote** John Kass, "Rahm Emanuel Should Hire Auditor to Dig Deep at Chicago Public Schools," *Chicago Tribune*, October 10, 2015.

299 **researchers found** Elaine M. Allensworth, Kaleen Healey, Julia A. Gwynne, and René Crespin, *High School Graduation Rates Through Two Decades of District Change: The Influence of Policies, Data Records, and Demographic Shifts* (Chicago: University of Chicago Consortium on School Research, 2016), 3.

299 **"schools have improved so much"** Whet Moser, "Are CPS Schools 'Crumbling Prisons'? The Data Say Otherwise," *Chicago Magazine*, June 2016, www.chicagomag.com/city-life/June-2016/Are-CPS-Schools-Crumbling-Prisons-The-Data-Says-Otherwise.

300 **Rauner was arguing** Tina Sfondeles and Fran Spielman, "Rauner Delivers One School Message in Chicago, Another Downstate," *Chicago Sun-Times*, June 7, 2016.

300 **Allensworth's report** Sfondeles and Spielman, "Rauner Delivers One School Message."

300 **"hitting remarkable highs"** Sfondeles and Spielman, "Rauner Delivers One School Message."

301 **"they actually learn"** Grossman, "4 CPS High Schools."

301 **"It put a lot of pressure on me"** Author interview, November 10, 2015.

301 **"believing in ourselves can also be our greatest accomplishment"** Fatima Salgado, quoted in "Words of Wisdom: 10 Inspirational Graduation Speeches," *Education Week*, July 11, 2012.

Epilogue

304 **shooting victims under the age of seventeen** Alex Bordens and Abraham Epton, "Young victims of violence in Chicago" chart, *Chicago Tribune*, http://apps.chicagotribune.com/news/local/young_victims.

305 **dominated the past two decades** Bill Gates, *Keynote Speech at the Council of the Great City Schools Annual Conference* video, Cleveland.com, 41:39, October 19, 2017, www.youtube.com/watch?v=ZEWsCWaQBHg.

306 **an explicit pivot away** Gates, *Keynote Speech.*

306 **more impactful and durable systemic changes** Gates, *Keynote Speech.*

307 **Freshman OnTrack in their states' accountability systems** "ESSA Plans: Explainer and Key Takeaways from Each State," *Education Week*, last updated April 28, 2018, www.edweek.org/ew/section/multimedia/key-takeaways-state-essa-plans.html.

308 **"cycles of learning to improve"** A.S. Bryk, "2014 AERA Distinguished Lecture: Accelerating How We Learn to Improve," *Educational Researcher* 44, no. 9 (2015): 473.

308 **Bryk characterizes this approach** Bryk, "Accelerating," 473.

308 **It is the opposite of the type of reforms** Bryk, "Accelerating," 468.

309 **"picking the right things to do"** Author interview, December 4, 2017.

309 **nation's school districts reported** U.S. Department of Education, Office of Planning, Evaluation and Policy Development Policy and Program Studies Service, "Issue Brief: Early Warning Systems" (Washington, DC, 2016), www2.ed.gov /rschstat/eval/high-school/early-warning-systems-brief.pdf.

309 **"It's really a fascinating story"** Author interview, December 4, 2017.

309 **early warning systems through networked communities** Author interview, December 4, 2017.

310 **inspector general accused him** Lauren Fitzpatrick, "Under Fire, CPS' Forrest Claypool Quits; Janice Jackson Replaces Him," *Chicago Sun-Times*, December 8, 2017.

310 **becoming the ninth CEO** Fitzpatrick, "Under Fire."

311 **Sarah Duncan said** Melissa Sanchez, "Hancock to Become a Selective Admissions School," *Catalyst*, October 1, 2014, chicagoreporter.com/hancock-become -selective-admissions-school.

312 **enrolled just 250 students** Juan Perez Jr. and Jennifer Smith Richards, "Can These Chicago High Schools Survive? Students Offered Fewer Choices, Resources in More Than a Dozen Near-Empty Schools," *Chicago Tribune*, November 29, 2017.

312 **to 147 different schools** Perez and Smith Richards, "Can These Chicago High Schools Survive?"

312 **cut by about $2.6 million** Perez and Smith Richards, "Can These Chicago High Schools Survive?"

313 **"design something to ensure"** Perez and Smith Richards, "Can These Chicago High Schools Survive?"

313 **average Chicago student actually learns more** S.F. Reardon, "Educational Opportunity in Early and Middle Childhood: Variation by Place and Age," *Stanford Center for Education Policy Analysis*, March 2018, cepa.stanford.edu/content/educational -opportunity-early-and-middle-childhood-variation-place-and-age.

ABOUT THE AUTHOR

Emily Krone Phillips is the communications director at the Spencer Foundation. She worked previously as an education reporter and as the communications director at the University of Chicago Consortium on School Research, where the Freshman OnTrack research originated and inspired her to write *The Make-or-Break Year*. She lives near Chicago.

PUBLISHING IN THE PUBLIC INTEREST

Thank you for reading this book published by The New Press. The New Press is a nonprofit, public interest publisher. New Press books and authors play a crucial role in sparking conversations about the key political and social issues of our day.

We hope you enjoyed this book and that you will stay in touch with The New Press. Here are a few ways to stay up to date with our books, events, and the issues we cover:

- Sign up at www.thenewpress.com/subscribe to receive updates on New Press authors and issues and to be notified about local events
- Like us on Facebook: www.facebook.com/newpressbooks
- Follow us on Twitter: www.twitter.com/thenewpress

Please consider buying New Press books for yourself; for friends and family; or to donate to schools, libraries, community centers, prison libraries, and other organizations involved with the issues our authors write about.

The New Press is a 501(c)(3) nonprofit organization. You can also support our work with a tax-deductible gift by visiting www.thenewpress.com/donate.